Language System and Its Change

Trends in Linguistics

Studies and Monographs 30

Editor
Werner Winter

Mouton de Gruyter
Berlin · New York · Amsterdam

Language System and Its Change

On Theory and Testability

by
Jadranka Gvozdanović

Mouton de Gruyter
Berlin · New York · Amsterdam

Mouton de Gruyter (formerly Mouton, The Hague)
is a Division of Walter de Gruyter & Co., Berlin.

Library of Congress Cataloging in Publication Data

Gvozdanović, Jadranka, 1947 –
Language system and its change.
(Trends in linguistics. Studies and monographs ; 30)
Bibliography: p.
Includes index.
1. Language and languages – Variation. 2. Linguistic change.
3. Nepal – Languages. 4. Typology (Linguistics)
I. Title. II. Series.
P120.V37G88 1985 410 85-21607
ISBN 0-89925-122-6 (alk. paper)

CIP-Kurztitelaufnahme der Deutschen Bibliothek

Gvozdanović, Jadranka:
Language system and its change : on theory and testability /
by Jadranka Gvozdanović. –
Berlin ; New York ; Amsterdam : Mouton, 1985.
(Trends in linguistics : Studies and monographs ; 30)
ISBN 3-11-010477-6
NE: Trends in linguistics / Studies and monographs

Printed on acid free paper.

Typesetting: Asian Research Service, Hong Kong. – Printing: Druckerei Gerike GmbH, Berlin. – Binding: Dieter Mikolai, Berlin. – Printed in Germany.

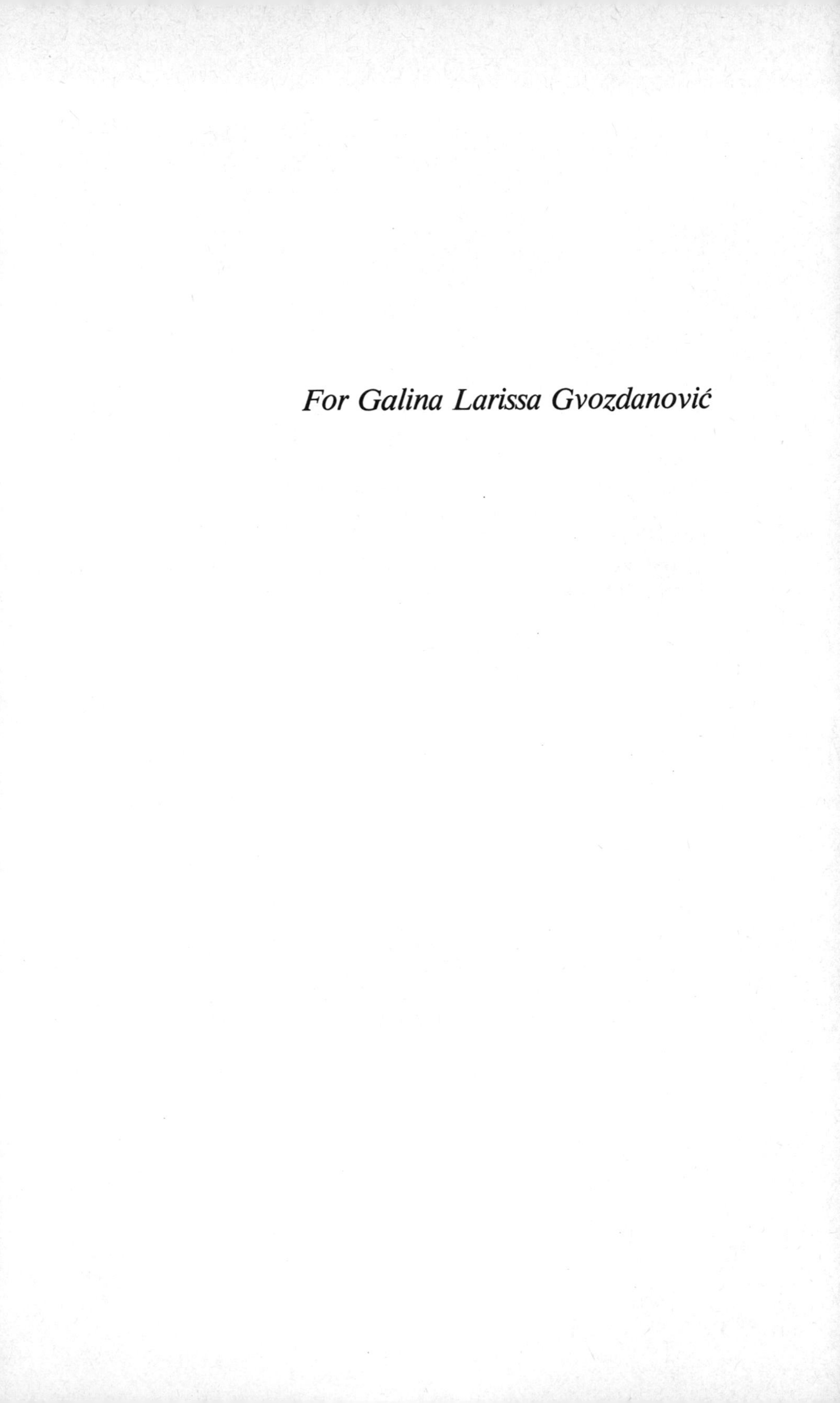

For Galina Larissa Gvozdanović

Note

I am thankful to the Alexander von Humboldt Foundation of the German Federal Republic for enabling me to carry out the research in Nepal, to the Linguistics Department of the University of Kiel for providing the available Tibeto-Burman data and advice, and to the Slavic Department of the University of Amsterdam for giving me a leave of absence in order to be able to carry out this research.

The present publication has been financed in part by the Alexander von Humboldt Foundation.

Abbreviations

du	'dual'
C.	'Central'
E.	'Eastern'
excl.	'exclusive'
incl.	'inclusive'
pl	'plural'
S.	'Southern'
sg	'singular'

NEPAL
EASTERN DEVELOPMENT REGION
SCALE
Kms 5 0 5 10 Kms.
N
CHINA
CHINA
INDIA
INDIA
INDIA
INDIA
JANAKPUR ZONE
SAGARMATHA
KOSI
MECHI
SOLU KHUMBU
Solu Salleri
OKHALDHUNGA
Okhaldhunga
KHOTANG
Diktel
UDAYAPUR
Gaighat
SIRAHA
Siraha
SAPTARI
Rajbiraj
SANKHUWASABHA
Khandbari
BHOJPUR
Bhojpur
DHANKUTA
Dhankuta
SUNSARI
Inarwa
Dharan
MORANG
Biratnagar
TAPLEJUNG
Taplejung
TEHRATHUM
Tehrathum
PANCHTHAR
Phidim
ILAM
Ilam
JHAPA
Chandragadhi
NEPAL
LOCATION OF
EASTERN DEVELOPMENT REGION
FAR WESTERN DEVELOPMENT REGION
MID WESTERN DEVELOPMENT REGION
WESTERN DEVELOPMENT REGION
CENTRAL DEVELOPMENT REGION
EASTERN DEVELOPMENT REGION
MAHAKALI
SETI
KARNALI
BHERI
RAPTI
DHAULAGIRI
GANDAKI
LUMBINI
BAGMATI
NARAYANI
JANAKPUR
SAGARMATHA
KOSI
MECHI
Eastern Development Region
LEGEND
International Boundary
Zonal Boundary
District Boundary
Development Boundary
Development Centre
Zonal Head Quarter
District Head Quarter

Contents

0. Introduction

In each language, we can observe variation along language-external and language-internal dimensions. Variation itself is a language-inherent phenomenon.

The first type comprises variation in space and time. Variation in space can be either horizontal, i.e., geographical, or vertical, i.e. social. Variation in time occurs when forms and/or meanings from different periods cooccur within the same language.

The second type comprises variation within one communication code, or between the explicit and elliptic codes in one speech community. This type of variation may also be called 'variability'.

Variation is characteristic of biological functions in general, language being one of them. And it is characteristic of variation that it is not unconstrained, but rather that it obeys constraints imposed by the system in which it occurs.

The constraints observable in variation are indicative of the organization of the language system, and can be used for testing hypotheses about that system. Only hypotheses which can stand such a test may be considered relevant to the language competence.

Language change arises from variability and obeys the same systematic constraints, at least in its initial stage. This is valid for language as much as it is for other communication means. In communication, mutual understanding is preserved only if each next step continues the essential part of the preceding one.

This is visualized in dance – another communication means – as holding both for form and meaning. And dance may be considered indicative because it is characteristic of its form that the dimensions of space and time are not only external, but also internal to it in the sense of movements in space and their rhythm. A sudden change of these movements conveys a change of meaning within one communication unit if at least one of the dominating principles of the form and of those of meaning is preserved, or otherwise it induces a break and a new communication unit.

What are the dominating principles constraining variation within one communication unit?

They can be hypothesized to be basic to the entire system.

This book develops procedures for establishing them for language.

1. Phonological Variation and Change in Relation to the System

1.1. Organization of the Sound System

The sounds of a language are elements of the forms of that language. And the forms are recognized as such by the native speakers if they are or can be associated with a meaning in a conventionalized way. Thus, *smurf* is a Dutch word since Dutchmen have invented the concept of a dwarf-like creature with good qualities and given it that name. Now every Dutchman can talk about it so that another Dutchman understands what is meant. Following the productive verb-from-noun formation pattern, the verb *smurven* can be formed and conjugated in order to denote a state or an action characterized by such features, and even prefixes may be added to it in order to denote additional details of such a state or action.

We can see that formal innovation follows the rules of the totality of the forms of that language (such as whether the language uses prefixes or suffixes), and that conceptual or meaningful innovation follows the rules of the concept formations of that language.

And the building elements of the form, the sounds of a language, follow the rules of sound formation and concatenation of that language.

What are the rules of sound formation and concatenation in language?

The relevant sounds of a language, i.e. those which are capable of distinguishing the forms of that language *ceteris paribus,* are assumed to be analysable in terms of distinctive features. The latter can be formulated in articulatory terms, such as *high* vs. *low* as referring to the tongue position in the production of vowels, or in acoustic terms, such as *diffuse* vs. *compact* as referring to the relatively low vs. high values of the first two formants produced by the aforementioned articulatory movements. There need not be a full correspondence between the articulatory and the acoustic features of a language.

Distinctive features are relative and their phonetic definitions are partly language-specific. Within these ramifications, their phonetic definitions must be left over to phoneticians.

The linguist is concerned with the role distinctive features play in language functioning.

It is only through that role that an indirect proof of their relevance can be obtained. The (by now generally accepted) hypothesis that speech sounds are sets of distinctive features can be put to a test only through testing properties of such sets by the presence vs. absence of the effects predicted by them.

One such property is the minimal number of the distinctive features participating in a set. Another property is the relation among the distinctive features of a set. It can be hypothesized that the related features cannot form sets in isolation from each other.

Let us first consider language evidence for the minimal number of distinctive features that can form a set recognizable as a speech sound.

Can a single distinctive feature form a speech sound? Yes, it can, as we know on the basis of floating tones e.g. in the African language Efik, or on the basis of the nasal relative clause marker e.g. in Old Irish.

Efik has a distinctive *high* vs. *low* tone, and a *rising* vs. *falling* tone, to be analysed as *low* + *high* and *high* + *low*, respectively. These sequences are due to an added floating tone, as a representative of a grammatical marker. For example, the original *low* tone of /kà/ in /à-kà/ 'you go' becomes rising through addition of a *high* tone in /à-kǎ/ 'you are going'.

The interesting feature of Efik is that addition of a floating tone is always accompanied by vowel lengthening (cf. Cook, forthcoming, and Ward (1933: 29)). The lengthened vowels can be seen as sequences. There are no other instances of vowel length in Efik.

We can see that tone as a single distinctive feature is capable of creating a distinctive feature set. In this set, the feature *vocalic* is added, and the remaining features are copied from the neighbouring syllable nucleus within the same grammatical unit. Apparently, a specification of a tone feature alone is capable of determining a vocalic, or a nonconsonantal, speech sound. There must consequently be a relation between tone and the feature specification either as *vocalic* or as *nonconsonantal* which makes them obligatorily cooccur within a speech sound. And it is apparently due to this relation that a single feature is capable of creating a distinctive feature set.

This is the kind of evidence language offers us for distinctive features and their sets.

Another piece of evidence is offered by the ability of distinctive features to change distinctive features of a neighbouring segment (and 'segment' is defined as a 'distinctive feature set') without themselves showing up, however. Such examples are also found with tone – e.g. the *high* tone associative marker in Efik causes a change from *low* to *high* on the initial syllable nucleus of the next following noun, rather than creating a *high* + *low* tone sequence with a corresponding additional vowel there – but the conditioning factors seem to show up more clearly with the feature *nasal,* such as the nasal relative marker in Old Irish.

In Old Irish, the feature *nasal* was used in order to mark a relative clause in the following cases (cf. Thurneysen (1946: 316-319)): when the antecedent designates the time at or during which the relative clause takes place, or the manner or degree of the content of the relative clause, or when the antecedent is a verbal noun of the verb of the relative clause, when it supplies the concept that constitutes the predicative nominative of the relative clause, less frequently when it specifies the source or cause of the action contained in the relative clause, and optionally (in place of a leniting relative clause), when the antecedent is felt as the object of the verb of the relative clause. The nasal relative marker of Old Irish precedes the verb and – as Thurneysen calls it – *"nasalizes its initial".* This means that it shows up as a segment (at least in writing, which is the only source for Old Irish) if the first segment (i.e. the first distinctive feature set) of the verb is originally a voiced one. If it is originally voiceless, it is voiced by the nasal feature, but the nasal feature itself is lost without forming a segment of its own. This can be illustrated by the following examples.

(1) The Old Irish nasal relative marker (from Thurneysen (1946: 316-319)):
hōre dēte (for tēte, d=nasalized t) Würzburg 11d7
'because he goes'
in tan ara llēgthar (11=nasalized 1) Würzburg 9b3
'when it is read out'
a-nno•n-derbid, Würzburg 22b24
'when ye approve'
nī nād•m-bia, Würzburg 13d17
'not that there will not be'
ōre do•n-ēcomnacht, Würzburg 1a1
'because he has imparted'.
((¯) denotes vowel length)

The first example above shows that the nasal feature voices an originally voiceless consonant, without itself showing up. The remaining examples illustrate its showing up as a segment if the initial segment of the verb is originally voiced. In these cases, it takes over the articulation place features of the following nonvocalic segment (even abandoning nasality when the following segment is a sonorant or an /s/, which means that it is also *non-vocalic,* and its specification for *voice* is nondistinctive in Old Irish, as it is in the nasal segments, too).

We can conclude that the feature *nasal* is capable of predicting the feature *consonantal,* or *nonvocalic,* in Old Irish. When it precedes a segment which already has this specification, and which is voiced, it forms a segment itself and takes over the remaining features from the next following segment. When it precedes a vocalic segment, on the other hand, it does not take over its remaining features. There is apparently a crucial discrepancy between *vocalic* and *nonvocalic* in relation to *nasal: nasal* appears to be related only to *nonvocalic,* but not to *vocalic.* When the feature *nasal* precedes a voiceless segment, it voices it without showing up itself. Apparently, *nasal* is incompatible with *voiceless* (or *nonvoiced*).

We can conclude that some features are mutually related in the segments in which they occur (such as *high* vs. *low* tone and *nonconsonantal,* or *nasal* and *nonvocalic*), and that some of the remaining ones are mutually incompatible (such as *nasal* and *voiceless*). For the remaining features (such as the articulation place features in the discussed languages), no relation could be established.

We are now justified in stating that speech sounds, also called segments, can be analysed in terms of distinctive features which have a restrictive and predictive value with respect to language behaviour such that it can be ascribed to language competence.

Distinctive features are phonetic dimensions which are partitioned by language into two or more sections. When they are partitioned into two by their physical nature (such as the phonetic dimension of *voice* is partitioned into *voiced* and *voiceless*), their language evaluation is always binary (i.e. in terms of [+voice] vs. [-voice]). When they are not partitioned into two by their physical nature (such as the phonetic dimension of *vowel height* is not), a language may evaluate them as binary (i.e. as [+high] vs. [-high] if it has only two vowel opening degrees), or in terms of more distinctions. I shall return to this point later.

As distinguished from relevance of a feature, a feature may also be irrelevant due to the remaining features involved in a given segment. Then a phonetic specification may still be found, but in a predictable way, or it may vary along the given phonetic dimension.

An example of a predictable feature specification is found in the Old Irish sonorants /m/, /n/, /l/ and /r/ (comprising the entire sonorant class in Old Irish), which are predictably *voiced,* and in /s/ in Old Irish, which is (presumably) predictably *voiceless,* as there is no /z/ in that language. The group of segments in Old Irish in which *voice* is nondistinctive appears to form a class, as shown by the nasalization rules. This class may be taken to illustrate that a predictable feature specification is not a third value, added to the two binary ones: there is not a unique phonetic reality attached to it. The only reason for these segments forming a class is the absence of a relevant *voice* specification in them, which is in the sonorants due to the combination with the remaining feature specifications relevant in them, and in /s/ due to a language-specific gap of a missing voiced counterpart.

In addition to paradigmatic predictability illustrated by Old Irish, which may either be due to relevant specifications of other distinctive features within the same distinctive feature set, i.e. segment, or to a language-specific gap, syntagmatic predictability, also called 'neutralization' or 'assimilation', occurs. It is a frequent case of feature irrelevance in a segment if the same feature is relevant in a contiguous segment. We can see that syntagmatic predictability occurs with respect to the same phonetic dimension in contiguous sets, whereas paradigmatic predictability occurs with respect to contiguous phonetic dimensions in the same set.

The Old Irish nasalization thus presents a piece of evidence in favour of distinctive features, their binary evaluation, and the fact that feature predictability is not a third value.

Following Saussure's (1916) concept of linguistic sign as consisting of a form and a meaning associated with it, and following Jakobson, Cherry and Halle's (1953) concept of distinctive features as being entirely based on oppositions and having no other meaning than that of mere otherness, we are on the basis of the test elaborated above, justified in conceiving distinctive feature specifications as signs indeed. Their form is defined with respect to a phonetic dimension, and their meaning is that of mere otherness, defined on the basis of opposition with a comparable sign, the form of which is defined as different along the same phonetic dimension. A distinctive feature specification as a sign in its totality is capable of distinguishing language forms *ceteris paribus*.

(2) Distinctive feature specifications as signs in the language system:

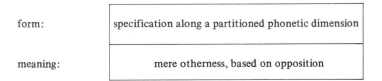

form:	specification along a partitioned phonetic dimension
meaning:	mere otherness, based on opposition

It follows from this concept of a distinctive feature specification as a sign that the sonorants and /s/ in Old Irish are not specified as [+voice] in the former case and [-voice] in the latter, but rather that the distinctive feature opposition [+voice] vs. [-voice] is irrelevant there: only the form of these signs is present, but not its meaning. The sign itself is consequently not there. And the very fact that these segments lack the sign for *voice* makes them form a single class, as stated above.

Given the approach advocated here by which a theory must be translatable into testable hypotheses, and in the sense of this testability, I assume that only signs which have a testable meaning and a testable form attached to it are relevant to language, as manifested through performance which reflects the relevant constraints imposed by competence. To the matter of competence and performance I shall return when discussing speech errors and the kind of evidence provided by them.

The assumption that only signs which have a testable meaning and a testable form attached to them are relevant to language, does not allow for feature changing rules as intervening between a meaning and its surface form in general, and in distinctive features in particular. It allows only for sign omittance in the process of derivation, and predictable form specifications.

In the latter respect, I differ fundamentally from Chomsky and Halle's (1968) usage of distinctive features in language analysis, but I do accept their basic concept of distinctive features as based on binary classifications, which is in itself derived from Jakobson's work. I also differ fundamentally from Jakobson's (e.g. 1949) allowance of a '±' specification, which merely shows a lack of sufficient analysis, and from his differentiating between a '–' specification and a lack of specification in a nontestable way, as we can see if we compare the Serbo-Croatian distinctive feature matrix as conceived by him in 1949, where no distinction between '–' and 'lack of opposition' was made, with the same matrix as revised by himself in 1962 in the reprint of the same article in his Selected Writings I, but with the introduction of '–' specifications in some distinctive feature sets where they have not been justified and even cannot be justified by the exclusive presence of oppositions.

(3a) The distinctive feature matrix of Serbo-Croatian, a South Slavic language (Jakobson (1949)):

	t	d	c	s	z	p	b	f	v	ć	đ	č	ğ	š	ž	k	g	x	n	m	ń	r	l	l′	i	u	e	o	a
vocality																						±	±	±	+	+	+	+	+
nasality																			+	+	+								
saturation										+	+	+	+	+	+	+	+	+			+			+			±	±	+
gravity						+	+	+	+											+						+		+	
contin-uousness			±	+	+			+	+			±	±	+	+			+					+	+					
voicing		+			+		+		+		+		+		+		+												

Add to the analytic records of /r/ and of any vowel:

	1	2	3	4
High-tone			+	+
Length		+		+

(3b) The same distinctive feature matrix, revised (Jakobson 1962):

	t	d	c	s	z	p	b	f	v	ć	đ	č	ğ	š	ž	k	g	x	n	m	ń	r	l	ľ	i	u	e	o	a
vocality																						±	±	±	+	+	+	+	+
nasality		–					–				–								+	+	+								
saturation	–	–	–	–	–	–	–	–		+	+	+	+	+	+	+	+	+	–	–	+		–	+			±	±	+
gravity	–	–		–	–	+	+	+	+	–	–			–		+	+	+	–	+					–	+	–	+	
continuousness	–	–	±	+	+	–	–	+	+	–	–	±	±	+	+	–		+				–	+	+					
voicing	–	+		–	+	–	+	–	+	–	+	–	+	–	+	–	+												

	1	2	3	4
High-tone	–	–	+	+
Length	–	+	–	+

It is, for example, not justifiable that /d/, /b/ and /đ/, and only those, be specified as [-nasal], as opposed to /n/, /m/ and /ń/, which are [+nasal]. There are, namely, two important differences between the former and the latter: the former are distinctively [-continuous] and [+voiced], whereas the latter are only predictably so. These signs are consequently present in the former distinctive feature sets, and absent in the latter. This discrepancy makes /d/, /b/ and /đ/ on the one hand, and /n/, /m/ and /ń/ on the other, not participate in minimal pair oppositions of the type /d/ vs. /n/, /b/ vs. /m/, and /đ/ vs. /ń/. There is consequently no ground for specifying /d/, /b/ and /đ/ as [-nasal].

The same can be said about Jakobson's specifying /k/ as [-continuous], and leaving /g/ unspecified for *continuousness:* only the former is apparently compared with /x/, which is [+continuous]. The problem is only that /k/ and /x/ are strictly speaking not mutually comparable in the sense of potentially forming a minimal pair, as Jakobson himself has left /x/ unspecified for *voicing,* whereas /k/ is [-voiced]. In Jakobson's specification, there is no minimal opposition between any two of the following three segments: /k/, /g/ and /x/. In such a situation, distinguishing between the presence of a specification and its absence on the basis of the organization of the matrix itself is arbitrary.

Other indications are needed when there is no minimal pair opposition involved. In a way comparable to establishing that /s/ in Old Irish is unspecified for *voice* because it forms one class with other segments unspecified for *voice* as far as nasalization goes, and this is not contradicted by the remaining language phenomena, we must ask ourselves whether /x/ can be said to form one class with the segments which are unspecified for *voice* (i.e. *voicing* in Jakobson's terminology) in Serbo-Croatian. And here the answer is clearly: no, it does not. This shows up clearly in the *voice* assimilation phenomena, by which the sign for *voice* is omitted from a segment if the following segment either contains that sign or undergoes the same omittance due to its further following segment. No omittance occurs if the following segment by itself does not contain that sign. A segment in which the sign for *voice* is omitted, takes over the form of that sign from the following segment. There is, however, no opposition possible. This means that in Serbo-Croatian, only sequences such as [tk], [sk], [dg] and [zg] can occur, and no *[dk], *[zk], *[tg] and *[sg]. Preceding /m/, /n/, /ń/, /l/, /l'/, /r/, /v/, /j/ or a vowel, on the other hand, either voiced or voiceless consonants can occur, and there is an opposition between them so that it is capable of distinguishing words *ceteris paribus.* And how about /x/? Preceding /x/, only voiceless consonants can occur in Serbo-Croatian. This means that /x/ in Serbo-Croatian is characterized by the sign [-voice] (or [−voicing] in Jakobson's terminology). The Serbo-Croatian /x/ must consequently be specified for *voice* in the matrix, and not left unspecified for it, on the basis of the following data illustrations.

(4) Consonantal *voice* distribution and assimilation in Serbo-Croatian:
[otkázati] 'to say off'
[odgòditi] 'to put off'
[otxòditi] 'to walk away'
[ȍtrova] 'he/she/it poisoned'
[ȍdrova] 'he/she/it pulled away'

The (´) diacritic denotes the rising tonal accent on a long vowel, (`) denotes the rising tonal accent on a short vowel, (ˆ) the falling tonal accent on a long vowel, and (ˆˆ) the falling tonal accent on a short vowel.)

And how about the specifications for *continuous,* in the given case with respect to /g/? These specifications are more difficult to trace, but a unique decision can still be reached in each case. In Serbo-Croatian, the only indication can be derived from the distribution of that feature within a syllable by which a sequence of two [−continuous] segments which is interrupted by one unspecified for *continuous* always contains a syllable with the nucleus on the segment unspecified for *continuous.* Examples of it are found not only with vowels, which are predictably *continuous,* but also with sonorants, including nasals, which are – at least in Jakobson's (1949) and Chomsky and Halle's (1968) analysis – *noncontinuous.* An example of a nasal forming a syllable nucleus is found in the Serbo-Croatian pronunciation of the name *Eisenhower* as [ȁjznhauer], with a vocalic [n̥]. And how about /g/ in this respect, which is according to Jakobson unspecified for *continuous,* too? The Serbo-Croatian example [òdgdje] 'where from' contains only two syllables, with the nuclei on [o] and [e], and shows that there is no reason for viewing /g/ as unspecified for *continuous* in Serbo-Croatian. On the basis of these data, it must be specified as [−continuous].

Jakobson's '±' specifications for *continuousness* in the case of [c], [č] and [ǧ] are a different matter. They are due to nondistinguishing between a single phonological segment and the corresponding sequence, the parts of which have been established independently in the system as well. Jakobson did not investigate the relation between [c] and [t] + [s], [č] and [t] + [š], and [ǧ] and [d] + [ž]. If he had done so, he would have noticed that these sequences occur only with an intervening morpheme boundary between the constitutive parts. Within a morpheme, only [c], [č] and [ǧ] occur. This means that there is complementary distribution between [c] and [t] + [s], [č] and [t] + [š], and [ǧ] and [d] + [ž]. As [t], [d], [s], [š] and [ž] have been independently established as distinctive segments in the system already (i.e. as /t/, /d/, /s/, /š/ and /ž/), we are justified in using them to resolve the

Serbo-Croatian [c], [č] and [ǧ] into /Ts/, /Tš/ and /Tž/, i.e. into sequences of a [-continuous] segment which is followed by a [+continuous], and on the understanding that the feature *voice* is then omitted from the first of these consonants due to the *voice* assimilation rule formulated above. A segment in which a feature sign is omitted due to syntagmatic predictability of its form and absence of an opposition possibility, is transcribed by means of a capital. (This procedure for dissolving affricates into the constitutive segments in the absence of an opposition with these segments within a morpheme has been outlined by Ebeling (1960: 67 etc.)) The matter of opposition is basic to the outlined procedure. In the total absence of opposition, we are justified in analysing such complex speech sounds in terms of the corresponding sequences, but language variation points to the possibility of analysing them as single segments as well, if there is only one distinctive feature differentiation involved, and if the given feature is specified in the order 'unmarked, marked' in the sequence. Then it is a case of a diphthong in the sense of Andersen (1972). And markedness can be directly derived from the phonetic feature specifications such that '+' = 'marked' and '–' = 'unmarked', unless the paradigmatic or the syntagmatic context dictates the opposite. This will be further elaborated in the section on markedness. For the time being it will suffice to say that in the total absence of /Ts/, /Tš/ and /Tž/ sequences in a language, [c], [č] and [ǧ] are potentially single segmental diphthongs. They are analysed as such, though, only if (new) /Ts/, /Tš/ and /Tž/ sequences appear in that language as well.

As to the '±' specification of /r/ for *vocality*, it is due to nondistinguishing between the sonorant /r/ and the vowel /r̥/. They are mutually opposed in Serbo-Croatian, though, as has been shown by Brozović (1967: 421) on the basis of the distinction between *Istro* [ȉstro] 'vocative singular of *istra*, a peninsula in Croatia' and *istro* [ȉstr̥o] 'he/she/it wiped out'. The former is [-vocalic], and only the latter occurs as a syllable nucleus (i.e., the first example above has two syllables, and the second one has three syllables), and can be characterized by tone and vowel length. An extensive discussion of the distinctive features involved can be found in Gvozdanović (1980a: 113f.).

The remaining '±' specifications of Jakobson's are due to analysing the phonetic dimensions called *vocality* and *saturation* as containing only one distinctive feature opposition within a dimension, whereas there are rather two distinctive feature oppositions involved: [+vocality] vs. [-vocality] and [+consonantality] vs. [-consonantality] in the former case, and [+compact] vs. [-compact] and [+diffuse] vs. [-diffuse] in the latter. (This was later correctly understood by Jakobson, Fant and Halle (1952).) On the basis of these distinctive feature oppositions, the remaining '±' specifications can be resolved. The way in which they are resolved is not undiscussible in the case of *vocality* and *consonantality,* as *consonantality* is in fact a 'cover feature', i.e. a classificatory one, without a single phonetic correlate, as correctly established by Vennemann and Ladefoged (1973). Most authors analyse /l/ and /l'/ as [+vocalic, +consonantal], and they do the same with /r/. For Serbo-Croatian, this does not hold for /r/ anyhow, as we have seen above. And how about /l/ and /l'/ in that language? Well, they are different from /r/ in their capacity of forming a syllable nucleus in the pronunciation of foreign names such as *Vltava*, which is in Serbo-Croatian rendered as [vl̥̀tava], with a vocalic [l̥]. This vocalic [l̥] is apparently only a positional variant of the nonvocalic [l], as no opposition between them is found. It is consequently a single phonological segment, and not two opposed ones. In this respect, /l/ resembles /n/ in Serbo-Croatian, which can also show up as a syllable nucleus, as illustrated by the example [ȁjznhauer] mentioned above.

Classificatorily, it is reasonable to distinguish the segments which participate in *voice* assimilation from those which never participate in it on the basis of *consonantal*, itself a classificatory feature. The consequence is that /l/, /l'/, /m/, /n/, /ń/, /r/, /v/ and /j/ in Serbo-Croatian are [-consonantal]. As to specifying the [-consonantal] segments with respect to *vocalic,* only those which are opposed to a vowel with the same remaining features must be specified as [-vocalic]. In Serbo-Croatian, only /r/, /v/ and /j/ are consequently [-vocalic], whereas /l/, /l'/, /m/, /n/ and /ń/ are unspecified for *vocality.* Only the latter, and not the former, show up as syllable nuclei in the absence of a contiguous vowel; but if there is a contiguous vowel, it will automatically be the syllable nucleus and not the sonorant. This shows that /l/, /l'/, /m/, /n/ and /ń/ lack the sign for *vocality,* and can assume the form of that sign exclusively depending on the surrounding.

On the basis of these considerations, and if length and tone are taken into account, as they are capable of systematically distinguishing the forms of Serbo-Croatian *ceteris paribus* – and for tone, acoustic and perceptual data point to relevant contours rather than levels (cf. Gvozdanović (1980a)) – the following acoustic matrix of Serbo-Croatian can be presented. The application of the principles outlined above shows several systematic distinctions between the Ijekavian, or western, variant of Serbo-Croatian, and the Ekavian, or eastern, variant. They must be accounted for in the matrix.

(5) The distinctive feature matrix of Serbo-Croatian, if features are systematically viewed as signs; Ijekavian Serbo-Croatian (acoustic features):

	p	b	f	t	d	s	z	ć	đ	š	ž	k	g	x	m	n	ń	l	ľ	v	j	r	ȑ	r̂	r̀	ŕ	ȉ	î	ì	í	ȅ	ê	è	é	ȁ	â	à	á	ȍ	ô	ò	ó	ȕ	û	ù	ú
vocalic																				–	–	–					+	+	+	+	+	+	+	+	+	+	+	+	+	+	+	+	+	+	+	+
consonantal	+	+	+	+	+	+	+	+	+	+	+	+	+	+	–	–	–	–	–	–	–	–	–	–	–	–																				
compact				–	–	–	–	+	+	+	+	+	+	+		–	–	–	–		+										–	–	–	–	+	+	+	+	–	–	–	–				
diffuse	+	+	+	–	–	–	–								+	–	–	–	–	+							+	+	+	+	–	–	–	–					–	–	–	–	+	+	+	+
acute	–	–	–	+	+	+	+	+	+	+	+	–	–	–	–	–	+	–	+	–	+	+	+	+	+	+	+	+	+	+	+	+	+	+					–	–	–	–	–	–	–	–
nasal															+	+	+	–	–	–	–	–																								
continuous	–	–	+	–	–	+	+	–	–	+	+	–	–	+																																
voiced	–	+	–	–	+	–	+	–	+	–	+	–	+	–																																
long																							–	+	–	+	–	+	–	+	–	+	–	+	–	+	–	+	–	+	–	+	–	+	–	+
rising																							–	–	+	+	–	–	+	+	–	–	+	+	–	–	+	+	–	–	+	+	–	–	+	+

[c] = /Ts/, [č] = /Tš/, and [ǧ] = /Tž/ (in T, *voice* is omitted due to predictability). /x/ = between [x] and [h]. In the Ekavian variant, [ć] = /tj/, [đ] = /dj/, [ń] = /nj/, and [l'] = /lj/. In /ȑ/, /ȓ/, /r̀/ and /ŕ/ in both variants, either the features *long* and *rising* are specified, or the feature *vocalic*; an opposition with the [-vocalic] /r/ occurs only when preceding a vowel, and in that position, vowel length and tone are omitted (cf. Gvozdanović (1980a: 113f.)).

In comparison with Gvozdanović (1980a: 124), *vocalic* has been omitted from /l/, /l'/, /m/, /n/ and /ń/, and *continuous* from /l/, /l'/, /m/, /n/, /ń/ /v/, /j/ and /r/, and [-voiced] added to /x/, due to the fully systematic analysis outlined above. (The absence of [-compact, -diffuse] in /ȅ/, /ê/, /è/, /é/, /ȍ/, /ô/, /ò/ and /ó/ in Gvozdanović (1980a: 124) was due to a printer's error, now corrected.)

I have elaborated the Serbo-Croatian phonological analysis here in order to show that a solution for every single problem can be reached if distinctive features are consistently viewed as signs. And I have elaborated it here in order to show that the whole of a sound system fits together, the distinctive feature specifications of each set and its distributional properties. The view on distribution as reflecting the oppositions in a language has been advocated by Ebeling (1960), and as reflecting the distinctive features involved in the specification of sets by Andersen (1969). In addition to their methodological findings, I have proposed here a method for establishing which features are paradigmatically predictable (i.e. nonrelevant to a set), and which are distinctive (i.e. relevant to a set) in cases where neither phonetic incompatibility nor concomitance is involved.

1.2. Distinctive Feature Definitions

As I have stated above already, the definition of the form of the distinctive features must be left over to phoneticians, within the ramification of oppositions on which their meaning is based. Oppositions refer to the entire system and are by that property relative, not absolute.

Distinctive features must be defined phonetically in terms of relative values.

The distinctive features to be used in this study are based on Jakobson and Halle (1956) for the acoustic features, and on Chomsky and Halle (1968) for the articulatory ones, with modifications to be mentioned below.

(6) Acoustic distinctive features (Jakobson and Halle (1956: 29-32)):
Sonority features

1. *Vocalic/nonvocalic:* acoustically – presence vs. absence of a sharply defined formant structure; genetically – primary or only excitation at the glottis together with a free passage through the vocal tract.
2. *Consonantal/nonconsonantal:* acoustically – low vs. high total energy; genetically – presence vs. absence of an obstruction in the vocal tract.
3. *Compact/diffuse:* acoustically – higher vs. lower concentration of energy in a relatively narrow, central region of the spectrum, accompanied by an increase vs. decrease of the total amount of energy; genetically – forward-flanged vs. backward-flanged.
4. *Tense/lax:* acoustically – higher vs. lower total amount of energy in conjunction with a greater vs. smaller spread of the energy in the spectrum and in time; genetically – greater vs. smaller deformation of the vocal tract – away from its rest position.
5. *Voiced/voiceless:* acoustically – presence vs. absence of periodic low frequency excitation; genetically – periodic vibrations of the vocal cords vs. lack of such vibrations.
6. *Nasal/oral:* acoustically – spreading the available energy over wider vs. narrower frequency regions by a reduction in the intensity of certain (primarily the first) formants and introduction of additional (nasal) formants; genetically – mouth resonator supplemented by the nose cavity vs. the exclusion of the nasal resonator.
7. *Discontinuous/continuant:* acoustically – silence (at least in frequency region above vocal cord vibration) followed and/or preceded by spread of energy over a wide frequency region (either as burst or as a rapid transition of vowel formants) vs. absence of abrupt transitions between sound and such a silence; genetically – rapid turning on or off of source either through a rapid closure and/or opening of the vocal tract that distinguishes plosives from constrictives or through one or more taps that differentiate the discontinuous liquids like a flap or trill /r/ from continuant liquids like the lateral /l/.
8. *Strident/mellow:* acoustically – higher intensity noise vs. lower intensity noise; genetically – rough-edged vs. smooth-edged.
9. *Checked/unchecked:* acoustically – higher rate of discharge of energy within a reduced interval of time vs. lower rate of discharge within a longer interval; genetically – glottalized (with compression or closure of the glottis) vs. nonglottalized.

Tonality features

10. *Grave/acute:* acoustically – concentration of energy in the lower vs. upper frequencies of the spectrum; genetically – peripheral vs. medial.

11. *Flat/plain:* acoustically – flat phonemes [i.e. segments, in the terminology used here (J.G.)] in contradistinction to the corresponding plain ones are characterized by a downward shift or weakening of some of their upper frequency components; genetically – the former (narrowed slit) phonemes [i.e. segments (J.G.)] in contradistinction to the latter (wider slit) phonemes are produced with a decreased back or front orifice of the mouth resonator, and a concomitant velarization expanding the mouth resonator.
12. *Sharp/plain:* acoustically – sharp phonemes [i.e. segments (J.G.)] in contradistinction to the corresponding plain ones are characterized by an upward shift of some of their upper frequency components; genetically – the sharp (widened slit) vs. plain (narrower slit) phonemes exhibit a dilated pharyngeal pass, i.e. a widened back orifice of the mouth resonator; a concomitant palatalization restricts and compartments the mouth cavity.

Investigation of African and Asian languages shows us, however, that more features are needed for a full phonological analysis of the various inventories. Specifically, [+rhotacized] vs. [-rhotacized], defined by Ladefoged (1975: 266) as based acoustically on the lowering of the frequency of the third formant, and genetically a.o. on the retroflex tongue position, is found a.o. in Indo-Aryan, Ewe, Araucanian etc.; [+click] vs. [-click] is found e.g. in Zulu (cf. Ladefoged (1975: 260)); and [+creak] vs. [-creak] is a laryngeal feature occurring in Tibeto-Burman languages, analysable as complementary to [+checked vs. [-checked] defined under 9 in the above list, as it equals acoustically a low frequency periodic excitation, produced genetically by the vibration of a small section of the vocal folds (cf. Lehiste (1970: 58)); so-called 'pharyngeal' segments are according to Ladefoged (1975: 298) complementarily distributed with 'velarized' segments in the languages of the world, but according to Chomsky and Halle (1968: 305) they are distinctive in the Caucasian language Ubykh; it depends on the evaluation of Ubykh whether 'pharyngealized' must be accounted for in the distinctive feature list separately of 11 and 12 above. And there are possibly still other cases.

Linguistic analysis in the sense of the methodology presented above is crucial to accepting a phonetic form as a distinctive feature in all cases. By this analysis, so-called 'breathy' segments do not have a separate feature, but either contain the feature *tense* defined under 4 in the above list, or can be analysed as contiguous to /h/ (both possibilities are found in Tibeto-Burman languages spoken in Nepal).

A clear example of features lacking in the acoustic list defined by Jakobson and Halle (1956) (and preceding it by Jakobson, Fant and Halle (1952)) are prosodic features. The fact that their phonetic specification is relative rather than absolute does not distinguish them from the remaining features defined above.

Prosodic features comprise those of length and tone. They can be distinctive in a language and must consequently be added to the inventory of universally possible features, what the above list attempts to be.

The prosodic feature *long* is distinctive in a language if there are long vowels systematically – and not complementarily – distinguished from the corresponding single short ones, and from the corresponding sequences of two short ones. If the long vowels are only complementarily distinguished from the corresponding single short ones, length is nondistinctive in that language. If the long vowels are not distinguished from the corresponding sequences of two identical short vowels – either because the latter sequences do not occur at all, or because they occur only across morpheme boundaries whereas the long vowels occur only within a morpheme – and if the corresponding short vowels have been established independently of the sequences as well, then we are justified in analysing the long vowels as the corresponding vowel sequences. Such a language does not have [+long] vs. [-long] as a distinctive feature, but only /VV/ = [V̄] and /V/ = [V] (if (V) is used to denote any vowel, and (‒) denotes vowel length). Such a language has phonetic, but no phonological length.

An example of a language in which long vowels are not distinguished from the corresponding vowel sequences is found in Slavonian Serbo-Croatian, where two identical vowels are always pronounced as a single long one, even if there is an intervening morpheme boundary between them, as can be seen from examples b and c presented under (7) below. In the absence of an opposition, we are justified in analysing the phonetically long vowels as phonological sequences, as shown below.

(7) Slavonian Serbo-Croatian long vowels, and their nondistinctness from the corresponding sequences (data from Ivšić (1913: 184)):

a. [gra] 'beans, nominative singular'
b. [grâ] 'beans, genitive singular'
c. [dóʼdit] 'to come, imperfective'.

Analysis:

a. /gra/
b. /grȁ-a/
c. /do-òd-i-t/.

((-) denotes a morpheme boundary; phonologically, (̏) denotes the high tone, and (̀) the low tone; in the variety presented here, tone is distinctive on one vowel of a prosodic word, with the exception of the vowel of the final short syllable.)

Only a language in which long vowels are systematically distinguished from the corresponding sequences of two short ones *ceteris paribus,* has [+long] vs. [−long] as a distinctive feature. An example of such a language is found in Neoštokavian Serbo-Croatian, forming the basis of the standard language, as can be illustrated by (8) below.

(8) Neoštokavian (i.e. Standard) Serbo-Croatian long vowels and their systematic distinction from the corresponding sequences:

a.	[zóna]	'zone'
b.	[zònālnī]	'zonal'
c.	[zoòloškī]	'zoological'
d.	[nína]	'Nin, genitive singular'
e.	[nînskī]	'pertaining to Nin'
f.	[nijìnski]	'Nijinsky'.

((´) denotes the rising tonal accent on a long vowel, (`) the rising tonal accent on a short vowel, (ˆ) the falling tonal accent on a long vowel, (̏) the falling tonal accent on a short vowel, and (¯) denotes vowel length.)

Analysis:

a. /zón-a/
b. /zòn-āln-ī/
c. /zoòlo-Šk-ī/
d. /nín-a/
e. /nîn-Sk-ī/
f. /niìn Sk-i/

((´) denotes the rising tone on a [+long] vowel, (`) the rising tone on a [−long] vowel, (ˆ) the falling tone on a [+long] vowel, (̏) the falling tone on a [−long] vowel, (−) denotes a [+long] vowel, and capitals denote that the feature [+voice] vs. [−voice] has been omitted.)

Phonetically, there seems to be a difference in duration between long vowels which are phonologically sequences and long vowels which are phonologically single segments in the languages of the world (cf. the data presented by Lehiste (1970: 33f.)). Long vowels which are phonologically sequences, are phonetically approximately twice as long as the corresponding short – phonologically single – ones. Long vowels which are phonologically long because they are opposed to the corresponding sequences, on the other hand, are phonetically approximately 1.5 times as long as the corresponding short ones.

Tone can be distinctive in one syllable nucleus of a prosodic word, or potentially in all syllable nuclei, but usually restricted on the basis of morphemes. Tone-bearing segments can be vowels and sonorants, which occur as syllable nuclei. A prosodic word, which is the domain of tone phenomena, contains one or more free morphemes and the surrounding bound ones, if any (on the understanding that clitics may be viewed as relatively bound morphemes as well). Even in languages without any general restriction on tone distribution, a bound morpheme may lack tone, or tone may be omitted due to a morpheme combination.

On the basis of the methodology outlined above, tone which is capable of distinguishing the forms of a language *ceteris paribus* must be viewed as a distinctive feature in that language, also if its occurrence is restricted to one syllable nucleus of a prosodic word – be it any syllable, or e.g. any nonfinal syllable, or any syllable except a final open one (all these possibilities are found in Serbo-Croatian dialects) – or a syllable at a prosodic word boundary (an example of it is found in the Jabem language of New Guinea as referred to by Greenberg and Kaschube (1976: 4), where the vowel of the first syllable of a prosodic word is specified as having either low or high tone, and the same pitch is predictable on all of the following vowels within the same prosodic word).

I have made here a terminological distinction between 'tone' as a phonologically distinctive feature, and 'pitch' as a comparable phonetic feature which, however, lacks the status of a sign because it is predictable due to another feature at the same or a higher level.

Jabem illustrates predictability due to another feature potentially at the same level, but in the given language at the next-higher level, namely that of the prosodic word, because tone in Jabem marks the prosodic word boundaries. Pitch predictability due to a feature clearly at the next-higher level is triggered by 'stress' or 'accent' (in this study, I shall use the term 'accent' in order to refer indiscriminately to what is understood by either of these terms). Accent was shown by Ebeling (1960) and by Hattori in the fifties (but available in English in 1973), to be a feature of the word, capable of distinguishing e.g. the Russian word [mukȧ] 'flour', with the accent on the second syllable, from the Russian word [mu̇ka] 'torture', with the accent on the first syllable. It was, however, still listed by Chomsky and Halle (1968: 300) among the features defining phonological segments, and only relatively recent work on phonological hierarchies (done e.g. by Selkirk (1980)) proposed to view accent as the property of being the strong syllable of the strong foot of a prosodic word. It must be added to this statement, however, that if the strong syllable contains a sequence as its nucleus, either part of that sequence can be specified for accent and marked accordingly by means of a high pitch and/or longer duration. This is a possibility, not a necessity. But it is relevant because no such possibility is found if only single segments (establishable by the methodology outlined above) occur as syllable nuclei.

If in a language with phonological sequences as syllable nuclei, and only in such syllables, a rising contour is opposed to a falling one, this can be ascribed to a differential accent specification either on the first or the second segment of a sequence. These pitch contours are in that case predictable from accent. If, however, either more contours are found, or if they are also found in syllables which contain only a single segment as the nucleus, then pitch is also distinctive at the level of the segment and must consequently be analysed as a phonological feature of tone.

An example of the first type, with pitch contours predictable from accent, is found in Čakavian Serbo-Croatian, e.g. of the Vrgada type presented below. An example of the second type, with three pitch contours in syllables containing a sequence as the nucleus, and two pitch levels in syllables containing a single segment as the nucleus, can be found in Southeastern Slavonian Serbo-Croatian. The second rising pitch contour differs in Cerna Slavonian Serbo-Croatian from the rest of Southeastern Slavonian Serbo-Croatian by a smaller and relatively irregular pitch rise in the second part, so that it can be assumed that the specification of the first part is phonologically relevant.

(9) Vrgada Čakavian Serbo-Croatian, with pitch contour predictable from accent (data from Jurišić (1966: 77f.)):

a. [vodȁ] 'water, nominative singular'
[vȍdu] 'water, accusative singular'
[rūkȁ] 'hand, nominative singular'
[rūkẽ] 'hand, genitive singular'
[rûku] 'hand, accusative singular'
[rũk] 'hand, genitive plural'.

(Phonetically, (̏) denotes the – only possible – falling accent on a short vowel as a syllable nucleus, (̂) denotes the falling accent on a long vowel as a syllable nucleus, (̃) denotes the neoacute accent on a long vowel, and (̄) denotes vowel length; (̂) is *high* – *low*, and (̃) is *low* – *high*, thus phonetically different from the Neoštokavian contours.)

Analysis:
a. /vod-á/
b. /vód-u/
c. /ruuk-á/
d. /ruuk-eé/
e. /rúuk-u/
f. /ruúk/

((ˈ) denotes accent, and (–), a morpheme boundary.)

(10a) Cerna in Southeastern Slavonian Serbo-Croatian, where the first vowel of a sequence can have either the *high* or the *low* tone, or no tone, and the second vowel, either the *high* tone or no tone (data based on Ivić (1958: 288)):

a. [vòda] Same translations as above.
b. [vȍdu]
c. [rūka] (in the final syllable
d. [rūke̋] optionally [rūkȇ])
e. [rûku] (in the final syllable
f. [rũk] optionally [rũk]).

((ˋˋ) denotes the falling accent on a short vowel as a syllable nucleus, (ˋ) the rising accent on a short vowel as a syllable nucleus, (ˆ) the falling accent on a long vowel as a syllable nucleus, (˞) a modified rising one, which is *low* and variably *high* afterwards, and (˜) the neoacute, which is high in its second part; and (¯) denotes vowel length.)

Analysis:
a. /vòd-a/
b. /vód-u/
c. /rùuk-a/
d. /ruuk-eé/ (optionally /ruuk-èe/)
e. /rúuk-u/
f. /ruúk/ (optionally /rùuk/).

((´) denotes the *high* tone, and (`) the *low* tone, following the tradition of tone level denotation e.g. in African languages; (–) denotes a morpheme boundary. The distributional possibilities are: V́, V̀, V, V́V, V̀V, VV́, VV.)

(10b) The rest of Southeastern Slavonian Serbo-Croatian, where the first vowel of a sequence can have either the *high* tone or no tone, and the second vowel, either the *high* or the *low* tone, or no tone (data based on Ivić (1958: 289f.)):

a. [vòda] Same translations as above.
b. [vȍdu]
c. [rúka]
d. [rūkȇ]
e. [rûku]
f. [rũk].

The same prosodic signs are used as in 10a above, with the exception of (˞), for which (´) is used instead.

Analysis:
a. /vòd-a/
b. /vód-u/
c. /ruùk-a/
d. /ruuk-eé/
e. /rúuk-u/
f. /ruúk/

((´) denotes the *high* tone, (`) the *low* tone, and (–) denotes a morpheme boundary. The distributional possibilities are: V́, V̀, V, V́V, VV́, VV̀, VV.)

Whereas the Vrgada Čakavian pitch contours are predictable from accent in the way shown above, and consequently not ascribable to a distinctive feature of tone, both types of Southeastern Slavonian must be analysed as having tone, and accent can then be viewed as predictable from it (as it phonetically in general equals a change of the pitch contour, cf. also Gvozdanović (1980: 17)).

How to analyse the Southeastern Slavonian *high* vs. *low* tone: as [+high] vs. [-high], or as [+low] vs. [-low]? The phonetic characterization may clearly point to one of the two opposed specifications as the '+' one by allowing for less variation than the opposed one – as it does in Standard Slovenian of the Ljubljana type, where the *low* tone allows for less variation than the opposed *high* one (cf. Toporišič (1967)), or in Cerna Southeastern Slavonian, where the (˘) tonal accent consists of a clearly specified first *low* part and an unclearly specified second *high* part, thus pointing to the analysis of the whole as V̀V, as shown above – but usually we must take the distributional considerations into account as well in order to establish which of the two possible solutions may be considered the correct one with respect to language behaviour. The distributional considerations to be taken into account are then to be modelled on the basis of those supported by the phonetic considerations. A model is consequently to be found in cases such as establishing whether a segment is specified for *voice* or not, if there is no opposition in a language, as there is none in the case of the Serbo-Croatian /x/ segment discussed above. The segment which shows up in the absence of an opposition is – unless predictable from the surrounding, in which case it does not contain the given sign – analysed as containing the '–' specification there where the phonetic dimension is clearly decisive for it. From that case, we are allowed to generalize and assume that the relevant specification showing up in the absence of an opposition equals the '–' one. And on the basis of this approach, we can now analyse the Cerna tones as based on [+low] vs. [-low] with the distributional restriction of the full opposition to the first part of the sequence and possibility of the '–' specification on the second part, and the remaining Southeastern Slavonian tones as based on [+low] vs. [-low] as well, but with the distributional restriction of the full opposition to the second part of the sequence and possibility of the '–' specification on the first part. The established phonetic difference between the two types is consequently due to a different distributional restriction of what is phonologically the same feature. And we can see that phonological feature specification corresponds with relative phonetic stability, indeed.

What kind of evidence do we have for the statement that a language restricting its tone distribution to a single syllable in a prosodic word, restricts it to a tone-bearing segment within the syllable nucleus, thus fiting in with the output of the segmentation phenomena demonstrated by the examples under (7) above? As distributional criteria are circular here, only phonetic and variational ones can be taken into account.

Phonetically, the Southeastern Slavonian pitch contours differ e.g. from the Neoštokavian Serbo-Croatian ones in that the former are phonetically clearly combinations of levels, whereas the latter are clearly contours: the Neoštokavian falling tone is characterized by a pitch peak within the first half of the duration, usually within the first third of the duration, whereas the rising tone is characterized by a pitch peak within the last third of the duration. This fits in with the segmental analysis, by which Slavonian long vowels are sequences, and Neoštokavian ones, single units, as shown under (7) and (8) above.

Variationally, the restriction of tone to one – independently established – segment in a syllable nucleus can be illustrated by tone development in Latgalian Latvian and Low Latvian, as distinguished from the remaining Latvian dialects.

The Baltic language Latvian is generally characterized by three pitch contours in syllables containing a long vowel or a diphthong as its syllable nucleus. The long vowels and diphthongs are phonologically sequences, and the contours are the following ones (cf. also Gvozdanović (1983d: 59, 83)): the so-called 'broken' tone, phonetically consisting of a *low* and a *high falling* part, the 'falling' tone, consisting of a *high* and a *low* part, and the so-called 'sustained' tone, which is presumably throughout *low*. Given the general implementation rule by which the pitch after a *low* tone automatically rises, and after a *high* tone automatically falls – taken into consideration in the analysis of Southeastern Slavonian as well – we can analyse the Latvian tones as follows: the broken tone = V̀V, the falling tone = V́V, and the sustained tone = VV̀. What kind of evidence do we have that this is a plausible analysis indeed, rather than viewing the entire tones as distinctive features? The evidence comes from variational treatment of these tones which relates them to two units.

Latgalian Latvian and Low Latvian have namely both eliminated one of the three pitch contours on syllable nuclei containing a sequence, but in a different way. Latgalian Latvian now has only the broken tone and the falling one, the sustained tone having merged with the latter (cf. Breidaks (1972: 94)). Low Latvian, on the other hand, now has only the broken tone and the sustained one, the falling tone having merged with the former. In other words, Latgalian now has an opposition between the broken contour (i.e. phonetically *low* + *high*) and the falling contour (i.e. phonetically *high* + *low*, historically originating from *high* + *low* and *low* + *low*). Low Latvian, on the other hand, now has an opposition between the broken contour (i.e. phonetically *low* + *high*, historically originating from *low* + *high* and from *high* + *low*, which could merge presumably due to the phonetic *low* + *high falling* specification of the broken tone) and the sustained contour (i.e. phonetically *low* + *low*).

The Low Latvian contours are apparently distinguished on the basis of the second part of the sequence, whereas the Latgalian Latvian contours can be distinguished on the basis of either part. The development seems to point to the second part as the relevant one in Latgalian Latvian, but the phonetic implementation points to the first part as the relevant one in so far as it is lengthened, and lengthening is a phonetic cue of accentedness, predictable on the basis of tone. Specifically, the first part of the broken contour is lengthened in Latgalian, whereas its second part is lengthened in Low Latvian, showing that this lengthening is not a generally predictable characteristic of the broken contour. It must consequently be viewed as significant.

Phonetically, the broken contour of Latgalian has a relatively stable specification, whereas the falling contour can vary considerably (according to Breidaks (1972)). This points to the broken contour as containing the '+' specification of the relevant feature. Given the relevance of the first part of the contour as established above, we can conclude that Latgalian Latvian has the tone feature [+low] vs. [-low], relevant to the first vowel of a sequence within a syllable nucleus. The [-low] tone allows for more variation, and this is why historically, too, the distinction between the *high* pitch of the first part of the falling contour and the *low* pitch of the first part of the sustained contour could be disregarded: the *low* pitch of the first part of the sustained contour was predictable (as it is in Latvian in general, where the second part is distinctive), and could presumably vary, too.

The contours of Low Latvian, on the other hand, are apparently distinguished on basis of the second part (which is the only different one between the broken and the sustained contours). Does it have the [+low] vs. [-low] tone there, or the [+high] vs. [-high] tone? The historical development, by which the distinction between the nondistinctive *high* (i.e. *high falling*) pitch of the second part of the broken contour and the nondistinctive *low* pitch of the second part of the falling contour could be disregarded (as these levels were predictable and presumably variable, given the relevant specification on the first part, as shown above for Latvian in general), point to the [+low] vs. [-low] tone as relevant on the segment of a syllable nucleus in Low Latvian.

To summarize: general Latvian has in syllables containing a sequence of two vowels or a vowel and a sonorant (represented by VV for all cases) the following possibilities: V̀V, V́V, VV̀ and VV; Latgalian Latvian has there: V̀V, V́V and VV; and Low Latvian has: VV̀, VV́ and VV.

Linguistic methodology is crucial for establishing the presence of a feature as a sign, but we can see that it is supported by phonetic and variational data.

Phonetic and variational data support the distinction between contours which are sequences of levels and contours which are single features as well. The distributional data fit in with the phonetic ones. An example of a distributional difference between the *rising* contour and the corresponding sequence of *low* + *high* levels (which I am further not able to evaluate) was given for the African language Kru by Fromkin (1974: 11f.). In Kru, successive high tones are lowered if they are preceded by a *low* tone, but they are not lowered if preceded by a *rising* tone. Fromkin concluded that contours can in principle be single features, distinguished from the corresponding sequences of levels.

I have shown for Neoštokavian Serbo-Croatian by means of perception tests (cf. Gvozdanović (1980a)) that the proposed analysis of the Neoštokavian contours as single features is not rejected by perception.

We can conclude that the features of tone can be either levels or contours, that they are reached at by means of the same methodology as the remaining features, and must consequently be included in the distinctive feature list. In addition to levels vs. contours, relevance of *concave* vs. *convex* contours assumed by Wang (1967) must further be investigated by means of the same methodology.

Acoustically, tone equals a fundamental frequency range, and genetically, it equals the rate of the vocal folds vibration, on the understanding that a relatively high rate corresponds with the *high* tone, and a relatively low rate with the *low* tone. In addition to these, *mid* may be a tone feature as well. For the contours as single features, the timing of the turning point of the fundamental frequency is relevant, in addition to its relevant height. And if *concave* vs. *convex* is relevant, too, this refers to the direction of the fundamental frequency change in addition to the turning point, and possibly also its height. Further genetic characteristics can be found in Lehiste (1970: 55 etc.).

The additional features defined above can be relevant in a language both acoustically and articulatorily.

As to the articulatory distinctive features, they have been defined by Chomsky and Halle (1968) as follows.

(11) Articulatory distinctive features (Chomsky and Halle (1968: 299-329)):

– *Major class features*

Sonorant-nonsonorant (obstruent); sonorants are sounds produced with a vocal tract cavity configuration in which spontaneous voicing is possible; obstruents are produced with a cavity configuration that makes spontaneous voicing impossible.

Vocalic-nonvocalic: vocalic sounds are produced with an *oral* cavity in which the most radical constriction does not exceed that found in the high vowels [i] and [u] and with vocal cords that are positioned so as to allow spontaneous voicing; in producing nonvocalic sounds one or both of these conditions are not satisfied.

Consonantal-nonconsonantal: consonantal sounds are produced with a radical obstruction in the midsaggital region of the vocal tract; nonconsonantal sounds are produced without such an obstruction.

– *Cavity features*

– *Primary strictures*

Coronal-noncoronal: coronal sounds are produced with the blade of the tongue raised from its neutral position; noncoronal sounds are produced with the blade of the tongue in the neutral position.

Anterior-nonanterior: anterior sounds are produced with an obstruction that is located in front of the palato-alveolar region of the mouth; nonanterior sounds are produced without such an obstruction. The palato-alveolar region is that where the ordinary English [š] is produced.

– *Features relating to the body of the tongue: high-nonhigh, low-nonlow, back-nonback.*

High-nonhigh: high sounds are produced by raising the body of the tongue above the level that it occupies in the neutral position; nonhigh sounds are produced without such a raising of the tongue body.

Low-nonlow: low sounds are produced by lowering the body of the tongue below the level that it occupies in the neutral position; nonlow sounds are produced without such a lowering of the body of the tongue.

Back-nonback: back sounds are produced by retracting the body of the tongue from the neutral position; nonback sounds are produced without such a retraction from the neutral position.

– *Rounded-nonrounded:* rounded sounds are produced with a narrowing of the lip orifice; nonrounded sounds are produced without such a narrowing.

– *Distributed-nondistributed:* distributed sounds are produced with a constriction that extends for a considerable distance along the direction of the air flow; nondistributed sounds are produced with a constriction that extends only for a short distance in this direction.

– *Covered-noncovered:* we shall assume that covered sounds are produced with a pharynx in which the walls are narrowed and tensed and the larynx raised; uncovered sounds are produced without a special narrowing and tensing in the pharynx.

– *Secondary apertures*

Nasal-nonnasal: nasal sounds are produced with a lowered velum which allows the air to escape through the nose; nonnasal sounds are produced with a raised velum so that the air from the lungs can escape only through the mouth.

Lateral-nonlateral: this feature is restricted to coronal consonantal sounds; lateral sounds are produced by lowering the mid section of the tongue at both sides or at only one side, thereby allowing the air to flow out of the mouth in the vicinity of the molar teeth; in nonlateral sounds no such side passage is open.

– *Manner of articulation features*

Continuant-noncontinuant (stop): in the production of continuant sounds, the primary constriction in the vocal tract is not narrowed to the point where the air flow past the constriction is blocked; in stops the air flow through the mouth is effectively blocked.

Release features: instantaneous release-delayed release: these features affect only sounds produced with closure in the vocal tract; there are basically two ways in which a closure in the vocal tract may be released, either instantaneously as in the plosives or with a delay as in the affricates; during the delayed release, turbulence is generated in the vocal tract so that the release phase of affricates is acoustically quite similar to the cognate fricative; the instantaneous release is normally accompanied by much less or no turbulence.

– *Supplementary movements*

Suction; clicks and implosives: since suction is produced by a downward movement of velar or glottal closures, it is necessary from a phonetic point of view to postulate two distinct suction features, one (the "click" feature) is associated with velar closure and the other (the "implosion" feature) with glottal closure; the clicks have primary constrictions in the dental and alveolar region, but there are also clicklike sounds which have a labial closure; moreover, there appear to be labiovelar suction sounds with glottal implosion.

Pressure: like most motions, pressure motions can be executed by the velar or by the glottal closure; we must therefore postulate two pressure features, a "velar pressure" feature and a "glottal pressure" feature; we shall refer to the latter by its traditional name "ejection", in view of its greater familiarity.

– *Tense-nontense* (lax): the feature "tenseness" specifies the manner in which the entire articulatory gesture of a given sound is executed by the supraglottal musculature; tense sounds are produced with a deliberate, accurate, maximally distinct gesture that involves considerable muscular effort; nontense sounds are produced rapidly and somewhat indistinctly;

in tense sounds, both vowels and consonants, the period during which the articulatory organs maintain the appropriate configuration is relatively long, while in nontense sounds the entire gesture is executed in a somewhat superficial manner.

– *Source features*

Heightened subglottal pressure: in discussions concerning tenseness it is usually observed that tense sounds are produced with greater subglottal pressure and that this fact accounts for the well-known presence of aspiration in the tense voiceless stops of many languages; since, however, the tenseness of the supraglottal muscles is evidently controlled by a different mechanism than is tenseness in the subglottal cavities, these two properties cannot be combined into a single phonetic feature; instead we must set up in addition to tenseness a feature of "heightened subglottal pressure".

Voiced-nonvoiced (voiceless): in order for the vocal cords to vibrate, it is necessary that air flow through them; if the air flow is of sufficient magnitude, voicing will set in, provided only that the vocal cords not be held as widely apart as they are in breathing or in whispering; as has been demonstrated in the various high-speed motion pictures of the vocal cords, glottal closure or a constriction of the glottis is not required for voicing; it is necessary only that the glottis not be wide open; on the other hand, vocal cord vibration will also result when the glottis is constricted, as long as there is an air flow of sufficient magnitude or the vocal cords are not held so tight as to prevent vibrating, as they are in the case of sounds produced with glottal constrictions.

Strident-nonstrident: strident sounds are marked acoustically by greater noiseness than their nonstrident counterparts; when the air stream passes over a surface, a certain amount of turbulence will be generated depending upon the nature of the surface, the rate of flow, and the angle of incidence; a rougher surface, a faster rate of flow, and an angle of incidence closer to ninety degrees will all contribute to greater stridency; stridency is a feature restricted to obstruent continuants and affricates; plosives and sonorants are nonstrident.

– *Prosodic features:* our investigations of these features have not progressed to a point where a discussion in print would be useful; some recent work by W. S-Y. Wang seems to us promising; for a report of some early results, see Wang (1967).

The citations present only the definitions offered by Chomsky and Halle (1968), not their full application or discussion. The same has been done with Jakobson and Halle's (1956) definitions.

The articulatory features defined by Chomsky and Halle appear to mirror to a large extent the acoustic features defined by Jakobson and Halle. This correspondence holds for the following pairs of articulatory and acoustic features:

articulatory (Chomsky and Halle (1968))	= acoustic (Jakobson and Halle (1956)):
vocalic-nonvocalic	*vocalic-nonvocalic*
consonantal-nonconsonantal	*consonantal-nonconsonantal*
coronal-noncoronal	*acute-grave* in consonants
anterior-nonanterior	*noncompact-compact* in consonants
high-nonhigh	*diffuse-nondiffuse*
low-nonlow	*compact-noncompact* in nonconsonants
back-nonback	*grave-acute*
rounded-nonrounded	*flat-plain*
nasal-nonnasal	*nasal-nonnasal*
lateral-nonlateral	*liquid* (Jakobson, Fant and Halle (1951: 19))
continuant-noncontinuant	*continuous-discontinuous*
release of the glottal closure	*checked-unchecked*
tense-nontense (lax)	*tense-lax*
voiced-nonvoiced	*voiced-voiceless*
strident-nonstrident	*strident-mellow*
distributed-nondistributed	*sharp-plain* (+ undefined *retroflex-nonretroflex*).

In addition to these, Chomsky and Halle have introduced the following features: *sonorant-nonsonorant,* in order to account for the distinction between vowels, glides, nasals and liquids as sonorant on the one hand, and stops, fricatives and affricates as nonsonorant on the other; *covered-noncovered,* in order to account for vowel harmony in West African languages which systematically distinguishes a narrowed and tensed pharynx from the absence of these characteristics; *instantaneous release-delayed release,* in order to distinguish between plosives and affricates; *suction,* in order to account for *clicks* and *implosives* of African languages; *pressure,* in order to account for *ejectives* found in India, in the Caucasus and in American Indian languages; *heightened subglottal pressure,* in order to account for aspirated stops – e.g. of Korean – which are not executed by the supraglottal musculature, but are rather due to subglottal pressure; and they have stated the necessity of adding *prosodic features* to the list, without being able to define them.

Both lists – the articulatory and the acoustic one – aim at presenting the distinctive features which are possible in the languages of the world. Each language chooses a set of distinctive feature oppositions out of the possible ones.

The authors of both lists assume that if a language has a distinctive sound (i.e. 'segment'), it is always due to the same distinctive feature constellation. For example, all of them classify vowels and liquids as vocalic, whereas glides, nasal consonants, and obstruents, as well as voiceless vowels and liquids, are nonvocalic. Also, liquids, nasal consonants and nonnasal consonants are consonantal, whereas all vowels and glides are nonconsonantal. (cf. the matrix in 1.4.) Finally, in Chomsky and Halle's (1968: 302f.) classification, this is crosscut by the feature opposition *sonorant-nonsonorant,* by which all vowels, glides, liquids and nasals are sonorant, whereas only nonnasal consonants are nonsonorant.

Language investigation shows, however, that the way in which these segments behave with respect to syllabicity is partly language-specific, and in a way which does not correspond with the boundary of either of those feature oppositions. Specifically, Rubach (1977: 76 etc.) showed that in the elliptic code in Polish, nasals more readily occur as syllable nuclei (i.e. as vocalic segments) than liquids do (under the same condition of a neighbouring unaccented vowel being omitted). He concluded (1977: 76) that as distinguished from English, "*in Polish liquids seem to be weaker than nasals: they do not become syllabic very readily and* [*r*] *in Polish is phonetically an obstruent; thus the strength order in Polish is the following: vowels – glides – nasals – liquids – fricatives – stops*".

I have shown in the preceding section already that in Serbo-Croatian, nasals syllabify as readily as do liquids. Glides, on the other hand, do not syllabify, because they are opposed to the corresponding vowels /i/ and /u/ in Serbo-Croatian.

These language-specific differences must be related to different distinctive feature specifications, due to the distinctive segments which are present in a given system.

I conclude that it is possible indeed to present a universal list of possible distinctive features employed in the inventories of the various languages of the world, but that it is not possible to present a universal classification of the attested distinctive segments in terms of distinctive features. For each case, the distinctive features involved must be established on the basis of the oppositions operative in the system, and by means of the methodology presented above.

The next matter I want to discuss are the cavity features "high", "low", "back", "anterior" and "coronal", defined by Chomsky and Halle in order to mirror the acoustic features "diffuse", "compact", "grave", "diffuse" in consonants, and "acute" in consonants, respectively. For vowels, the height and "back" vs. "front" features had been present in the traditional phonetic literature already, but Chomsky and Halle proposed to use these features, in addition to "anterior" and "coronal", for consonants as well, in order to replace the traditional articulation place features "labial", "dental", "alveolar", "palatal" and "velar". Except for the relation to the acoustic features, no clear motivation for this replacement can be found, and even the parallellism with the acoustic features is not a full one in this sense that "anterior and "coronal" are not applicable to vowels (with the exception of so-called retroflex vowels which are found in some languages of India, and classifiable as [+coronal]), whereas the acoustic features are in principle applicable to all the segments of a language. Furthermore, the articulation place features were not the only ones traditionally used for classifying non-vowels. Instead of these, also features based on the articulator, actively participating in the articulation, had been proposed in the literature. The features based on the articulator are: *labial* (with the lower lip as the articulator), *apical* (with the tip of the tongue as the articulator), *laminal* (with the blade of the tongue as the articulator), *central* (with the center of the tongue as the articulator), *dorsal* (with the back of the tongue as the articulator), and those involving the tongue root, apparently relevant to the West African vowel harmony for which Chomsky and Halle proposed the feature *covered-noncovered,* but which is according to Lindau (1975) *expanded-nonexpanded,* relating to the size of the pharynx.

By means of these features, Cohen *et al.* (1969, 4th: 43) had given the following classification of the Dutch consonants:

"labial": /v/, /f/, /b/, /p/, /m/;
"apical": /z/, /s/, /d/, /t/, /n/;
"dorsal": /γ/, /x/, (g), /k/, /ŋ/.

The first two columns consist of spirants, the second two ones of stops, and the fifth column consists of nasals. In addition to that, the first and third columns consist of voiced consonants, and the second and fourth columns of voiceless ones.

We can see that there is a basic difference between the features "labial", "apical" and "dorsal" on the one hand, and e.g. "voiced" vs. "voiceless" on the other. Whereas the latter consist of two opposed values and can directly be translated into a binary framework, the former consist of three values, which can be used in order to positively specify a segment, but the possibility of a negative usage (e.g. of replacing "apical" by [-labial, -dorsal]) is not by itself evident.

There is thus a basic difference between the traditional features and Chomsky and Halle's: the latter are conceived of as throughout binary, whereas the former are not evidently fully translatable into a binary framework.

The phonetically based view on nonbinarism of features where the phonetic substance does not dictate binarism, has been advocated by Ladefoged (1975: 239 etc.), who assumed that the articulation place features, i.e. "labial", "dental", "alveolar", "palatal" and "velar", and the vowel height features, i.e. "maximum", "4 height", "3 height", "2 height" and

"1 height" are in a principled way multivalued. In addition to these, he also considered "approximant" to be the third value of "stop", applicable to liquids, glides and vowels, as distinguished from the remaining two values, "stop" and "fricative", applicable to the remaining segments.

The crucial question for evaluating these proposals is: does a language ever classify features which are phonetically in principle multivalued in a binary way, and what kind of evidence can be found for that?

I have investigated this matter for Serbo-Croatian by applying the traditional phonetic features in the potentially multivalued cases (the feature "stop" not considering to be multivalued, due to predictability of the so-called value "approximant" in the segments in which it occurs), on the understanding that the Serbo-Croatian vowels do not offer a real test case for the vowel height features due to only three degrees of aperture relevant to them, which can in principle always be translated into two binary distinctive feature oppositions. A test case is provided only by segments which are phonetically classifiable by means of more than three characteristics, which means that a possible resolution into binary oppositions does not simply follow, but must rather be related to other feature characteristics observable in that language if any.

In Serbo-Croatian, the following phonetic features are relevant to classification:

a) articulator place features:
"labial": /p/, /b/, /f/, /m/, /v/;
"apical": /t/, /d/, /s/, /z/, /n/, /l/, /r/;
"laminal": /c/, /đ/, /š/, /ž/, /ń/, /ĺ/, /j/;
"dorsal": /k/, /g/, /x/, /j/;

b) articulation place features:
"labial": the same segments;
"alveolar": the same segments;
"palatal": the same segments;
"velar": the same segments.

(/f/ and /v/ are not considered to form a pair in Serbo-Croatian, as the former does participate in the voice assimilation rules, whereas the latter does not participate in them.)

We can see that there is a full classificatory parallellism between the articulator place features and the articulation place features. In Serbo-Croatian, either of them can form the basis of the analysis.

If we, however, consider parallelism with the acoustic features, then we can see that the acoustic features defined by Jakobson, Fant and Halle (1952) and Jakobson and Halle (1956) are applicable to the entire sound system of a language, whereas out of the articulatory phonetic features considered above, only the articulator place features are in principle applicable to vowels: vowels are formed without constrictions in the oral cavity, and consequently cannot be defined on the basis of the articulation place where a constriction is formed. Only the articulator place features can mirror the acoustic features defined above.

As to the rules of feature omittance, only the feature "apical" (or "alveolar") is omitted preceding a laminal (or palatal) (nonnasal) consonant. And it is omitted only in the nonlabial (and nondorsal) fricatives (i.e. continuants, in Chomsky and Halle's terminology) preceding a laminal (or palatal) consonant in Serbo-Croatian, as only laminal consonants are allowed in that position. The rule by which the phonetic feature "apical" (or "alveolar") is omitted can be illustrated by the Serbo-Croatian examples *mast* 'fat, nominative singular' vs. *mašću* 'fat, instrumental singular', with the distinction between /s/ and /š/ automatically omitted preceding /ć/ (as directly reflected by the script in the given examples).

The omittance of "apical" when there is no opposition to "laminal" is a relevant indication for considering "apical" as [-laminal]; and the dependence of this rule on the specification as "nonlabial" is a relevant indication for considering "apical" as [-labial] as well. "Laminal" and "labial" are consequently both evaluated as binary in Serbo-Croatian, and "apical" is apparently analysed in that language as [-labial, -laminal]. If one would like to write a rule for the omittance of the opposition between [-laminal] and [+laminal] in the given environment, the rule would have the following shape:

$$[\alpha\,\text{laminal}] \rightarrow [\phi\,\text{laminal}] \;/\; \begin{bmatrix} \text{+consonantal} \\ \text{-labial} \\ \text{+continuant} \end{bmatrix} \_\_\_\_ \begin{bmatrix} \text{+consonantal} \\ \text{+laminal} \end{bmatrix}.$$

(Note the difference between this notation, with an explicit difference between distinctive and predictable specifications, and generative notation, by which the predictable specification as [+laminal] would show up in the rule, instead of [ϕ laminal]. Here it is specified by means of a general rule that in cases of sign omittance, the form is taken over from the following segment of the same major class.)

On the basis of these findings, and given the fact that the articulator place features are usable for vowels as well, whereas the articulation place features are not, I have proposed an articulatory feature matrix of Serbo-Croatian (1980a: 123) in which the features "labial" and "laminal" are used as binary. The same has been tentatively proposed for "dorsal" in the vowels, in order to distinguish /a/ as [-dorsal] from /o/, which is [+dorsal], and assuming that omittance of this feature can account for the back realization of /a/ found in various Serbo-Croatian dialects. Strictly speaking, though, there is no support for this analysis within the standard language, so I propose now to omit the specification of /a/ as [-dorsal]. And the same holds for its originally proposed specification as [-laminal], in opposition to /e/, which is [+laminal]. I now propose to leave /a/ unspecified for both these features, and to have only the positive specifications for vowels.

(12) The distinctive feature matrix of Serbo-Croatian, if features are systematically viewed as signs; Ijekavian Serbo-Croatian (articulatory features, including the articulator place features):

	p	b	f	t	d	s	z	ć	đ	š	ž	k	g	x	m	n	ń	l	l′	v	j	r	ȑ	ȓ	r̀	ŕ	ȉ	î	ì	í	ȅ	ê	è	é	ȁ	â	à	á	ȍ	ô	ò	ó	ȕ	û	ù	ú
vocalic																				−	−	−					+	+	+	+	+	+	+	+	+	+	+	+	+	+	+	+	+	+	+	+
consonantal = obstruent	+	+	+	+	+	+	+	+	+	+	+	+	+	+	−	−	−	−	−	−	−	−	−	−	−	−																				
labial	+	+	+	−	−	−	−								+	−		−		+	−	−	−	−	−	−																	+	+	+	+
laminal				−	−	−	−	+	+	+	+					−	+	−	+		+	−	−	−	−	−	+	+	+	+	+	+	+	+												
dorsal												+	+	+							+						+	+	+	+									+	+	+	+				
nasal															+	+	+	−	−	−	−	−																								
continuant	−	−	+	−	−	+	+	−	−	+	+	−	−	+																																
voiced	−	+	−	−	+	−	+	−	+	−	+	−	+	−																																
long																							−	+	−	+	−	+	−	+	−	+	−	+	−	+	−	+	−	+	−	+	−	+	−	+
rising = stiff vocal cords																							−	−	+	+	−	−	+	+	−	−	+	+	−	−	+	+	−	−	+	+	−	−	+	+

[c] = /Ts/, [c] = /Tš/, and [ǧ] = /Tž/ (in T, *voice* is omitted due to predictability). /x/ = between [x] and [h]. In the Ekavian variant, [ć] = /tj/, [đ] = /dj/, [ń] = /nj/, and [ĺ] = /lj/. In /ȑ/, /r̂/, /r̀/ and /ŕ/ in both variants, either the features *long* and *rising* are specified, or the feature *vocalic;* an opposition with the [-vocalic] /r/ occurs only when preceding a vowel, and in that position, vowel length and tone are omitted (cf Gvozdanović (1980a: 113f.)). In comparison with Gvozdanović (1980a: 123), *vocalic* has been omitted from /l/, /l'/, /m/, /n/ and /ń/, and *continuant* (there: *continuous*) from /l/, /l'/, /m/, /n/, /ń/, /v/, /j/ and /r/, and [-voiced] added to /x/ due to its behaviour in the *voice* assimilation rules.

The status of *stiff vocal cords* (cf. Halle and Stevens (1971)) must further be investigated.

In Serbo-Croatian, *vocalic* and *consonantal* are mutually exclusive. This follows from potential syllabicity of its sonorants which are not opposed to a vowel *ceteris paribus.* Consequently, in both matrices of Serbo-Croatian, if a segment has the '+' specification for one of these features, the '-' specification of the other feature is predictable and thus omitted as a sign.

As to the relation between the proposed articulatory features of Serbo-Croatian and the acoustic ones, the following correspondencies can be established:

articulator place feature	=	acoustic feature
labial-nonlabial		*diffuse-nondiffuse*
laminal-nonlaminal		*acute, compact – noncompact* (in consonants)
		acute – *nonacute* (in vowels)
dorsal		*compact* (in consonants)
		no unique correlate in vowels, *noncompact.*

We can see that a direct relation between the articulator place features and the acoustic ones can be established exactly in those articulator place features which behave as binary with respect to the assimilation rules, whereas it is missing exactly in the feature which does not behave as binary in the syntagmatic rules. I take it as a proof of the correctness of the proposed analyses.

In addition to this, we can observe that the distinction between [+laminal] and [-laminal] is relevant in the [-labial] segments, whereas it is predictable in the [+labial] ones. No such relation holds between any other two conceivable feature oppositions, i.e. not between *labial* and *dorsal,* and also not between *laminal* and *dorsal,* in whatever direction. And in the case of asymmetry between *labial* and *laminal,* the direction of the asymmetry is relevant, too: we cannot reverse it, as *labial* is distinctive both in the

[+laminal] and [-laminal] segments. The established asymmetry consequently has the following shape:

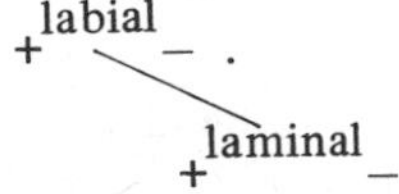

We can see that it equals hierarchy, such that *labial* is the dominating feature opposition, and *laminal* the subordinate one.

This leads to the conclusion that hierarchy is a relevant way in which a language can pattern the phonetic substance. In the absence of hierarchy, the phonetic substance is directly reflected by the language, and phonetically potentially multivalued features then show up as characterized by a single specification for each value, which corresponds with their nonparticipation in any of the potential language hierarchies.

This answer can be given to the controversy between Ladefoged's (1975) assumption that some features are always multivalued, and Chomsky and Halle's (1968) (as well as Jakobson and Halle's (1956)) assumption that all the distinctive features of a language are by necessity binary. The answer is that some features are potentially multivalued, and that it is a matter of the organization of a given language whether they are evaluated by that language as binary, or left unevaluated, in which case they are patterned as multivalued, directly reflecting the phonetic substance.

Hierarchy may thus be assumed to be a basic principle of ordering characteristic of the language system. In some cases, it is given by the phonetic substance in the sense of universal incompatibilities, such as incompatibility of the features *strident* and *vocalic*, but in a relevant amount of cases it is due to a language specific ordering.

Hierarchy equals asymmetrical ordering between two distinctive feature oppositions which is established whenever a feature opposition is distinctive in combination with one term (i.e. one distinctive specification) of another feature opposition, and predictable (or incompatible) with its other term.

This definition of hierarchy is in accordance with Brøndal's (1943) "principle of compensation", on which e.g. Andersen's (1975) definition of hierarchy was also based. There is a difference between the two approaches, however, in that mine is a restrictive – and thus testable – one. The approach advocated by Brøndal and Andersen views hierarchy as related to markedness and states that it is usually not the case that the terms of a subordinate opposition are combined with the marked term of the dominating one unless they are also combined with its unmarked term. Even if markedness is viewed as directly related to the phonetic specifications, my definition differs fundamentally from Brøndal's and Andersen's by stating that hierarchy is established only if the terms of one opposition are combined with one term of another opposition, but not with both its terms. In other words, I define hierarchy exclusively as equalling asymmetry, which can be established for each case on the basis of the distinctive feature system. Brøndal's and Andersen's definitions, on the other hand, allow the possibility of a hierarchy even if there is a full symmetry between two distinctive feature oppositions. For example, such a case would be established for *grave-acute* and *compact-diffuse* in a language which has *grave compact, grave diffuse, acute compact* and *acute diffuse* vowels, but on the basis of the system itself it would be impossible to establish which is the dominating feature opposition and which the subordinate one, and thus no testable hypotheses could be derived from it.

In my approach, hierarchy is defined exclusively on the basis of asymmetrical ordering. I assume that this is the only case of nontrivial ordering which can hold for pairs of distinctive feature oppositions (and possibly be transitive in addition). And by 'nontrivial' I mean 'not universally predictable from the phonetic substance', in other words, I am measuring it against its organizational value for the distinctive feature system.

Given this definition of hierarchy as equalling asymmetrical ordering, the following cases of feature hierarchy can be established for Serbo-Croatian on the basis of the matrices presented under (5) and (12).

(13) Articulatory distinctive feature hierarchies in Serbo-Croatian:

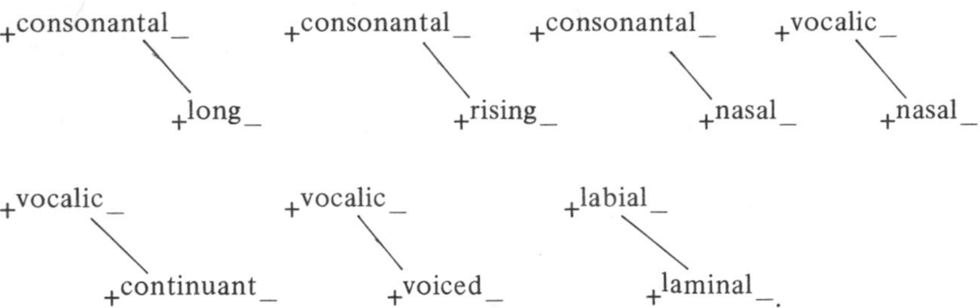

(14) Acoustic distinctive feature hierarchies in Serbo-Croatian:

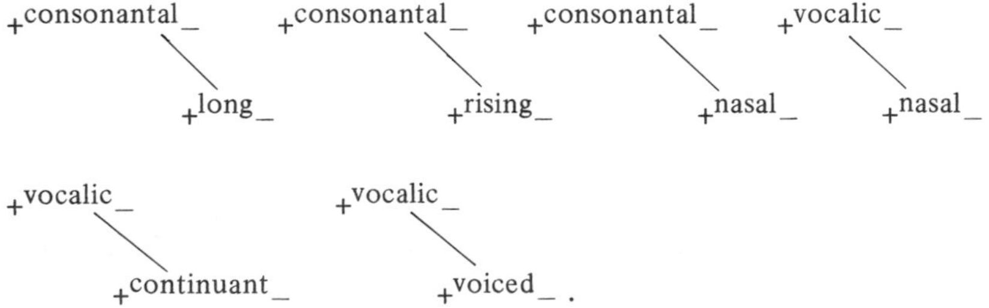

The remaining distinctive feature oppositions are either unordered or symmetrically ordered (the latter is found in the acoustic feature oppositions *compact* and *diffuse*), which are phonetically patterned within the same dimension.

We can see that ordering of the articulatory features is to a large extent parallelled by ordering of the acoustic ones: the only exception is found exactly in the articulation place features *labial* and *laminal,* which are ordered in the articulatory features, but their acoustic correlates are not mutually ordered. This points to a necessity of further investigating those features as to their adequacy.

Out of the ordered features (i.e. feature oppositions, as shown above), the articulatory features *long, nasal, voiced, labial* and *laminal* may in principle be unordered (i.e. relevant without restriction to only a group of the distinctive segments of a language); the same holds for the acoustic features *long, voiced,* and *nasal* (note that relevance of *acute* vs. *grave* only in the noncompact vowels is not analysed as a case of hierarchy, because the same restriction does not hold for the consonants, where the given feature oppositions are relevant, too).

It may be assumed on the basis of the asymmetrical treatment of the feature opposition *acute-nonacute* in the consonants and vowels that for the nonconsonants, this feature should presumably be replaced by *nongrave-grave.* If this is done, then the following acoustic hierarchy can be established (for the consonants only, but now in general for the system, as it is after the revision only in the consonants that the feature *acute-nonacute* plays a role):

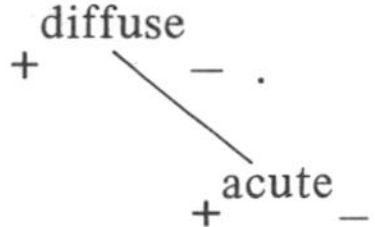

This hierarchy parallels the

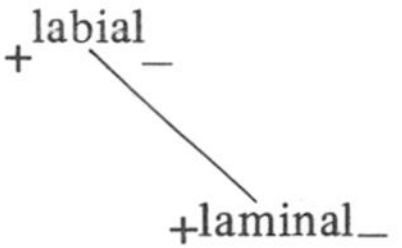

one in the articulatory features, and may be viewed as a serious candidate for the correct solution.

What kind of language data do we have in order to evaluate the proposed replacement of [+acute] vs. [-acute] by [-grave] vs. [+grave] in the [-consonantal] segments?

The indication comes again from the same consonant assimilation rule as already used for evaluating the "apical" segments in terms of distinctive features. Namely, the given rule can be formulated acoustically as omittance of the feature signs [+compact] and [-compact] in the [+acute,+continuous] segments, but only in the [+consonantal] ones, even though in the original conception neither of these feature oppositions could be analysed as related to the feature opposition [+consonantal] vs. [-consonantal]. In the revised conception, on the other hand, the rule can be formulated without reference to *consonantal,* and still automatically account for the absence of assimilation preceding a sonorant as e.g. in *sjedim* 'I am sitting', *sljepoća* 'blindness' or *snježan* 'snowy', and its presence in *mašću* 'instrumental singular of *mast,* fat' as discussed above. This may consequently be considered a plausible solution.

Still, this kind of motivation based on rules is in itself not free of circularity. Only independent variational facts can deliver the proof.

In the case of *acute* vs. *grave* as determining the vowel system of Serbo-Croatian, borrowings point to *grave* as being phonetically the more restricted one, indeed, because originally central vowels in borrowings are rendered in Serbo-Croatian as /i/, not as /u/. This holds even for the unround back central vowel [ɨ], so that the Russian name *Tynjanov* [tɨńànəf] is rendered in Serbo-Croatian as *Tinjanov* [tińánof], as it does also for the round central vowel [ü], which is rendered in Serbo-Croatian as [i], e.g. in the French borrowing *bureau* [büro], pronounced in Serbo-Croatian as [bȉrō], with the sounds and the tonal accent characteristic of the Serbo-Croatian system.

If *acute* and *grave* would be symmetrical, and thus equally possible in the classification, then one would expect a cut-off point in the middle of the phonetic dimension comprising [i] - [ü] - [ɨ] - [u], by which [ü] of the borrowings would be rendered as [i], and [ɨ] as [u]. What we find in Serbo-Croatian instead is an asymmetry by which /u/ is contrasted with the rest. This asymmetry within a distinctive feature opposition equals presence of a characteristic in the one case vs. its absence in the other case, with relatively more variation allowed in the former than in the latter case.

Only on the basis of such evidence we are justified in (re)analysing the Serbo-Croatian vowels as [+grave] vs. [-grave]. And we have an additional evidence of binarism as related to asymmetry within a distinctive feature opposition.

Note that the methodology proposed here follows the principles outlined by Winter as early as 1959, by which syntagmatic combination possibilities give the relevant indications as to paradigmatic evaluation of distinctive features. The importance of Winter's contribution was originally disregarded, though, and the relevance of the issue became clear only a decade later.

The main hypothesis for further phonological research can now be formulated as follows: the phonological system of a language exhibits asymmetrical ordering between the two terms of a distinctive feature opposition, and between two distinctive feature oppositions, which is to a language-specific extent imposed onto the phonetic substance, constraining it in a relevant way.

This hypothesis can be tested on the basis of constraints observable in variability and various types of language variation.

1.3. Variability in Relation to Asymmetry Within and Between Distinctive Feature Oppositions

As I have stated in the Introduction already, language variation occurs along horizontal (i.e. geographical) and vertical (i.e. social) dimensions, which can be mutually related in this sense that a variant characteristic of a geographic region can be associated with a given social group also independent of that region. Examples of it are found in standard languages which are based on a geographical region and at the same time associated with the higher social groups. When discussing variation, I shall not elaborate on these dimensions, but only state that they are relevant to the location of a phenomenon and the direction of change connected with it.

In addition to the horizontal and vertical variation, there is also variability, which I have defined in the Introduction as restricted to variation between (or among) codes within one speech community. It goes without saying that the codes within a speech community are related to the vertical dimension, and through it possibly also to the horizontal one, but I shall leave also these considerations out of the picture while discussing code differences, and restrict myself to stating that the dimensions defined above cause further subdifferentiation of the two main codes, the explicit and the elliptic one. So I shall be referring to variability only in terms of observable differences between the explicit code, used in formal speech situations, and the elliptic one, used in informal speech situations.

Does variability give any specific evidence for asymmetry within a distinctive feature opposition and asymmetry between distinctive feature oppositions?

Evidence for asymmetry within a distinctive feature opposition can be found in the Standard Dutch pronunciation of /v/, /z/ and /γ/, which are in the explicit code opposed to /f/, /s/, and /x/, respectively, as *voiced* vs.

voiceless. In the elliptic code, on the other hand, the pronunciation of the former varies between *voiced* and *voiceless,* whereas the pronunciation of the latter is always voiceless. From this we can conclude that in the elliptic code, /v/, /z/ and /γ/ are left unspecified for the distinctive feature *voiced*, whereas /f/, /s/ and /x/ are specified as [−voiced]. The absence of a sign for *voiced* in the former case accounts for the observed variability. Its absence accounts also for the full merger in some areas and social groups.

The variable pronunciation of /v/, /z/ and /γ/ in Standard Dutch shows that the *voiced* vs. *voiceless* opposition between /v/ and /f/, /z/ and /s/, and /γ/ and /x/ is an asymmetrical one, because one of the terms of the opposition has a constant specification, connected with a constant phonetic correlate, whereas the specification of the other term can be omitted, and its phonetic correlate is correspondingly variable if it is omitted indeed.

Code-triggered omittance of a distinctive feature specification parallels paradigmatic absence of a distinctive feature specification in that it is the '+' specification which may be absent, at least, if this is not contradicated by syntagmatic constraint.

The Dutch pronunciation of /v/, /z/ and /γ/ in the elliptic code as distinguished from the explicit one shows that the elliptic code differs from the explicit one by distinctive feature omittance, constrained in the sense of asymmetry within an opposition.

Another characteristic of the elliptic code in Dutch emerged from Blom and Van Uys's (1966) and Koopmans-van Beinum's (1980) studies of vowel contrast reduction in free conversation, as compared with the same vowels in isolated words. Koopmans-van Beinum (1980: 151) concluded that *"viewing the acoustic and perceptual data in combination . . . points to a decrease of contrast for unstressed vowels* [i.e. vowels in words in unstressed position, as stated precedingly in the author's text] *in free conversation which shows up on the one hand in a great degree of centring or neutralization, on the other in a certain amount of clustring in 'front vowels' and 'back vowels'".* On the other hand, when asked to generate acoustically the optimal Dutch vowels, the informants investigated by Blom and Van Uys appeared to generate them with all the maximal distinctions possible. This shows that the explicit code, with all the possibly relevant distinctions in a system, and the elliptic code, with a reduced number of distinctions, form a part of the competence of the same speakers, and that they can consequently be viewed as mutually related in a systematic way.

The possibility to omit some, but apparently not all the distinctive features in the elliptic code, must consequently be related to the different roles played by those features in the organization of the distinctive feature sytem. In order to investigate this, consider the entire distinctive feature matrix of Standard Dutch.

(15) Articulatory distinctive feature matrix of Standard Dutch:

	p	b	f	v	t	d	s	z	k	(g)	x	γ	h	j	l	r	m	n	ŋ	w	ɑ	a	ɛ	($\bar{\epsilon}$)	e	I	i	ə	ʌ	($\bar{\Lambda}$)	ö	ü	ɔ	($\bar{ɔ}$)	o	ò	u
vocalic													−	−	−	−	−	−	−	−	+	+	+	+	+	+	+	+	+	+	+	+	+	+	+	+	+
consonantal	+	+	+	+	+	+	+	+	+	+	+	+	−	−	−	−	−	−	−	−																	
low																					+	+	−	−	−			−	−	−	−		−	−	−		
high																							−	−	−	+	+	−	−	−	−	+	−	−	−	+	+
back	−	−	−	−	−	−	−	−	+	+	+	+	+	−	−	−	−	−	+	−			−	−	−	−	−	−	−	−	−	−	+	+	+	+	+
round																					−	−	−	−	−	−	−	−	−	−	+	+					
tense																					−	+	−	−	+	−	+	−	−	+	+	+	−	−	+	−	+
coronal	−	−	−	−	+	+	+	+						−	+	+	−	+		−																	
nasal																−	+	+	+																		
continuant	−	−	+	+	−	−	+	+	−	−	+	+	+	+	+	−	−	−	−	+																	
voiced	−	+	−	+	−	+	−	+	−	+	−	+																									
long																							−	+					−	+			−	+			

The occurrence of (g), ($\bar{\epsilon}$), ($\bar{\Lambda}$) and ($\bar{ɔ}$) is restricted to borrowings. /ò/ is used only in the northern and eastern areas, and not in the main, central areas. /ɑ/ and /a/ are assumed to be unspecified for *back,* following Cohen et al. (1969, 2nd: 43). Dutch diphthongs [ɛi], [ɑu] and [ʌü] are phonologically sequences, as there is no opposition between these diphthongs and the corresponding sequences.
The sonorants /j/, /l/, /r/, /m/, /n/, /ŋ/ and /w/, and in addition to them /h/, are considered to be [-consonantal] on the basis of comparable classificatory arguments as in Serbo-Croatian, which are not contradicted by the phonetic ones. They are [-vocalic] as they are incapable of forming syllable nuclei (e.g. *Eisenhower* is in Dutch pronounced as [ájzənhauər]). I derive the different specification of /l/ and /r/ for *continuant* from the Dutch pronunciation of *melk* 'milk' either as [mɛlk] or [mɛ́lək], but of *merk* 'mark' only as [mɛ́rək].

(16) Articulatory distinctive feature hierarchies in Dutch:

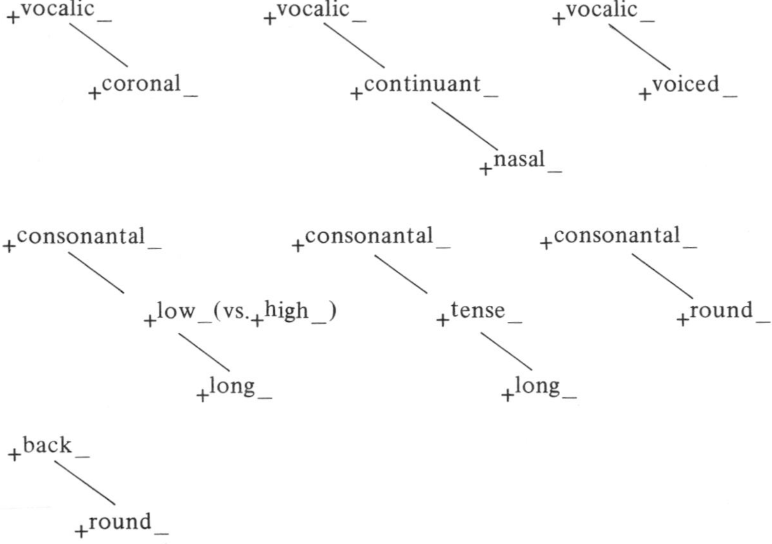

The remaining distinctive feature oppositions are either unordered, or – if patterned within one phonetic dimension – symmetrically ordered. Symmetrical ordering is found in the case of *low* vs. *high,* where the '+' specification of one of them makes the '–' specification of the opposite feature predictable. Due to the proposed analysis of the sonorants, by which /r/ and /l/ cannot be claimed to be [+vocalic] in comparison with the nasals and glides, which are [-vocalic], and also not [+consonantal] in comparison with the glides, which are [-consonantal], but rather all of them are assumed to be [-vocalic, -consonantal], the distinctive feature oppositions *vocalic* and *consonantal* can also be viewed as symmetrically ordered, but this is more of a classificatory than a purely phonetic matter. And its classificatory nature can be justified in view of *consonantal* being basically a classificatory feature.

Except for the marginally occurring nonlow lax long vowels (ɛ̄), (ʌ̄) and (ɔ̄) (not present in Blom and Van Uys's and Koopmans-van Beinum's materials), which further extend two of the existing hierarchies as can be seen above, we can see that within the Dutch vowels, only one distinctive feature hierarchy holds, by which [+back] vs. [-back] is the only dominating vowel feature opposition. And this matches exactly with the findings of the phoneticians mentioned above by which *back* vs. *front* is the only vowel feature relatively well preserved in free conversation, representing the elliptic code in Dutch as defined above. The fact that this is supported by acoustic and perceptual data has its distinctive feature correlate in the mirrorring of the articulatory feature *back* by the acoustic feature *grave*.

On the basis of these variability data, showing relevance of asymmetrical patterning between distinctive feature oppositions, we can now formulate the following hypothesis about the constraints it exerts:

- a specification for a subordinate or unordered feature opposition can be changed or omitted without any consequence for its dominating or other feature oppositions,

  but
- a change or omittance of a specification for a dominating feature opposition has consequences for its subordinate one(s) which follow from the asymmetrical implication holding between them.

1.4. Phonological Speach Errors in Relation to Asymmetry Within and Between Distinctive Feature Oppositions

Another type of variability, neither aiming at being communicated nor resulting from communication, but still apparently giving relevant indications as to the organization of the language system, are speech errors.

That speech errors 'do not just happen, but are caused', has been noticed by Meringer (1908) already, and later further investigated by Morton (1964), Cohen (1966), Nooteboom (1969), Fromkin (1971) and others. Especially

Cohen pointed to errors as indicative of linguistic units in speech monitoring, and Fromkin's further research along the same lines presented data on their relevance at all levels, viz. distinctive segments, morphemes, words, and higher-level units, as processing units in speech production and perception. Segmental errors were shown a.o. by Fromkin to involve either only one distinctive feature or a limited number of them. Fromkin hypothesized that there might be some hierarchy involved, but did not investigate it further.

I shall investigate now the matter of segmental speech errors in relation to distinctive feature hierarchy defined as asymmetrical ordering as formulated above, on the basis of the general hypothesis (following Cohen and others) that speech errors do not just happen, but are caused by the mechanisms of speech production and perception, and constrained by the underlying language system. And I shall do so on the basis of segmental error data collected in spontaneous American English by Fromkin (1971) and Shattuck-Hufnagel and Klatt (1979), and explicitly discussed in relation to a lacking adequate linguistic model by the latter authors.

Shattuck-Hufnagel and Klatt (1979) studied 1620 spontaneous segmental errors and compared the most frequent nonvocalic intrusions (i.e. the segments actually realized) with their targets (i.e. the corresponding segments aimed at). For example, in 'I have pretty mell decided', the target [w] of 'well' was replaced by the intrusion [m] of 'mell'. The authors found that manner of articulation (i.e., stop, fricative, sonorant, or nasal – in their terminology distinguished) and voicing are significantly more likely to be preserved than place of articulation, and that most single-feature errors involve a change of the articulation place only. Additionally, significantly more errors involved a change of [s] to [ʃ] or [tʃ], and of [s] to [tʃ], than vice versa. (Note that their [ʃ] equals my [š], and their [ʒ], my [ž].) They ascribed the latter phenomenon to a palatalization mechanism characteristic of English. They compared their data with those collected by Fromkin (1971) containing 1369 errors and obtained comparable results in this sense that significant asymmetry was observed for [s] and [t], which are more often targets, and for [ʃ] which is more often the intrusion. They computed the total chi-square values for both sets of nonvocalic error data (which will be reproduced below) and obtained the values of 61.1 and 80.2, respectively, which are both significant at the .001 level. (In other words, there is .1% chance that the obtained result would show up if there is no asymmetry between the targets and the intrusions involved.) However, when the palatalization errors in the sense of [ʃ] and [tʃ] being more often intrusions than targets were subtracted from the matrices, the chi-square values became nonsignificant (i.e. not reaching significance at the .05 level). Shattuck-Hufnagel and Klatt could not reach any explanation on the basis of the preceding distinctive feature models (for which they relied on Jakobson (1941), Trubetzkoy (1958, 2nd), and Chomsky and Halle (1968)).

What we are facing here is a sample-independent different treatment of the articulation place features in speech errors, and the question of how these features are related to the other features in speech errors, and how they are related to the other features in the phonological system of American English.

In order to investigate the relations among the distinctive features in speech errors, let us examine the most common nonvocalic confusions in the corpus collected by Shattuck-Hufnagel and Klatt, as compared with that collected by Fromkin.

(17) Error rates for the most common nonvocalic confusions in the sample of 1620 errors collected by Shattuck-Hufnagel and Klatt at MIT (i.e. Massachusetts Institute of Techonology), as compared with those of 1369 errors collected by Fromkin at UCLA (i.e. University of California, Los Angeles). From Shattuck-Hufnagel and Klatt (1979: 49).

Shattuck-Hufnagel & Klatt (MIT)						Fromkin (UCLA)		
Pairs			⇒	⇐	Sum	⇒	⇐	Sum
[r]	:	[l]	86	67	153	37	42	79
[s]	:	[ʃ]	68	33	101	32	9	41
[p]	:	[f]	40	35	75	23	25	48
[m]	:	[n]	34	34	68	27	23	50
[w]	:	[r]	37	27	64	8	10	18
[k]	:	[t]	28	23	51	18	16	34
[p]	:	[k]	31	16	47	25	22	47
[s]	:	[θ]	28	19	47	2	10	12
[s]	:	[t]	25	21	46	11	10	21
[f]	:	[s]	23	21	44	9	11	20
[n]	:	[l]	27	14	41	13	11	24
[t]	:	[p]	22	16	38	26	20	46
[w]	:	[m]	18	13	31	4	5	9
[l]	:	[y]	17	12	29	5	5	10
[d]	:	[b]	14	10	24	15	11	26
[d]	:	[dʒ]	11	11	22	9	3	12
[w]	:	[l]	13	7	20	3	6	9
[m]	:	[r]	17	3	20	5	4	9
[b]	:	[g]	11	9	20	15	12	27
			Total:		941			547

The distinctive features involved must be established against the background of the articulatorily and acoustically defined matrices of American English. My analysis of the articulatory distinctive feature matrix is based on Chomsky and Halle (1968), and that of the acoustic one on Jakobson, Fant and Halle (1952). I assume the same set of segments for both matrices, and thus modify Jakobson *et al.'s* segment inventory, who do not mention /r/ and /x/, and Chomsky and Halle's inventory, who list /kʷ/, /gʷ/ and /hʷ/ as single segments instead of sequences. I furthermore consider the analysis of [ŋ], [c], [tʃ] and [dʒ] as sequences justifiable. Following Jakobson *et al.*, I propose to replace [+voice] vs. [-voice] in the consonants of English by [-tense] vs. [+tense]. Due to the fact that vowels are not at issue in the error data under investigation, and in order to avoid discussing general methodological differences as compared with Chomsky and Halle which have led them to postulating also vowels which are not justifiable on the basis of the methodology outlined here, I shall restrict myself to presenting only the nonvocalic (i.e. nonsyllabic) parts of the matrices.

(18a) Articulatory distinctive feature matrix of the nonvocalic segments of English (based on Chomsky and Halle (1968)):

	j	w	r	l	p	b	f	v	m	t	d	θ	ð	n	s	z	ʃ	ʒ	k	g	χ	h
vocalic	–	–	+	+	–	–	–	–	–	–	–	–	–	–	–	–	–	–	–	–	–	–
consonantal	–	–	+	+	+	+	+	+	+	+	+	+	+	+	+	+	+	+	+	+	+	–
high	+	+	–	–	–	–	–	–	–	–	–	–	–	–	–	–	+	+	+	+	+	
back	–	+	–	–	–	–	–	–	–	–	–	–	–	–	–	–	–	–	+	+	+	–
low																						+
anterior			–	+	+	+	+	+	+	+	+	+	+	+	+	+						–
coronal			+	+	–	–	–	–	–	+	+	+	+	+	+	+	+	+				
round	–	+																				
tense	–	–	–	–	+	–	+	–	–	+	–	+	–	–	+	–	+	–	+	–	+	+
continuant					–	–	+	+	–	–	–	+	+	–	+	+	+	+	–	–	+	+
nasal					–	–	–	–	+	–	–	–	–	+	–	–	–	–	–	–	–	–
strident					–	–	+	+	–	–	–	–	–	–	+	+	+	+	–	–	–	–

(18b) Acoustic distinctive feature matrix of the nonvocalic segments of English (based on Jakobson *et al.* (1952)):

	j	w	r	l	p	b	f	v	m	t	d	θ	ð	n	s	z	ʃ	ʒ	k	g	χ	h
vocalic	–	–	+	+	–	–	–	–	–	–	–	–	–	–	–	–	–	–	–	–	–	–
consonantal	–	–	+	+	+	+	+	+	+	+	+	+	+	+	+	+	+	+	+	+	+	–
compact	–	–	+	–	–	–	–	–	–	–	–	–	–	–	–	–	+	+	+	+	+	+
diffuse	+	+																				
grave					+	+	+	+	+	–	–	–	–	–	–	–	–	–	–	–	–	–
flat	–	+																				
tense	–	–	–	–	+	–	+	–	–	+	–	+	–	–	+	–	+	–	+	–	+	+
continuant					–	–	+	+	–	–	–	+	+	–	+	+	+	+	–	–	+	+
nasal					–	–	–	–	+	–	–	–	–	+	–	–	–	–	–	–	–	–
strident					–	–	+	+	–	–	–	–	–	–	+	+	+	+	–	–	–	–

For the sake of clarity, let me state explicitly that these matrices are redundancy free in this sense that predictable feature specifications have been left out. A feature specification is considered predictable whenever the opposite specification cannot occur in combination with a given specification of another distinctive feature. For example, given the fact that all of the [+high] segments are [-anterior], the latter specification is considered redundant in combination with the former specification. On the other hand, [+high] is not predictable in combination with [-anterior], as can be seen from the segment /r/, which is [-high, -anterior]. This is why the feature *high* (terminologically equalling [±high], so I shall proceed now to use the latter type of denotation) has been specified in all cases, and the feature *anterior* (i.e. [±anterior]) only in combination with [-high].

Given this specification of the distinctive feature matrices of English, we can now proceed to analyse the segmental speech errors reported by Shattuck-Hufnagel and Klatt in terms of articulatory and acoustic distinctive feature oppositions. In the discussion, I shall systematically distinguish between a distinctive feature opposition (e.g. [±vocalic]) and a distinctive feature specification (e.g. [-vocalic], or [+vocalic]). Whenever I say that a change of a distinctive feature opposition implies a change of another distinctive feature opposition, I refer by that to a change of either the '+' or the '–' specification of a given feature opposition into the opposite specification, implying a change of the specification of another feature opposition relevant to the given segment into the opposite specification. For example, it will be stated below that a change of [±high] implies a change of [±anterior] in the consonantal segments. This means that whenever [-high] changes into [+high] or vice versa, the specification of [±anterior] changes from [+anterior] into [-anterior] or vice versa. This is found in the following exchanges: [s] – [ʃ], [t] – [k], [p] – [k], [d] – [dʒ], and [b] – [g], in either direction. On the other hand, a change of [±anterior] has no consequences for [±high], as can be seen from the [r] – [l] and [m] – [r] exchanges, in either direction.

In the following survey, I shall analyse the speech errors discussed by Shattuck-Hufnagel and Klatt entirely in terms of the distinctive feature oppositions involved. It can be seen that some errors involve only one distinctive feature opposition. The errors involving more than one distinctive feature opposition form two groups. The first group of such errors is characterized by distinctive feature oppositions which are mutually unrelated, and the second group is characterized by distinctive features for which an implicational relation holds in the sense described above. This is found both in articulatorily based and in acoustically based distinctive feature oppositions.

(19a) Articulatory distinctive features involved in the errors (from Gvozdanović (1983b: 134)):

- single feature oppositions: [±anterior], [±coronal] and [±strident];
- feature oppositions either as single or independently joining other feature oppositions: [±continuant] and [±nasal];
- feature oppositions implying a change of another feature opposition as described above: [±vocalic] implies [±continuant] and [±nasal] (if distinctive in either of the segments), [±consonantal] implies either [±high] or [±low]; [±back] implies [±high], unless [±consonantal] is changed, too, and [±high] implies [±anterior] in the [+consonantal] segments.

(19b) Acoustic distinctive features involved in the errors (from Gvozdanović (1983b: 135)):

- single feature oppositions: [±grave], [±compact] and [±strident];
- feature oppositions either as single or independently joining other feature oppositions: [±continuant] and [±nasal];
- feature oppositions implying a change of another feature opposition in the errors: [±vocalic implies [±continuant] and [±nasal] (if distinctive in either of the segments), and [±consonantal] implies either [±diffuse] or [±compact].

We can conclude that there are clear differences among the distinctive feature oppositions involved in the errors. Some distinctive features (i.e. feature oppositions) are more often involved than others, and especially the articulatorily based feature [±anterior] is the one most frequently involved because it can occur as the only distinctive feature involved, or be implied by a change of [±high], which is itself implied by [±consonantal], and may be implied by [±back], too. The next most frequently involved distinctive feature opposition is that of [±continuant]. Among the acoustically based features, [±compact] and [±continuant] are the ones most frequently involved.

The significant asymmetry established by Shattuck-Hufnagel and Klatt according to which significantly more errors involved a change of [s] to [ʃ] or [tʃ], and of [t] to [tʃ], than vice versa, can now be reanalysed as involving the articulatorily based distinctive feature oppositions [±anterior] and [±continuant], and the acoustically based distinctive feature oppositions [±compact] and [±continuant] (in [tʃ], specification of [±continuant] occurs in the order '–, +', which was signalled by Andersen (1972) as universally characteristic of diphthongization processes; markedness in relation to distinctive feature specifications will be discussed in a following section).

Is there any relation among the distinctive feature oppositions of English which can account for the observed asymmetry in speech errors? Let us try to relate it to hierarchies in the sense of asymmetrical patterning between distinctive feature oppositions defined in the preceding chapters.

If we examine the distinctive feature matrices of English presented above, we can see a recurring regularity in which some feature oppositions are relevant only for one term of another feature opposition, but not for both its terms.

In the articulatory matrix of English, [±continuant], [±nasal], and [±strident] are distinctive in the [-vocalic] segments but predictable in the [+vocalic] ones; [±low] and [±round] are distinctive in the [-consonantal] segments but predictable in the [+consonantal] ones; [±anterior] is distinctive in the [-high] segments but predictable in the [+high] ones, and [±anterior] and [±coronal] are distinctive in the [-back] segments but predictable in the [+back] ones.

In the acoustic matrix of English, [±continuant], [±nasal], [±grave] and [±strident] are distinctive in the [-vocalic] segments but predictable in the [+vocalic] ones, and [±diffuse] and [±flat] are distinctive in the [-consonantal] segments but predictable in the [+consonantal] ones. This equals the hierarchies presented under (20a) and (20b) below, established exclusively on the basis of the distinctive feature matrices of English (i.e. independently of the observed errors).

(20a) Hierarchies in the articulatory features of English (from Gvozdanović (1983b: 139)):

[±vocalic] dominates [±continuant], [±nasal] and [±strident];
[±consonantal] dominates [±low] and [±round];
[±high] dominates [±anterior], and
[±back] dominates [±anterior] and [±coronal].

(20b) Hierarchies in the acoustic features of English (from Gvozdanović (1983b: 139)):

[±vocalic] dominates [±continuant], [±nasal], [±grave] and [±strident];
[±consonantal] dominates [±diffuse] and [±flat].

The remaining distinctive feature oppositions of English are unordered. If we now compare the patterning established as holding for the distinctive feature matrix of English with the patterning established as causing segmental errors discussed above, we can conclude that the feature hierarchy restricts speech errors in a relevant way. In the segmental errors, a specification for a subordinate or an unordered feature opposition can be changed without consequences for other distinctive features, whereas a change of a dominating feature opposition triggers corresponding changes of its subordinate feature oppositions (to which other subordinate or unordered feature oppositions can be added). The only exception so far is found in [±back], which does not trigger [±coronal] if [±high] is involved, too. This may be due to the fact that no hierarchy holds for [±high] and [±coronal]. But it is also possible that the feature oppositions [±anterior] and [±coronal] have to be revised.

Coming back to the problem formulated by Shattuck-Hufnagel and Klatt, namely why [ʃ] and [tʃ] were intrusions in a significantly higher number of cases than their corresponding targets [s] and [t], we are now able to formulate an answer to it. In both cases, there is a change of [+anterior] into [−anterior], i.e. from marked into unmarked, if markedness is viewed as directly related to the phonetic specifications in the absence of any relevant paradigmatic or syntagmatic feature context, as will be shown in the section on markedness below. But why did this change take place exactly in the case of [±anterior]? Because it is the only feature opposition which is subordinated to two other feature oppositions, viz. [±high] and [±back]. This means that it stands twice as much chance to be 'taken along' with another feature opposition, i.e. whenever one of its dominating feature oppositions changes, it must change as well. In addition to this, it can change independently of the remaining feature oppositions, as all subordinate feature oppositions can. [±anterior] is thus 'special' in the system on independent grounds of phonological patterning as outlined above, and it is exactly this patterning which apparently constrains speech errors in a relevant way.

1.5. Variation and Language Change in Relation to Asymmetry Within and Between Distinctive Feature Oppositions

1.5.1. On the basis of observable constraints on variability analysed in 1.3., I have formulated a general hypothesis by which a change of a subordinate or unordered feature opposition has no consequences for the remaining feature oppositions, whereas a change of a dominating feature opposition always does have consequences for its subordinate one(s). This hypothesis appeared not to be rejected by another area of variability, namely speech errors, but rather to be able to account for observable phenomena in a relevant way, indeed.

As it is generally assumed that variation results from language change which has its origin in variability, we can expect the same constraints to be operative in language change, and thus to be observable in variation as well.

What do we know about phonological change?

We know that speech production may influence change in universally predictable ways (hence its 'naturalness', cf. Hooper (1976)), due to asymmetry of the speech organs (cf. Martinet (1955)) or ease of articulation (cf. Jespersen (1922)). The articulatory phenomena characteristic of speech production are translated into shifts in the acoustic space (cf. Labov, Yaeger and Steiner (1972)), which occur in universally predictable ways, unless they are prevented by speech perception, reflecting the underlying language system.

There are two main phonological reasons why sound shifts may be prevented:

a) because the slots that would become filled by a sound change are filled already, and/or

b) because the distinctive feature patterning of a given system restricts the possibilities of feature changes.

Given the fact that distinctive speech sounds are analysed in terms of distinctive features, the first reason is included in the second one. The second reason, that of feature patterning, may have consequences not only for the effectuation of a given change, but also for its direction. Let us examine it on the basis of the hypothesis about constraints imposed by the distinctive feature patterning as formulated at the beginning of this section. And let us do it by examining effectuation of phonetically motivated principles of vowel shifts, assumed to be generally valid.

Labov, Yaeger and Steiner (1972: 106) formulated the following general principles of vowel shifting:

I: in chain shifts, tense or peripheral vowels rise (mid tense vowels may develop either ingliding or upgliding diphthongs (op.cit.: 228));

II: in chain shifts, lax or nonperipheral vowels usually fall, particularly the lax nuclei of upgliding diphthongs:

III: in chain shifts, back vowels move to the front.

These general principles are constrained, as can be seen from Kajkavian Serbo-Croatian concerning the first two principles, and Hungarian concerning the third one. Are the involved constraints of a general nature?

The vowel system underlying Kajkavian dialectal differentiation can be reconstructed as indicated in (21), following Ivić (1968: 58f.).

(21a) Reconstruction of the Kajkavian vowel system, following Ivić (1968: 58f.):

i u
ọ
e o
ȩ ȧ

(These vowels could be distinctively either long or short. The long ones can be considered 'peripheral', and the short ones 'nonperipheral'. Whenever length is irrelevant to a development, I make no reference to it.)

(21b) Developments of /ọ/ in Kajkavian, spoken in western Croatia in Yugoslavia:

(a) /ọ/ → /o/ in the northern and northeastern areas;

(b) /ọ/ → /u/ in the western and eastern areas;

(c) /ọ/ remains preserved in most parts of the central area

(d) /ọ/ → /oʉ/ if long, and /u/ if short (in Bednja either short or rising) in the northern and western parts of the central area;

(e) /ọ/ → /o/ if long, and /ọ/ → /u/ if short; original long /o/ → /uo/ and long /e/ → /ie/ in Ključ and Koškovec.

The Kajkavian developments show that both peripheral and nonperipheral vowels may either rise or fall in chain shifts. They may either merge with other vowels or remain distinct. There is a tendency for peripheral mid vowels to rise in diphthongization, but in different ways (further left unexplained by Labov, Yaeger and Steiner), as can be seen from a comparison of the systems of the type (d) with those of (e): /ọ/ is diphthongized as /ou/, and /o/ as /uo/. The same regularity holds for Slovenian (cf. Rigler (1967: 133f.)). Following Andersen's (1972) definition of diphthongization as due to a distribution of feature specifications in the order 'unmarked, marked' within a segment (and viewing markedness as directly related to the phonetic specifications unless either the paradigmatic or the syntagmatic feature context indicates the opposite), we can see that in the /ọ/ → [ou] diphthongization, the values of [±diffuse] (or [±high] in the articulatory terminology) are distributed in the order assumed by Andersen as directly reflecting the distinctive phonetic specifications (i.e. in the order '–, +', irrespectively of [±compact], or [±low], which is redundant in such segments – at variance with Andersen's own analysis of comparable phenomena). In the /o/ → [uo] diphthongization, on the other hand, it is due to the distinctive [–compact] (or [–low]) specification of the given segment that [+diffuse] (or [+high]) is treated as 'unmarked', and [–diffuse] (or [–high]) as 'marked'. This can account for the [+diffuse, –diffuse] (or [+high, –high]) diphthongization in the /o/ → [uo] case, in accordance with Andersen's analysis.

The Kajkavian types of diphthongization show that specification with respect to [±diffuse] (or [±high]) is subject to variation, whereas in such cases specification with respect to [±compact] (or [±low]) is not. Is there anything that makes [±compact] (or [±low]) 'special'?

In the systems of the type (e), where the latter feature opposition was relevant to diphthongization of the segments distinctively specified for it, an asymmetry connected with this feature opposition can also be observed.

In those systems, the opposition between [-grave] and [+grave] (or [-back] and [+back]) vowels is operative only in the distinctively and redundantly [-compact] (or [-low]) ones, but not in the [+compact] (or [+low]) ones. This asymmetry equals a hierarchical relation, in which [±compact] (or [±low]) is the dominating feature opposition, and [±grave] (or [±back]) the subordinate one. This then makes [±compact] (or [±low]) 'special' in comparison with [±diffuse] (or [±high]): the former is a dominating feature opposition, whereas the latter is not.

(22) Kajkavian systems of the type (e): – distinctive feature hierarchy:

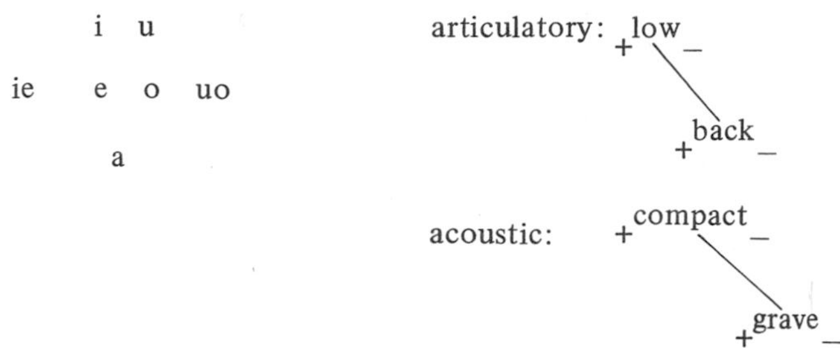

The Kajkavian data show that if a sound change involves a segment which is distinctively specified for a dominating feature opposition, this feature specification remains preserved, whereas other feature specifications change. (Those patterned within the same phonetic dimension must also take the dominating feature opposition into account in the sense of markedness reversal as illustrated above, by which [+diffuse] is apparently evaulated as 'unmarked' in the context of [-compact], whereas it is evaluated as 'marked' in the absence of such a relevant context.)

We can see that the Kajkavian data fit into the same picture of constraining principles as do the Dutch data discussed in 1.3. above, thus giving support to the same hypothesis.

The third principle of vowel shifting formulated by Labov, Yaeger and Steiner stated that back vowels shift to the front. Greenberg (1966: 514) listed this shift among diachronic universals indeed, and stated in particular that in unconditional sound change, *"of the two vowels /i/ and /ü/, /i/ may originate from /ü/ but not /ü/ from /i/"*. However, in Hungarian from the tenth to the fifteenth centuries we do encounter rounding of front vowels (cf. Kálmán (1972)), as a consequence of which /ü/ did originate from /i/. Why not vice versa? The fact that there was an open slot in the /ü/ position (because the original /ü/ was lowered to /ö/) obviously cannot give an answer as to why this open slot was not filled from the /u/ side, in a 'natural' phonetic way.

The only answer can be found in the fact that Hungarian already had rounded vowels at the point at which the change took place. This means that preceding the change, the Hungarian system had the following asymmetrical feature patterning:

(23a) the articulatory feature patterning of Hungarian preceding the /i/ → /ü/ change

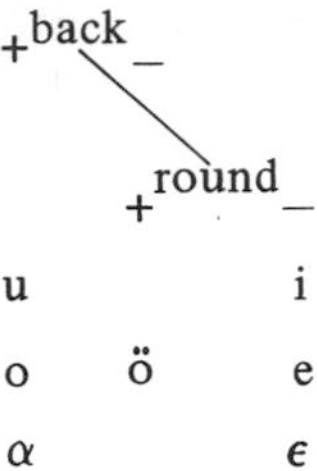

(23b) the acoustic feature patterning of Hungarian preceding the /i/ → /ü/ change

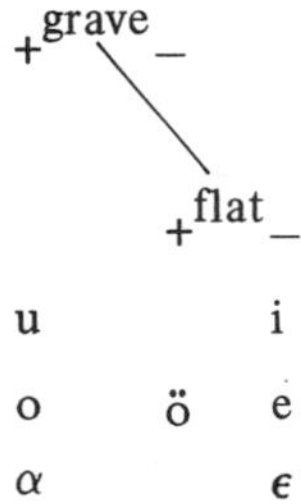

We can observe a feature hierarchy in Hungarian, which occurs in an isomorphous way both in the articularily based and the acoustically based features. By this hierarchy, [±back] is dominating and [±round] subordinate in the articulatory vowel features, and [±grave] is dominating and [±flat] subordinate in the acoustic ones.

What would a change of /u/ into /ü/ have entailed? A change of a relevant dominating feature specification.

And what did the change of /i/ into /ü/ entail? A change of a relevant subordinate feature specification, under preservation of the relevant dominating one. (By 'relevant' I mean throughout 'distinctive for the given major set of segments', in casu: vowels.)

We can see that sound change is constrained by the existing feature hierarchy. But strictly speaking, this effect can be shown to be generally valid only if it is absent whenever feature hierarchy is absent, too.

In the same period or somewhat earlier than Hungarian had the change of /i/ into /ü/, Dutch had the predicted change of /u/ into /ü/. And the relevant difference between Dutch and Hungarian at that stage was indeed that preceding the change, Dutch did not have any round front vowels, whereas Hungarian did have them. This means that Dutch did not have any feature hierarchy between [±back] and [±round] (or [±grave] and [±flat]) preceding the change, whereas Hungarian did have that hierarchy. This is why the Dutch change was an unconditional one, and it followed the general phonetic principle formulated by Labov, Yaeger and Steiner.

Following the change, both languages did have the given hierarchy. And once the hierarchy was there in Dutch, it exerted influence on further development. Thus marginal Dutch local dialects (i.e. Dendervallei, the surroundings of Leuven, Belgian Limburg, Egmond-aan-Zee, and Vlieland, cf. Weijnen (1968: 36)) later eliminated the round front vowels by unrounding them (i.e. /ü/ → /i/ and /ö/ → /e/), not by defronting them. In other words, they eliminated the subordinate feature specification of the round front vowels, but preserved the dominating one.

Once feature hierarchy is present in a system, its constraining influence cannot be disregarded by change which is based on the sound system, and thus unconstrained by the meaningful units of that language. Only change which is based on meaningful units – and constrained by them correspondingly – can disregard feature hierarchy, as I shall show in the next subsection.

1.5.2. There is a basic difference between sound change which is based on the sound system, and sound change which is based on meaningful units. Whereas sound change which is based on the sound system reflects its organization in the sense of constraints imposed by the existing hierarchies (such that a change of a dominating distinctive feature specification triggers a change of its subordinate one or ones, but not *vice versa*), sound change which is based on meaningful units reflects the organization of the lexicon, the syntax or the morphology of the changing system, its productivities, or similarities in general. Sound change based on the meaningful units of a language may disregard the existing phonological hierarchies.

The difference between change based on the sound system and change based on meaningful units can be illustrated by two different possibilities of eliminating round front vowels in a language: either by making them unround front, or by making them round unfronted, i.e. round back. In both cases, one of the two distinctive features involved in round front vowels, namely either [±round] or [±back], is eliminated, but in the first case it is [±round] which is eliminated, and in the second case, [±back]. And there is a basic difference between the two eliminations.

We have seen in the preceding subsection that round front vowels are characterized by distinctive feature specifications for [±back] and [±round] in such a way that [±back] is the dominating feature and [±round] the subordinate one. Unrounding of round front vowels equals elimination of the subordinate feature specification. Defronting of round front vowels, on the other hand, equals elimination of the dominating feature specification, but preservation of the subordinate one. The former type of change reflects the organization of the phonological system, whereas the latter type of change does nor reflect it. The latter type of change can only be based on meaningful units – we can hypothesize. If so, then other types of constraints must be demonstrably present in the latter type of change.

I have come to understand those regularities by studying the Kajkavian dialect of the Yugoslav city of Zagreb, which is my own native dialect. The Zagreb Kajkavian dialect is based on the Kajkavian dialect of the surroundings and influenced by the standard Serbo-Croatian language, which is based on the Neoštokavian dialect. As a result of this influence, Zagreb Kajkavian has eliminated the round front vowels which are still found in at least some of the surrounding Kajkavian local dialects in two ways: either by changing them into unround front vowels (i.e. /ü/ → /i/ and /ö/ → /e/) or by changing them into round back ones (i.e. /ü/ → /u/ and /ö/ → /o/). The regularity underlying these two types of elimination of rounded front vowels can be illustrated by the following examples.

(24) Elimination of round front vowels in Zagreb Kajkavian:

original Kajkavian	Zagreb Kajkavian	Standard Serbo-Croatian	
[künštler]	[kinštler]	[umjetnik]	'artist'
[kük]	[kuk]	[kuk]	'hip'

These two Kajkavian words have a different origin: whereas [künštler] is a borrowing from German, [kük] is a word of Slavic origin. Standard Serbo-Croatian has its own derivative pendant of the first word, and an equivalent of the second one. This means that on the basis of its lexicon, Standard Serbo-Croatian could not have influenced the Zagreb Kajkavian pronunciation of the first word, whereas it could have influenced the pronunciation of the second word. In the absence of a lexical conditioning of sound change in the course of adaptation (by which the Kajkavian words were adapted to the similar Standard Serbo-Croatian ones by changing /ü/ and /ö/ into /u/ and /o/), phonological conditioning took place determining that the dominating feature specification cannot be changed without consequences for the subordinate one, and that – consequently – if only one feature specification is to be changed, it can only be the subordinate one. Hence the change of /ü/ into /i/, and of /ö/ into /e/.

The fact that sound change which is based on meaningful units need not follow the restrictions imposed by the organization of the sound system holds for the lexicon as much as it does for morphology and syntax. The regularity which is operative here aims at relating one meaning to one form. This is a restrictive tendency, too.

Next to conditioning sound change, the tendency of having one form attached to one meaning may have a preservative effect as well. This is attested not only in spoken language, but also in writing within a given scribal tradition. What we often encounter in manuscripts is preservation of the unchanged lexical form of the word, whereas sound change may be found in desinences. A concrete example of it is found in the Slavic manuscript *Code Slave 11* of the National Library of Paris, dating from the end of the fourteenth century. Its scribe presumably did not distinguish between /ẹ/ and /i/, but he continued to distinguish them in the writing of lexical stems (apparently knowing how they used to be spelled), whereas he sometimes interchanged them in desinences and particles.

The mechanism of sound change is always restricted by the existing system in one way or another. Whatever the source of sound change may be – the trial-and-error process of language acquisition (termed 'abduction' by Andersen (1973)), adaptation, or expressive formation, the initial stage of sound change reflects the organization of the changing system. This may be overlayered by later stages, but it may also remain overtly visible, as in the prosodic system of the Serbo-Croatian local dialect of Dubrovnik.

In the sixteenth century, the Serbo-Croatian dialect of Dubrovnik was basically Štokavian (with Čakavian influences due to a population mixture), but of an older type than the Neoštokavian dialect, which had undergone a series of phonological and morphological innovations preceding that period. One of those innovations was a regressive accent shift which yielded the rising tonal accent, as opposed to the unshifted falling tonal accent, occurring only in the initial position of a prosodic word (for a definition of the prosodic word, cf. Gvozdanović (1980a: 12)). The final syllable never had the accent, as there was a prosodic word boundary there. The Neoštokavian system could (as it still can) be analysed as having tone, with the accent predictable from tone and prosodic word boundaries. The rising vs. falling tone of Neoštokavian occurred on long and short vowels, the long ones being single phonological segments due to their opposition to the corresponding sequences (cf. also Gvozdanović (1983d: 68)). Each vowel formed a syllable nucleus.

Dubrovnik was different from that. Its poetry from that time shows that a syllable nucleus could contain two vowels as well (cf. e.g. [meu] 'between', which counted as one syllable). The long vowels of the local dialect of Dubrovnik were not opposed to the corresponding sequences, which means that they could themselves be analysed as sequences. At that time, the local dialect of Dubrovnik did not distinguish tone in short syllable nuclei (consisting of a single vowel), but only in long ones (consisting of a vowel sequence as its nucleus), which could have the accent either on the first or on the second vowel of the syllable nucleus.

In the sixteenth and seventeenth centuries, Dubrovnik underwent socio-linguistically conditioned extensive Neoštokavian influences. One of them triggered the accent retraction, which started in word-final syllables. The retracted accent was rendered as rising on the prefinal syllable if that syllable was long. If it was short, there was no tonal distinction. Originally short prefinal syllables were lengthened under the retracted accent if the final syllable was short. Only in that case did they become rising. The output of the first stage of the accent retraction correspondingly agreed with the existing system.

(25a) Neoštokavian in the sixteenth century:

[vòda]	/vòda/	'water, nominative singular'
[vòdē]	/vòdē/	'water, genitive singular'
[vȍdu]	/vȍdu/	'water, accusative singular'
[lòpata]	/lòpata/	'spade, nominative singular'
[gláva]	/gláva/	'head, nominative singular'
[glávē]	/glávē/	'head, genitive singular'
[glâvu]	/glâvu/	'head, accusative singular'
[pítala]	/pítala/	'ask, feminine active past participle'.

(̀) denotes the rising tone on a short vowel, (̏) denotes the falling tone on a short vowel, (́) denotes the rising tone on a long vowel, (̂) denotes the falling tone on a long vowel, and (̄) denotes vowel length.

(25b) Dubrovnik in the sixteenth century:

[vóda]	/voo̍da/
[vȍdē]	/vo̍dee/
[vȍdu]	/vo̍du/
[lopȁta]	/lopa̍ta/
[gláva]	/glaa̍va/
[glávē]	/glaa̍vee/
[glâvu]	/gla̍avu/
[pītȁla]	/piita̍la/.

The same translations as above. In the phonological notation, (') denotes the accent.

In the further course of the developments, the accent retraction proceeded into all positions, and the pronunciation rules of Neoštokavian were taken over by which a long vowel was systematically differentiated from the corresponding sequence. In the final result, tone emerged as a vowel feature in the same way as in Neoštokavian. The result of the first stage of the development was preserved and rendered as the rising tone on a long vowel and the falling tone on a short one, respectively.

(25c) Dubrovnik after the change:

[vóda]	/vóda/
[vȍdē]	/vȍdē/
[vȍdu]	/vȍdu/
[lòpata]	/lòpata/
[gláva]	/gláva/
[glávē]	/glávē/
[glâvu]	/glâvu/
[pítala]	/pítala/.

The same translations and notation as in (25a).

1.5.3. Sound change is not only constrained paradigmatically, i.e. by the feature hierarchy relevant in the given system. It is also constrained syntagmatically, i.e. by the segmentation of the involved segments, as demonstrated by the Dubrovnik case presented in (25a) above.

Phonological segments are sets of distinctive features – and this is why they are directly related to the feature patterning. Following Ebeling (1960: 67), I define the phonological segment as a set of distinctive features for which the fact that they are grouped together is relevant in this sense that the same features constitute different linguistic forms according as they are grouped together differently. At this point I must add, however, that even this grouping is constrained by the existing hierarchies and relatively free only in so far as it concerns the unordered feature oppositions.

We have seen on the basis of the Dubrovnik case discussed above that the initial stage of sound change obeys the segmentation principle characteristic of the system undergoing the change. At the next stage, the same principle may either be preserved or changed. Its preservation can be taken as a proof of the relevance of the existing segmentation principle.

Preservation of the original segmentation principle, but change of the prosodic one, is found in Southeastern Slavonian Serbo-Croatian, discussed under 1.2. above. In Slavonian Serbo-Croatian, there is no systematic distinction between long vowels and the corresponding sequences; each sequence of two identical vowels is pronounced as a single long vowel, even if there is an intervening morpheme boundary between them, as shown by (7) in section 1.2. above.

Slavonian in general, and particularly Southeastern Slavonian, underwent Neoštokavian influences. In the period directly preceding the Neoštokavian influence, Slavonian had phonetic rising and falling tonal accents only on long syllable nuclei, where they were due to a differential accent placement either on the first or on the second vowel of a sequence. These phonetic tonal accents differed from the Neoštokavian ones by a pitch break between the high-pitched part and the low-pitched part of a long syllable nucleus having a tonal accent (cf. Ivšić (1911: 151 etc.)). This breaking reflects the segmentation principle.

As a result of the Neoštokavian influence, Southeastern Slavonian retracted the accent from any short syllable. In Cerna, this also optionally affected any final vowel (be it a single one or the second part of a sequence), and obligatorily any single vowel of a syllable, and elsewhere, this affected only single vowels, not those forming the second part of a sequence. Anyhow, the retracted accent was reinterpreted as the low tone, and the unretracted accent as the high tone. The low vs. high tone is a vowel feature there, as is also shown by its phonetic realization (cf. also Ivić's somewhat different notation (1958: 291)).

(26) Southeeastern Slavonian equivalents of the Neoštokavian and Dubrovnik ones:

Cerna:		rest of Southeastern Slavonian:	
[vòda]	/vòda/	[vòda]	/vòda/
[vodẽ], [vodẽ]	/vodeé/, /vodèe/	[vodẽ]	/vodeé/
[vȍdu]	/vódu/	[vȍdu]	/vódu/
[lòpata]	/lòpata/	[lòpata]	/lòpata/
[glāva]	/glàava/	[gláva]	/glaàva/
[glā̃vẽ], [glāvẽ]	/glaaveé/, /glaavèe/	[glāvẽ]	/glaaveé/
[glȃvu]	/gláavu/	[glȃvu]	/gláavu/
[pītali]	/pìitali/	[pítali]	/pìitali/

The same translations as in (25a). Phonetically, (` ) denotes the short rising tonal accent, ( ̏ ) the short falling one, ( ´ ) the long rising one, ( ̑ ) the long falling one, ( ˜ ) the neoacute, and ( ˉ ) the Cerna new rising one, as in (10a) and (10b) above. Phonologically, ( `) denotes the low tone, and (´) the high tone.

The segmentation principle of a given language is its principle of linear feature ordering. At least at its initial stage, sound change is constrained by the existing linear ordering of the distinctive features of the language undergoing the change.

1.5.4. We have seen that paradigmatic and syntagmatic feature ordering accounts for constraints observable in sound change which cannot – or cannot fully – be accounted for by the articulatory or acoustic space and empty phonological slots in it.

How about so-called strength hierarchies formulated by Foley (1977) as determining the direction of change? Specifically, Foley analysed sound shifts in terms of strengthening and weakening along the following parameters:

(27) Scales of increasing phonological strength formulated by Foley (1977):

(ρ)

stops	spirants	nasals	liquids	glides	vowels →
1	2	3	4	5	6

(β)

voiced spirants	voiced stops	voiceless stops	voiceless spirants,	affricates, double stops →
1	2	3	5	

(ω)

i	u
e	o
	a →
1	2

(η)

ü	ö	
i	e	
u	o	a →
1	2	3

Language specific scales, relating to the articulation place:

(α) Romance:

velars	dentals	labials →
1	2	3

Germanic:

velars	labials	dentals →
1	2	3

Foley assumed that the basic phonological units are not distinctive sounds (or segments) but rather the relations among them presented above, and that the direction of sound change can be predicted in terms of these relations, viz. that the weakest elements of a group are the first ones to weaken, and strongest elements the first ones to be strengthened.

If we look at Foley's parameters, we can see that they directly reflect the distinctive features involved, which are and have always been conceived of as relative terms. The (ρ) parameter reflects the distinctive feature oppositions [±continuant], [±nasal], [±consonantal] and [±vocalic], the (β) parameter reflects [±voiced] and [±continuant], the (α) parameter reflects on a language-specific basis [±back], [±coronal] and [±anterior] in the articulatory features, and [±compact] and [±acute] in the acoustic ones, the (ω) parameter reflects the articulatory feature opposition [±back] and the acoustic one [±grave] (with the exception of /a/, which has a language-specific treatment in this respect), and the (η) parameter reflects the articulatory distinctive features [±high] and [±low], and the acoustic ones [±diffuse] and [±compact].

How can the statement that the strength hierarchies are entirely translatable in terms of distinctive features be put to a test? In two ways. Firstly, distinctive features have been shown in 1.2. to be partly language-specific.

If the strength hierarchies reflect them, they must also be language-specific to the extent that the distinctive features are. And secondly, distinctive features have been shown above to exert constraints on variability and variation in terms of asymmetrical patterning. If the strength hierarchies reflect them indeed, they must follow the constraints imposed by the asymmetrical ordering also in cases which are unpredicted by the proposed strength scales.

Variability data pointing to a language-specific treatment of nasals on the strength scale have been presented by Rubach (1977: 76). And variational data pointing to a different treatment of /b/, /d/ and /g/ on the same scale in Danish dialects have been presented by Smith (1981).

(28) Development of /b/, /d/ and /g/ in Danish dialects (from Smith (1981: 592)):

	b	d	g
a) Vensyssel (N. Jutland)	β	ϕ	γ
b) Mors (N. Jutland)	β	r	γ
c) C.C.E. Jutland	v	r/ϕ	γ
d) S.E. Scania	v	d	g/dʒ
e) Fünen	w	δ	w.

		stop	fricative	liquid	glide	deletion
Vensyssel		b	——→			
		d	——	——	——	——→
		g	——→			
Mors		b	——→			
		d	——	——→		
		g	——→			
C.C.E. Jutland		b	——→			
		d	——	——→	– – –	– – –→
		g	——→			
S.E. Scania		b	——→			
		d				
		g				
Fünen		b	——	——	——→	
		d	——→			
		g	——	——	——→	

In Vensyssel, Mors and C.C.E. Jutland, the [+coronal] (or [+acute]) [+consonantal, -continuant]) segment became [+continuant, -consonantal], whereas the [-coronal] (or [-acute]) ones became only [+continuant]. In S.E. Scania, only the [-coronal, +anterior] (or [-acute, -compact]) [-continuant] segment became [+continuant]. In Fünen, on the other hand, the two [-coronal] (or [-acute]) [-continuant, +consonantal] segments became [+continuant, -consonantal], whereas the [+coronal] (or [+acute]) [-continuant, +consonantal] segment became only [+continuant], but remained [+consonantal].

All of the investigated changes, unpredicted by Foley's strength hierarchies, appear to have increased the number of distinctive feature hierarchies in the systems, thus increasing predictability. The exact direction of change appears not to be fully predictable though. In the Danish dialects, predictability of [±consonantal] and/or [±continuant] has been introduced as attached differentially to an articulation place feature, and differences in the latter account for the observed variation.

The fact that sound change is not fully predictable, but rather a matter of the language learner's guessing about the analysis of the language input he is getting, and on the basis of the general rules about the organization of the language system he has internalized, has been termed 'abduction' by Andersen (1973). The constraints imposed by the feature hierarchies I have elaborated here apparently belong to the general rules about language systems internalized by the language learner. And it is a matter of abduction indeed that the direction of sound change cannot be fully predicted on the basis of general rules.

Finally, let me discuss another type of change unpredicted by Foley, and pointed at by Harlow (1983) as presenting a problem against the background of Foley's strength scales. It concerns nasal changes in Polynesian languages. They go, namely, in different directions, viz. the dental nasal /n/ merges with the velar nasal /ŋ/ in Colloquial Samoan yielding the velar nasal /ŋ/, /ŋ/ merges with /n/ in the Bay of Plenty Maori yielding the dental nasal /n/, and /ŋ/ merges with /k/ in the South Island Maori yielding the velar consonant /k/. Harlow discussed these changes in terms of Foley's weakening and strengthening hierarchies, and stated that the /n/ → /ŋ/ change can be analysed as weakening, and /ŋ/ → /n/ as strengthening, but that there are problems analysing the /ŋ/ → /k/ change in Foley's terms. This is why I am going to elaborate the Maori changes here (leaving the Samoan one for the discussion about markedness in the next section).

The discussion of the Maori changes of /ŋ/ in terms of the distinctive features involved which I am going to present here makes sense only if Harlow's analysis of /ŋ/ as a single segment (and not a sequence of a nasal and a velar) is correct indeed. It may be assumed to be correct on the basis of Harlow's (1983: 100) observation about the absence of clusters there, but strictly speaking it must be further investigated.

In order to be able to discuss the elimination of /ŋ/ in the Bay of Plenty Maori (henceforth: MAB) and the South Island Maori (henceforth: MAS), I shall first present a distinctive feature analysis of the Maori which still has the velar nasal /ŋ/. The acoustic analysis of the Maori phonological system was forwarded to me by Harlow in a letter dated July 20, 1981. I shall present it here with minor modifications due to predictability, and leaving the distinctive feature [±acute] for the vowels – as they are not at issue at the moment anyhow, and further data on their feature evaluation are not available to me – and add the corresponding articulatory analysis (based on Chomsky and Halle (1968)).

(29a) The articulatory features of Maori:

	i	e	a	o	u	p	t	k	m	n	ŋ	h	r	f	w
consonantal						+	+	+	+	+	+	+	–	+	–
vocalic	+	+	+	+	+								–		–
high	+	–		–	+										
back	–	–		+	+										
low			+												
anterior						+		–	+		–	–		+	+
coronal						–	+	–	–	+	–	–	+	–	–
nasal						–	–	–	+	+	+				
continuant						–	–	–	–	–	–	+		+	

(29b) The acoustic features of Maori:

	i	e	a	o	u	p	t	k	m	n	ŋ	h	r	f	w
consonantal						+	+	+	+	+	+	+	–	+	–
vocalic	+	+	+	+	+								–		–
diffuse	+	–		–	+										
compact		–	+	–		–	–	+	–	–	+	+	–	–	–
acute	+	+		–	–	–	+		–	+			+	–	–
nasal						–	–	–	+	+	+				
continuant						–	–	–	–	–	–	+		+	

The following distinctive feature hierarchies can be established for Maori on the basis of the presented matrices.

(30a) The articulatory distinctive feature hierarchies of Maori:

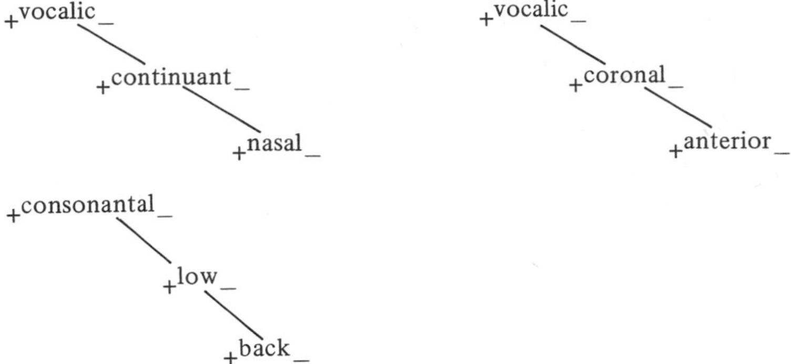

(30b) The acoustic distinctive feature hierarchies of Maori:

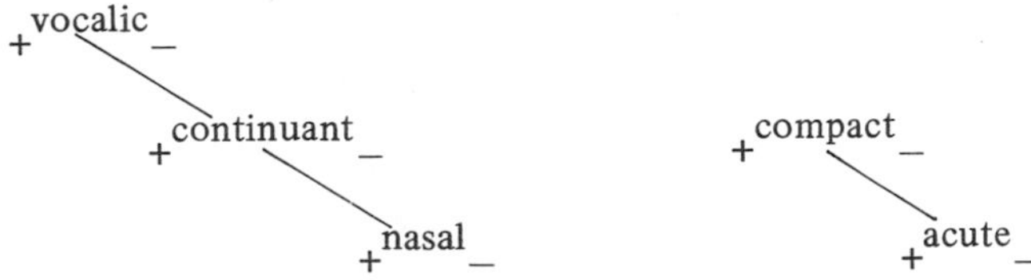

([±compact] and [±acute] are unordered with respect to [±vocalic] and [±consonantal], but the usage of [±acute] for the vowels must further be investigated.)

We can see that in the determination of hierarchies, a '–' specification is grouped together with the absence of a specification. This is a case of markedness, to be discussed in the next section, by which both are treated as unmarked in the absence of a relevant feature context.

What did the nasal changes entail for the feature hierarchies?

The Bay of Plenty Maori eliminated /ŋ/ by letting it merge with /n/. Due to this change, MAB has now the following feature hierarchies.

(31a) The articulatory distinctive feature hierarchies of the Bay of Plenty Maori following the /ŋ/ → /n/ change:

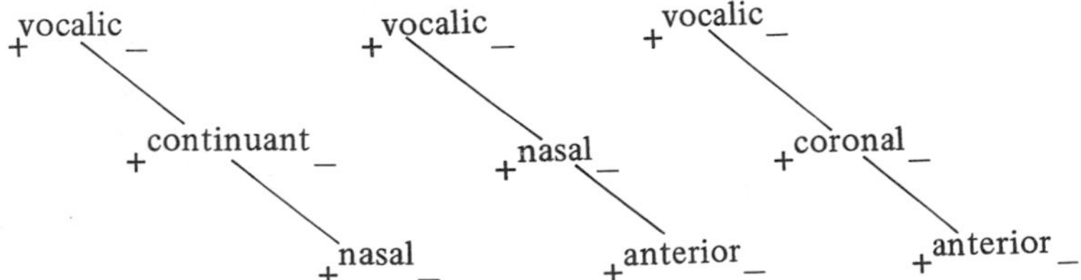

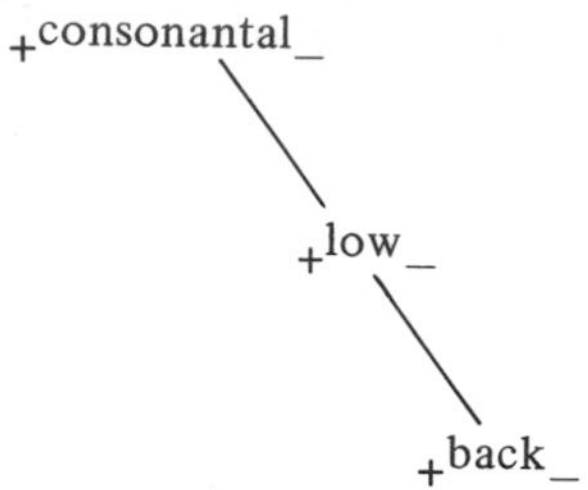

(31b) The acoustic distinctive feature hierarchies of the Bay of Plenty Maori following the /ŋ/ → /n/ change:

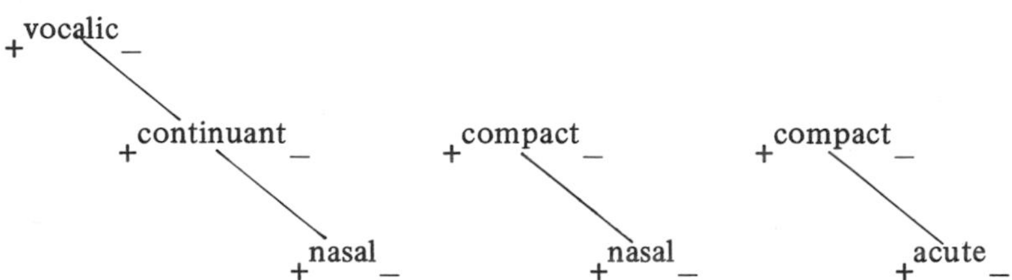

In the articulatory features, MAB had a change of the dominating feature [±coronal] in the context of [+nasal], and its subordinate feature [±anterior] changed, too, and became subordinate with respect to [±nasal] as well. In the acoustic features, MAB had a change of the dominating feature [±compact] in the context of [±nasal], and its subordinate feature [±acute] changed, too. In the acoustic features, the (already) dominating feature [±compact] became dominating with respect to [±nasal] as well, but the discrepancy between the articulatory and the acoustic features must further be investigated.

The MAB change of /ŋ/ into /n/ has increased the amount of predictability in both the articulatory and the acoustic features, without violating the constraints imposed by the existing hierarchies.

The South Island Maori (MAS) eliminated /ŋ/ by letting it merge with /k/. It was a change of [+nasal] into [-nasal] in the context of [+consonantal, -coronal, -anterior, -continuant] in the articulatory features, and a change of [+nasal] into [-nasal] in the context of [+consonantal, +compact, -continuant] in the acoustic features. The resulting segment inventory of MAS is the same as that of MAB, and the resulting feature hierarchies are consequently the same, too. This shows that the same structural change can be reached by different processes, which are predictable only to the extent that they do not involve a dominating distinctive feature opposition without involving its subordinate one(s).

1.5.5. We have seen in the preceding subsections that phonological constraints on sound change are based on the syntagmatic ordering (i.e. the segmentation) valid for the language undergoing sound change, and on the paradigmatic ordering (i.e. the hierarchies) valid for the distinctive feature system of that language.

These orderings underlie the phonological constraints on sound change discussed in the literature such as rule transparency as formulated by Kiparsky (1982, 2nd: 75), and add restrictiveness to them. They also underlie the strength hierarchies established by Foley (1977) and can account for phenomena for which strength hierarchies cannot account.

Finally, the principles of paradigmatic feature ordering established above underlie the abductive mechanism of sound change defined by Andersen (1973) and show why sound change cannot be merely inductive (i.e. based on the language data) or merely deductive (i.e. based on the general principles of ordering). The phonological system of a language is as a rule only partially ordered. And only the ordered parts of the system are by nature restrictive, and the restrictions imposed by them can be satisfied in various ways, as we have seen above.

1.6. Markedness and Ordering at Various Levels

I have been referring to markedness on several occasions in the preceding sections, but there are still so many unsolved problems about markedness that a full survey seems necessary at this point. The vexed status of markedness can be well understood on the basis of Winter's (1982) discussion of how inconclusive markedness is if conceived of as universal and based on phonetic and distributional criteria. As distinguished from these substantive properties, Winter pointed to formal ones as providing a conclusive criterion. He conceived of formal properties as directly related to the linguistic form: a more complex form is marked, and a less complex one, unmarked.

It is the idea of markedness as based on a formal criterion that I am going to further elaborate here. Although the formal criterion underlying markedness is related to the surface form, I hope to show that this relation is not always a straightforward one, and that it can be fully understood only if all the relations of the same level within a given language are taken into account.

In order to make the background of my discussion more clear, I shall first give a survey of markedness in structural phonology (under 1.6.1.) and then in generative phonology (under 1.6.2.), in the order as the ideas about markedness developed. Then I shall discuss system-internal properties of sound change yielding marked segments, which cannot be accounted for in terms of the preceding approaches (under 1.6.3.), and finally I shall propose to view markedness as related to the asymmetrical patterning discussed in the preceding sections (under 1.6.4.). It should be noted that both the correct solution and the possible incorrect elaborations originate from the first formulation of markedness as worded by Trubetzkoy in 1930.

1.6.1. The history of markedness in linguistic theory, and specifically in phonology, goes back to Trubetzkoy, who formulated it as follows in a letter to Jakobson in 1930: *"Statistics has nothing to do with it. And the essence lies in the so-to-speak 'intrinsic content' of the correlation. Apparently any (or might it not be 'any'?) phonological correlation acquires in the linguistic consciousness the form of a contraposition of the presence of a certain mark to its absence (or the maximum of a certain mark to its minimum)."* And Jakobson answered: *"I am coming increasingly to the conviction that your thought about correlation as a constant mutual connection between a marked and unmarked type is one of your most remarkable and fruitful ideas. It seems to me that it has significance not only for linguistics but also for ethnology and history of culture, and that such historico-cultural correlations as life ~ death, liberty ~ nonliberty, sin ~ virtue, holidays ~ working days, etc., are always confined to relations α ~ non-α, and that it is important to find out for any epoch, group, nation, etc., what the marked element is."* (Both citations are from Jakobson and Waugh (1979: 90f.).)

These first formulations conceived of markedness as partly system-specific, but they lacked a criterion for establishing when markedness is present in a system and when it is not (cf. Trubetzkoy's formulation *"or might it not be 'any'?"*). The same problem was posed again – and remained unanswered – half a century later at a conference on markedness, where Basbøll (1981: 60) correctly stated: *"it seems quite evident that we are still far from being able to give a reasonable algebra of markedness which agrees with the external conditions to be placed upon such a theory"*.

So let us examine the answers that have been formulated by the structuralists first.

Trubetzkoy (1958, 2nd: 73 etc.) established markedness whenever the phonetic implementation is characterized by the presence of a mark (e.g. voicing) in one of the members of a correlation, and by its absence in the other member (i.e. absence of voicing). He called such correlations 'private oppositions'. They are determined by the phonetic substance, but they can occur also independent of (though not contradictory to) the phonetic substance – if determined by the organization of the system. He did not answer the question of when phonetically nonprivative correlations are modelled as privative by the organization of the phonological system. Neither did he fully answer the question of how we may know whether a phonetically nonprivative correlation is modelled phonologically as privative or not.

There are two indications as to markedness. One of them is allowance of more distinctions in connection with one term of the opposition than in connection with its other term. The first term is then viewed as unmarked. This idea, in a nutshell formulated by Trubetzkoy already, underlies the principle of asymmetrical ordering elaborated here. The second indication is that of neutralization, or sign omittance of a distinctive feature in the terminology used in this study. In the positions of neutralization, the unmarked term shows up. It [*sic;* the correct formulation should be rather 'its phonetic specification', J.G.] is either predictable by the neutralizing segmental context (e.g. a voiced segment is unmarked in the context of a voiced segment), or by the evaluation of the segment itself in the system (in which case a voiceless consonant is by itself unmarked, and not its voiced counterpart). Trubetzkoy thus derived conclusions about markedness from phonetic and distributional criteria (assuming that they are related to the system), but understood that markedness is a systematic characteristic.

Jakobson (1949 etc.) further developed these phonological principles by fully analysing distinctive segments in terms of binary distinctive features, and applied markedness to the entire distinctive feature system. Whereas his distinctive feature analysis based on phonetic feature correlates and binary oppositions holding between them was a revolutionary contribution to phonological theory, his application of markedness to the entire system had a drawback of lacking a criterion for establishing which feature specifications are predictable. And this is crucial in his approach because it considers '–' and predictable (either '+' or '–') specifications unmarked, whereas '+' specifications are marked.

This can be illustrated by Jakobson's (1962, 2nd: 421) usage of the feature specifications [+nasal] and [–nasal] in the matrix of Serbo-Croatian, as discussed in 1.1. (following chart 3b) above. Whereas in the original version of the given paper all of the '–' and predictable specifications, considered unmarked, were left unspecified, in the second edition of the paper, Jakobson attempted at making a difference between '–' and predictable specifications in the matrix, thus not basing it any more on markedness. But the attempted difference between '–' and predictable specifications was inconclusive, as I have shown above already, and this means that Jakobson's notion of markedness, not revised in the intervening period, was inconclusive as well.

In the course of the development of his distinctive feature theory (from 1949 to 1962, in the given example), Jakobson thus came to the correct insight that those feature specifications which are distinctive, be they plusses or minusses, must be distinguished from predictable ones in the matrix, and also that the distinction between plusses and minusses is relevant with some of the remaining distinctive features. However, he neither explicitly nor implicitly answered the questions of 'which distinctive features' and 'how to establish them'. This is why he could not fully develop the markedness theory, which hinges on those questions.

Later approaches to phonological markedness kept tackling the same questions of how to derive markedness from phonetic and distributional characteristics, and how to relate these characteristics to the organization of the distinctive feature system. I shall concentrate here on proposals of how to relate markedness to the organization of the distinctive feature system, because sufficient understanding of this aspect has been a missing link since the beginnings of the phonological theory.

1.6.2. Starting from phonetic and distributional characteristics, generative phonology investigated which distinctive features are relevant to unmarkedness of other distinctive features by making them predictable. And came to several possible solutions, because a system-internal procedure for establishing markedness vs. unmarkedness was lacking. A direct derivation of markedness from phonetic and distributional characteristics depends on which segment or segments are to be considered fully unmarked, and for this there is only a high probability, not a necessity, that *in casu* /a/ (in Chomsky and Halle's (1968) approach), or /a/ and /t/ (in Kean's (1980) and later generative approaches) are to be considered unmarked. Due to their phonetic characteristics these segments are usually the first ones to occur in language acquisition, and they are the most spread ones in the languages of the world. But why /a/ and /t/, and e.g. not /a/ only? Even the answer to this cannot be derived directly from phonetic and distributional characteristics, but it depends on whether the entire system is conceived of as affected by markedness, or its separate parts.

In the absence of system-internal criteria, phonetic and distributional characteristics lead to different sets of markedness conventions, as can be illustrated by those for the unmarked value of [±anterior] proposed by Chomsky and Halle (1968), Kean (1980) and Van Lessen Kloeke (1981). Assumed to be universal, these rules, should account also for English /l/, /p/, /b/, /f/, /v/, /m/, /t/, /d/, /θ/, /ð/, /n/, /s/ and /z/, which are according to Chomsky and Halle (1968: 177) [+anterior], whereas the remaining segments are [-anterior]. Which of them are unmarked for [±anterior]?

(32a) The markedness convention for the unmarked value of [±anterior] according to Chomsky and Halle (1968: 406):

$$[\text{u anterior}] \rightarrow \begin{cases} [-\text{anterior}] \; / \; \begin{bmatrix} \overline{} \\ +\text{high} \\ +\text{coronal} \\ \alpha\,\text{continuant} \end{bmatrix} & \text{(a)} \\ [+\text{anterior}] & \text{(b).} \end{cases}$$

(32b) The markedness convention for the unmarked value of [±anterior] according to Kean (1980: 23):

$$[\text{u anterior}] \rightarrow [+\text{anterior}] \; / \; \begin{bmatrix} \overline{} \\ +\text{consonantal} \end{bmatrix} .$$

(32c) The markedness convention for the unmarked value of [±anterior] according to Van Lessen Kloeke (1981: 400):

$$[\text{u anterior}] \rightarrow [+\text{anterior}] \; / \; \begin{bmatrix} \overline{} \\ -\text{high} \end{bmatrix}$$

Finally, let me mention that all the three conventions differ from the structural one, which may be formulated as in (32d).

(32d) The markedness convention for the unmarked value of [±anterior] in structural phonology:

$$[\text{u anterior}] \rightarrow \begin{cases} [-\text{anterior}] & \text{(a)} \\ [\ \text{anterior}] & \text{(b)} \end{cases}$$

(b), where [anterior] denotes either predictable presence or absence of a specification for [±anterior].

What does the markedness theory predict? That language acquisition, language change, and speech errors will occur in the direction from marked into unmarked, unless other conditioning factors are involved. If it is to have the status of a scientific theory, the markedness theory must be falsifiable by its predictions, and falsified if contradictory language data are found.

Language acquisition gives only a partial support to the markedness conventions proposed in the theory. Even the first segments to be acquired are not always /a/ and /t/, but may be /a/ and a labial stop, as established by Jakobson (1962, 2nd: 357).

Speech errors give even less support. Kean (1981: 583ff.) discussed the spontaneous errors in American English which were reported by Shattuck Hufnagel and Klatt (1979) and established that 31% of these errors cannot be accounted for by the rules. Kean concluded that the proposed markedness theory is plausible in a statistically significant number of cases.

The unaccounted cases are of crucial importance here. If they contain a regularity which cannot be accounted for by the theory, then the theory is falsified in this respect. If, on the other hand, they do not contain any regularity, then they need not falsify the theory.

As we have seen in 1.4. above, there was a relevant asymmetry in Shattuck-Hufnagel and Klatt's data by which [t] was replaced by [ʃ] or [tʃ], and [s] by [ʃ] in a significantly higher number of cases than vice versa. In other words, there was a significant tendency to change [+anterior] into [-anterior] in the [-back, +coronal] segments, which also changed from [-high] into [+high].

The relevant asymmetry observed in the speech errors is counterpredicted by Kean's and Van Lessen Kloeke's conventions for the unmarked value of [±anterior], and must be taken as a basis for rejecting the given conventions within the requirements posed on a scientific theory. If these language data are not accepted as a falsification by the given authors, then their markedness conventions do not have the status of a theory.

As to Chomsky and Halle's markedness conventions, we have seen under (32a) above that [-anterior] is unmarked a.o. in the context of [+high], whereas [+anterior] is unmarked in the remaining cases in the consonants. In the speech error data discussed above, there was a significant asymmetrical change of [+anterior] into [-anterior], and of [-high] into [+high]. Given the specification as [+high], then [-anterior] is unmarked indeed, but how do we arrive at the change of [-high] into [+high]? Especially, how do we arrive at it in view of the markedness convention for the unmarked value of *high*, by which it is [+high] in the context of either the marked or the unmarked value of *anterior*?

(32e) The markedness convention for the unmarked value of [±high] according to Chomsky and Halle (1968: 405):

$$[\text{u high}] \rightarrow \left\{ \begin{array}{ll} [-\text{high}] \,/ \begin{bmatrix} \overline{\qquad\quad} \\ \text{u anterior} \\ \text{u back} \end{bmatrix} & \text{(a)} \\ [+\text{high}] \,/ \left\{ \begin{array}{l} \begin{bmatrix} \overline{\qquad\quad} \\ \text{m anterior} \end{bmatrix} \\ \begin{bmatrix} \overline{\qquad\quad} \\ \text{u anterior} \\ \text{m back} \end{bmatrix} \end{array} \right. & \begin{array}{l} \text{(b)} \\ \\ \text{(c)} \end{array} \end{array} \right.$$

According to Chomsky and Halle's conventions, both [+anterior, -high] and [-anterior, +high] are unmarked, and there is no way to derive the asymmetry observed in the speech errors by which the latter occur in a significantly higher number of cases than the former. Chomsky and Halle's markedness conventions must consequently be considered inadequate in this respect.

The structuralist conception of markedness cannot account for the observed asymmetry either, for two reasons. Firstly, the observed asymmetry consists of a change from marked into unmarked (in the case of [±anterior]) and a change from unmarked into marked (in the case of [±high]) which apparently go together even though the first one is predicted and the second one unpredicted by the structuralist markedness theory. Secondly, there is no way to predict in the structuralist markedness theory that exactly this change will occur significantly more often than other conceivable changes involving the direction from marked into unmarked. The structuralist markedness conventions must consequently be considered inadequate as well.

The only way out is to consider markedness in connection with the entire distinctive feature system as relevant to the direction of change. This idea, already present in Chomsky and Halle's, Kean's and Van Lessen Kloeke's approaches, acquires a falsifiable elaboration only if related to distinctive feature hierarchy in the sense of asymmetrical ordering, as defined above.

I define markedness as derivable from the phonetic specifications in the structuralist sense, unless a specification for a dominating feature opposition patterned within the same phonetic dimension is relevant to a given segment. In the latter case, markedness reversal can take place.

Markedness reversal can be illustrated by the Kajkavian vowel system of Ključ and Koškovec discussed under 1.5.1. above, where [±compact] is a dominating distinctive feature opposition, and this has consequences for [±diffuse], which is patterned in the same phonetic dimension, in this sense that in the [-compact] segments, it is [+diffuse], and not [-diffuse], which is unmarked, whereas the opposite term is marked. In addition to this paradigmatically conditioned markedness reversal, which should be put to a test as potentially universal, there is also syntagmatic markedness reversal, depending on the specification for the same distinctive feature opposition in the neighbouring segment. Syntagmatic markedness reversal is at best a universal potentiality, not a necessity.

In the speech errors discussed above, the specification of [±anterior] changed from marked into unmarked. And it is due to the phonetically limited space of this change that the [-back] segments changed in this way became [+high]. This does not reject the hypothesis formulated at the end of 1.3. above, namely, that a change of a subordinate feature opposition need not have consequences for the dominating one. Here it does have a consequence for it, due to the phonetically allowable space, but it is not a necessity within the system, only an accident due to the articulation possibilities in that given case. Only the fact that [±anterior] will change most of all the distinctive feature oppositions due to its being the only one which is twice subordinated, and that it will change from marked into unmarked, is predicted by the organization of the distinctive feature system of American English.

1.6.3. The next step is to further test my proposal to view the change from marked into unmarked as relevant to variation only within the constraints imposed by the feature hierarchy of a given system. I shall do so by discussing a change from the dental consonant /t/ into the velar consonant /k/ in the Polynesian languages Hawai'ian, Colloquial Samoan, and possibly also Luanguia (for which the sources do not seem to be reliable, cf. Harlow (1983: 101)), which is either unpredicted or counterpredicted by all of the preceding approaches to markedness. In order to be able to test my proposal, and see what the given change has brought about in the system, we must take the entire distinctive feature matrices into consideration. The data on the distinctive segments of Hawai'ian and Samoan have been forwarded to me by Harlow (cf. also Harlow (1983: 101 etc.)), for which I am proposing an articulatory and an acoustic distinctive feature analysis in order to establish whether regularities to be observed are of a general or a feature-idiosyncratic nature. This is especially relevant in view of the potentially vexed status of [±acute] for the vowels, which I am not able to evaluate.

(33a) Articulatory distinctive features of Hawai'ian preceding the /t/ → /k/ change:

	i	e	a	o	u	p	t	ʔ	h	m	n	l	w
consonantal						+	+	+	+	+	+	+	−
vocalic	+	+	+	+	+								−
high	+	−		−	+								+
low		−	+	−									
back	−	−		+	+								+
anterior						+		−	−	+			
coronal						−	+	−	−	−	+	+	
nasal						−	−	−		+	+		
continuant						−	−	−	+	−	−	+	

(33b) Articulatory distinctive features of Hawai'ian following the /t/ → /k/ change:

	i	e	a	o	u	p	k	ʔ	h	m	n	l	w
consonantal						+	+	+	+	+	+	+	−
vocalic	+	+	+	+	+								−
high	+	−		−	+								+
low		−	+	−									
back	−	−		+	+								+
anterior						+	−	−	−	+			
coronal										−	+	+	
nasal						−	−	−		+	+		
continuant						−	−	−	+	−	−	+	
glottalized							−	+					

(34a) Acoustic distinctive features of Hawai'ian preceding the /t/ → /k/ change:

	i	e	a	o	u	p	t	ʔ	h	m	n	l	w
consonantal						+	+	+	+	+	+	+	−
vocalic	+	+	+	+	+								−
diffuse	+	−		−	+								+
compact		−	+	−		−	−	+	+	−	−	−	
acute	+	+		−	−	−	+			−	+	+	−
nasal						−	−			+	+		
continuant						−	−	−	+	−	−	+	

(34b) Acoustic distinctive features of Hawai'ian following the /t/ → /k/ change:

	i	e	a	o	u	p	k	ʔ	h	m	n	l	w
consonantal						+	+	+	+	+	+	+	−
vocalic	+	+	+	+	+								−
diffuse	+	−		−	+								+
compact		−	+	−		−	+	+	+	−	−	−	
acute	+	+		−	−					−	+	+	−
nasal						−				+	+		
continuant						−	−	−	+	−	−	+	
glottalized							−	+					

If we look at the entire system, the change of /t/ into /k/ becomes much better understandable than if we look at it as an isolated phenomenon. In terms of the entire system, it appears to be directly related to the originally predictable glottalization of /ʔ/ which became distinctive by the introduction of the unglottalized velar stop /k/.

In the articulatory features, the /t/ → /k/ change was a change of [+coronal] into [−coronal] in the context of [−continuant, −nasal], by which [−coronal] became predictable and thus eliminated there. In the acoustic features, it was a change of [+acute] into [−acute] in the context of [−continuant, −nasal], by which [−acute] became predictable and thus eliminated there. In both sets of features, [±glottalized] was introduced in the same environment.

The /t/ → /k/ change in Hawai'ian was a change of a marked feature specification into the corresponding unmarked one in the structuralist sense. At the same time, a new unmarked feature specification (i.e. [−glottalized]) was introduced as opposed to the existing potentially marked (i.e. [+glottalized]) one.

This change can be viewed in terms of markedness only after the examination of the entire system. If looked at separately, it is by no means clear whether e.g. in the acoustic features it should be viewed as a change of [-compact] into [+compact], i.e. from unmarked into marked, or a change of [+acute] into [-acute], i.e. from marked into unmarked. The actual change was both, as a matter of fact. The difference which can be understood only in terms of the entire system is that a change of a marked feature specification into the corresponding unmarked one eliminates a distinctive feature from a given set of segments (in this case, [±acute] from the [-continuant, -nasal] segments), whereas a change of an unmarked feature specification into the corresponding marked one need not in itself equal any such elimination. Elimination of a distinctive feature opposition from a set of segments equals increasing predictability, and thus potentially also hierarchy. So let us examine the distinctive feature hierarchies of Hawai'ian preceding and following the /t/ → /k/ change.

(35a) Asymmetrical ordering of articulatory features in Hawai'ian preceding the /t/ → /k/ change:

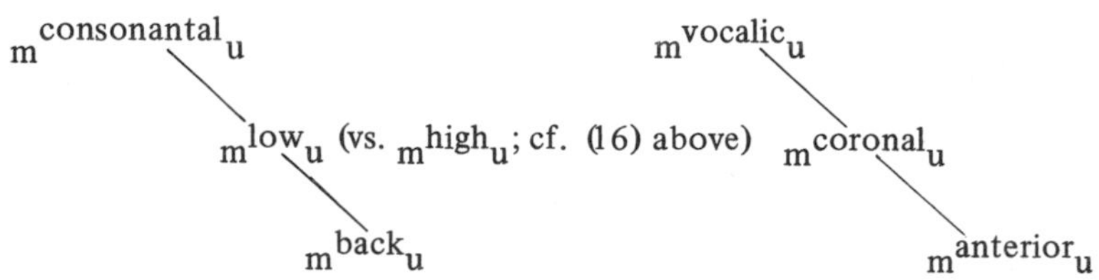

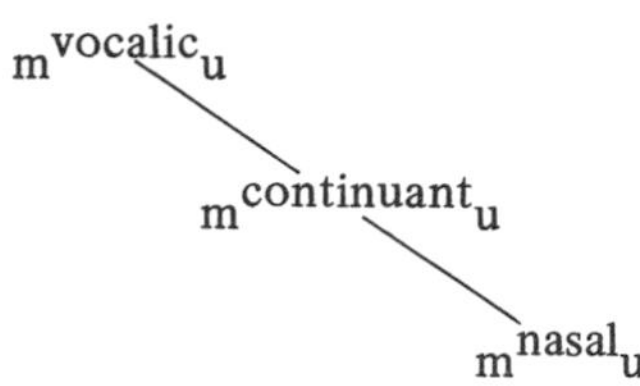

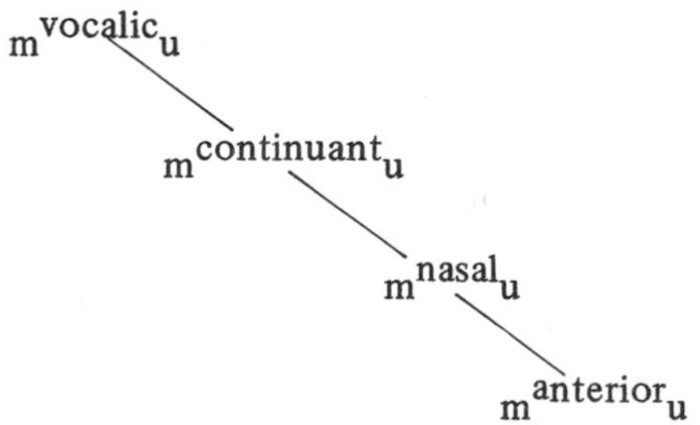

(35b) Asymmetrical ordering of articulatory features of Hawai'ian following the /t/ → /k/ change:

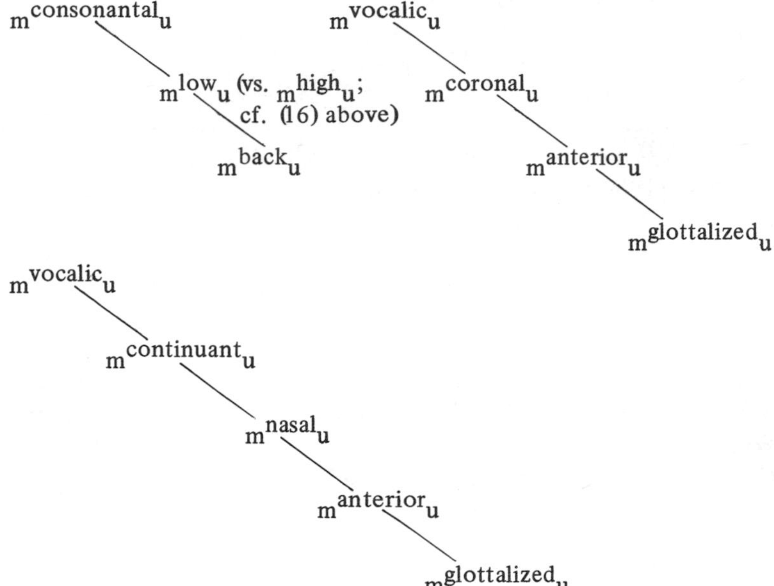

(35c) Asymmetrical ordering of acoustic features in Hawai'ian preceding the /t/ → /k/ change:

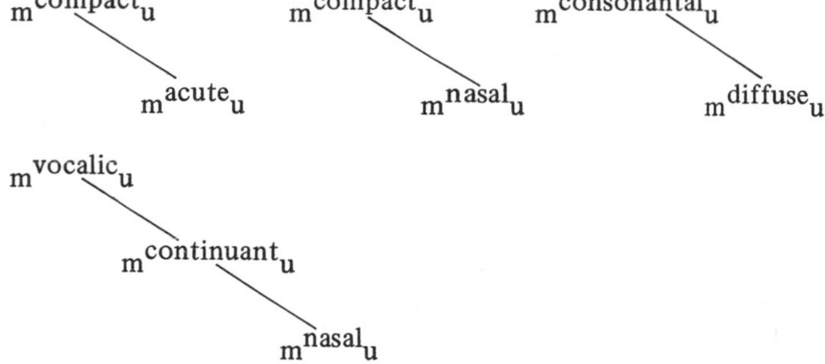

(35d) Asymmetrical ordering of acoustic features in Hawai'ian following the /t/ → /k/ change:

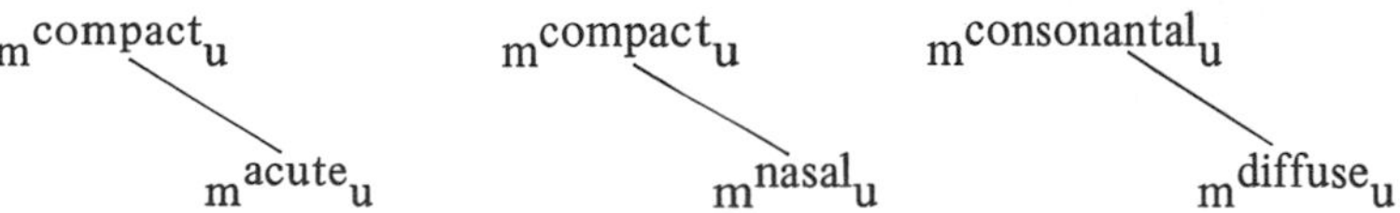

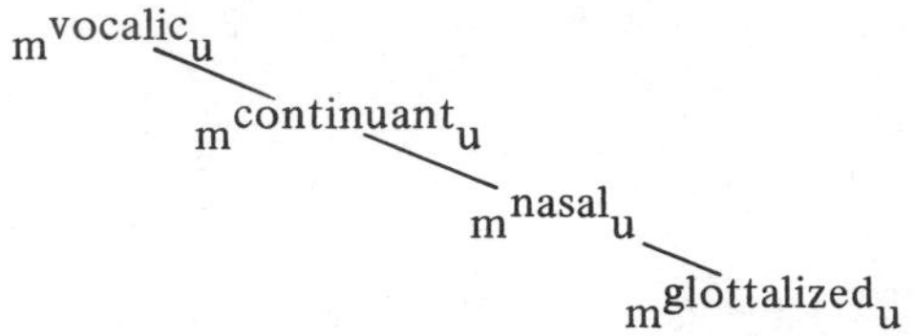

We can see that the /t/ → /k/ change in Hawai'ian has introduced a new distinctive feature opposition (i.e. [±glottalized]) into the system, but that this new distinctive feature opposition has entered an asymmetrical relation with another, already existing, distinctive feature opposition. Due to asymmetrical patterning, partial predictability holds for [±glottalized] in the system of Hawai'ian, which may be viewed as a systematic compensation for the increase of complexity brought about by a new distinctive feature opposition.

How can this be compared with the Colloquial Samoan change of /t/ into /k/, which was parallelled by a change of /n/ into /ŋ/, as compared with Formal Samoan?

(36a) Articulatory distinctive features of Formal Samoan:

	i	e	a	o	u	p	t	ʔ	m	n	ŋ	s	l	f	v	(j	w)
consonantal	+					+	+	+	+	+	+	+	+	+	+	–	–
vocalic	+	+	+	+	+											–	–
high	+	–		–	+											+	+
low		–	+	–													
back	–	–		+	+											–	+
anterior						+		–	+		–			+	+		
coronal						–	+	–	–	+	–	+	+	–	–		
nasal						–	–	–	+	+	+						
continuant						–	–	–	–	–	–	+	+	+	+		
voice														–	+		

(36b) Articulatory distinctive features of Colloquial Samoan:

	i	e	a	o	u	p	k	ʔ	m	ŋ	s	l	f	v	(j	w)
consonantal						+	+	+	+	+	+	+	+	+	–	–
vocalic	+	+	+	+	+										–	–
high	+	–		–	+										+	+
low		–	+	–												
back	–	–		+	+										–	+
anterior						+	–	–	+	–			+	+		
coronal											+	+	–	–		
nasal						–	–	–	+	+						
continuant						–	–	–	–	–	+	+	+	+		
voice													–	+		
glottalized							–	+								

(36c) Acoustic distinctive features of Formal Samoan

	i	e	a	o	u	p	t	ʔ	m	n	ŋ	s	l	f	v	(j	w)
consonantal						+	+	+	+	+	+	+	+	+	+	−	−
vocalic	+	+	+	+	+											−	−
diffuse	+	−		−	+											−	+
compact		−	+	−		−	−	+	−	−	+						
acute	+	+		−	−	−	+		−	+		+	+	−	−	+	−
nasal						−	−	−	+	+	+						
continuant						−	−	−	−	−	−	+	+	+	+		
voice														−	+		

(36d) Acoustic distinctive features of Colloquial Samoan:

	i	e	a	o	u	p	k	ʔ	m	ŋ	s	l	f	v	(j	w)
consonantal						+	+	+	+	+	+	+	+	+	−	−
vocalic	+	+	+	+	+										−	−
diffuse	+	−		−	+										−	+
compact		−	+	−		−	+	+	−	+						
acute	+	+		−	−						+	+	−	−	+	−
nasal						−	−	−	+	+						
continuant						−	−	−	−	−	+	+	+	+		
voice													−	+		
glottalized							−	+								

(I am not able to evaluate the phonological status of [j] and [w], which are assumed by Marsack (1962) to be distinctive, and by Harlow (personal communication) to be nondistinctive.)

In the articulatory features, the /t/ → /k/ and /n/ → /ŋ/ changes equalled changing [+coronal] into [-coronal] in the [-continuant] segments, by which [-coronal] became predictable there, and [±glottalized] was introduced in the [-continuant, −nasal] segments. In the acoustic features, these changes equalled changing [+acute] into [-acute] in the [-continuant] segments, by which [-acute] became predictable there, and [±glottalized] was introduced in the [-continuant, -nasal] segments.

The Colloquial Samoan change thus differed from the Hawai'ian one only by its less restricted environment: it took place in all the [-continuant] segments, not only the [-continuant, -nasal] ones.

(37a) Asymmetrical ordering of articulatory features in Formal Samoan:

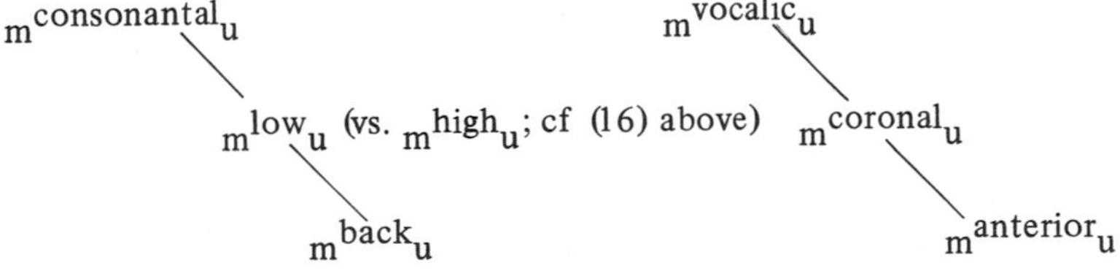

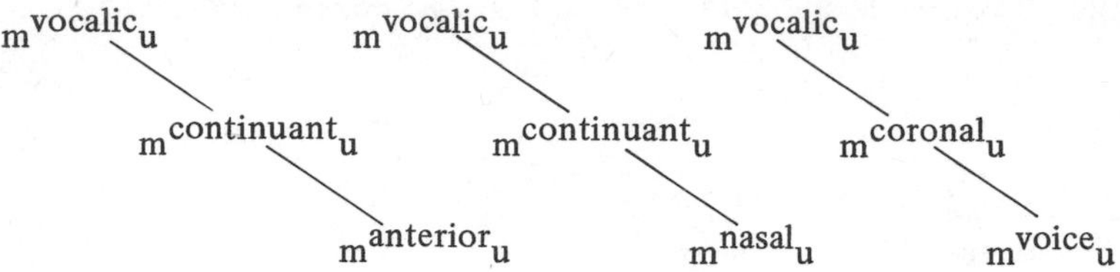

(37b) Asymmetrical ordering of articulatory features in Colloquial Samoan:

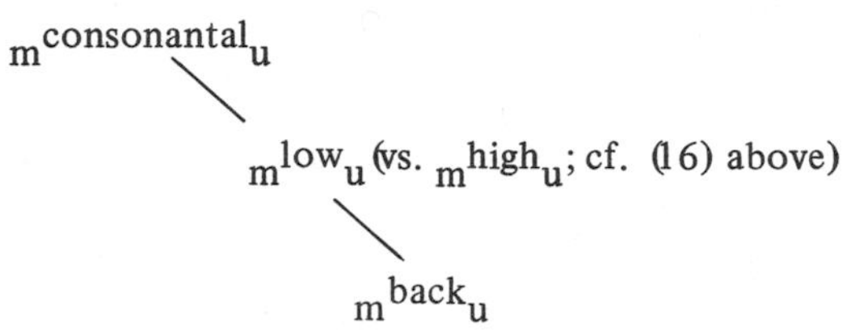

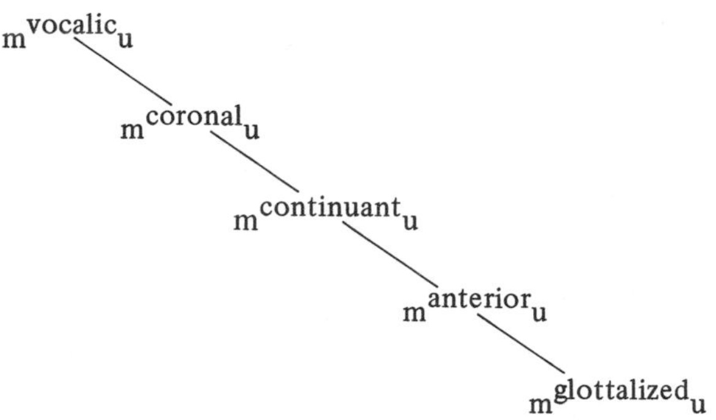

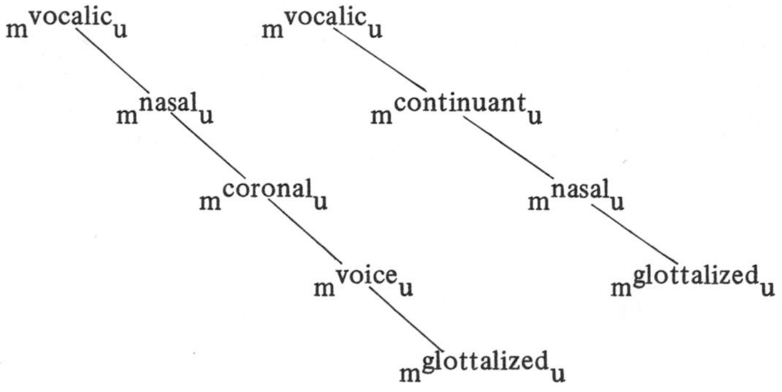

(37c) Asymmetrical ordering of acoustic features in Formal Samoan:

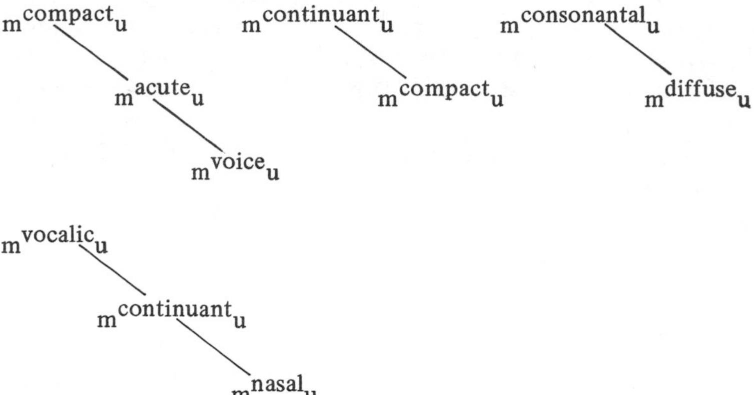

(37d) Asymmetrical ordering of acoustic features on Colloquial Samoan:

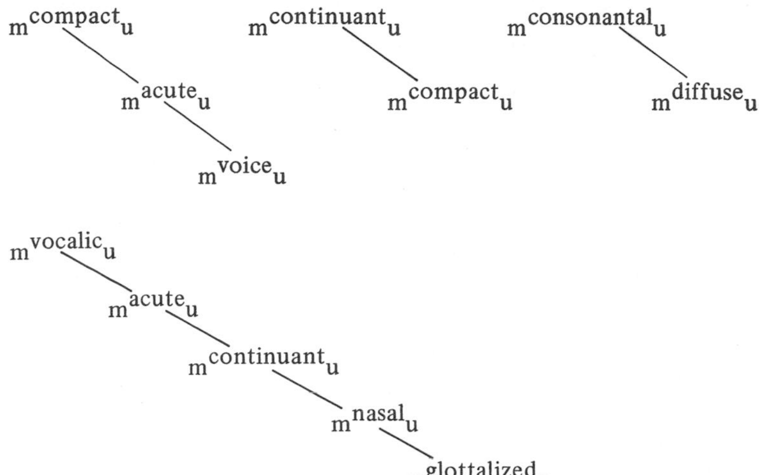

(It must further be investigated whether it is indeed the case that only in transitive asymmetrical ordering (such as *vocalic* → *acute* → *continuant* → *nasal* → *glottalized*), a feature may be distinctive exclusively in combination with a predictable specification of another feature opposition, whereas otherwise, asymmetrical ordering is established only if a feature is distinctive with '—' and predictable specifications of another feature opposition.)

Comparable to Hawai'ian, the /t/ → /k/ and /n/ → /ŋ/ changes in Colloquial Samoan have also introduced [±glottalized] into the system, and in addition to that increased predictability even more, by introducing transitivity between pairs of asymmetrically ordered features. So we can see that also in Colloquial Samoan, the increase of complexity caused by the introduction of a new distinctive feature was compensated for by letting the new distinctive feature enter an asymmetrical relation with an already existing distinctive feature.

We can conclude that markedness is relevant to the direction of change only if viewed against the background of the existing hierarchies. This holds for the phenomena discussed in this section as much as it does for those discussed in the preceding sections, also for those which are not so obviously related to the existing hierarchies, as for example diphthongization discussed in 1.5.1. above.

Markedness can be defined as asymmetry itself, which shows up within a distinctive feature opposition whenever there is phonetic presence of a specification in one of the terms and its absence in the other term, or whenever distributional phenomena treat one of the terms of the opposition in the same way as they treat the absence of a sign pertaining to the given distinctive feature.

In terms of the system, this asymmetry means that the marked term implies the existence of the unmarked one, but not *vice versa*.

To my knowledge, markedness within a dominating distinctive feature opposition cannot be reversed by a subordinate distinctive feature opposition, whereas markedness within a subordinate distinctive feature opposition can be reversed by a dominating one patterned within the same phonetic dimension. It occurs by necessity if the two distinctive feature oppositions are mutually exclusive, as illustrated by diphthongization in Kajkavian of Ključ and Koškovec discussed above.

1.7. Prosodic Hierarchy in Phonology

One of the main issues in the phonological theory of the past years has been hierarchical structuring of the phonological system, and the question of how these nonlinear hierarchical structures relate to linear sequences of phonological segments. This section reexamines the motivation for the proposed hierarchical structures, and modifies and further elaborates them in some cases.

1.7.1. In addition to distinctive features which form sets at the linearly ordered segmental level, the phonological representation has been recently assumed (cf. Selkirk (1980a)) to contain a fixed hierarchy of levels which can be defined as prosodic and characterized by a constituent structure as follows.

(38) Prosodic levels in phonology (cf. Selkirk (1980a)):
utterance
intonational unit
prosodic phrase
word
foot
syllable
segment.

An element at each level is composed of one or more elements at the next lower level. According to Kiparsky's (1981: 245) survey of the hierarchy, *"each level is represented in a formally parallel fashion, by means of binary trees, each nonterminal node branching into S(trong) and W(eak)".* Hence the term 'prosodic' for this hierarchy. In Kiparsky's approach, prosodic hierarchy equals phonological hierarchy, and he defines it as consisting of the following levels: phonological phrase, word, foot, syllable, and segment.

First of all, it must be investigated whether prosodic hierarchy must by necessity equal phonological hierarchy, as a part of a general quest for its definitory basis, which also questions the relation between prosodic hierarchy and morphological and syntactic structure. The latter come into the picture at the level of the word and at higher levels.

Secondly, it must be investigated whether prosodic constituency and prominence as related to it are independent of the remaining parts of the language structure indeed.

These questions must be investigated for each level stated by Selkirk and Kiparsky.

1.7.2. Even though the internal structure of the segment is crucial to a correct understanding of the structure of the higher levels, it has not been given the required attention in the analysis of the prosodic – or phonological – hierarchy. So, what is a distinctive segment and which distinctive features can minimally form it? On the basis of the investigation presented in the preceding sections, we are now able to formulate an answer to it.

The basis for a definition of the phonological segment has been laid down by Ebeling (1960: 67 etc.), who came to the insight that phonological segments are sets of distinctive features for which the fact that they are grouped together is relevant in this sense that the same features in the same order constitute different linguistic forms according as they are grouped together differently. We can now propose a reformulation of the part of this definition which refers to the order of the features. The paradigmatic order is given for a distinctive feature system in the sense of partial asymmetrical ordering, and it is liable to a differential grouping only in so far as it does not crosscut the dominance relation within a pair of asymmetrically ordered distinctive feature oppositions. The syntagmatic order, on the other hand, is liable to differential grouping to the extent that this is not prevented by the asymmetrical ordering, and that it does not include specifications of the same distinctive feature which occur in the order other than 'unmarked, marked', because only that order can be differentially grouped either into two segments or into one, whereas another order of specifications for the same distinctive feature can only be grouped into two segments. The order 'unmarked, marked' has been recognized as underlying diphthongization by Andersen (1972), and a phonetic diphthong can be analysed phonologically either as a single segment or a segment sequence, depending on whether it is opposed to the corresponding sequence (then it is a single segment) or not (then it is itself a sequence if its constituting elements have been established independently as well). And we have seen in the preceding section that the evaluation either as 'unmarked' or 'marked' is derivable from the phonetic specifications, unless markedness reversal is triggered by a dominating distinctive feature opposition which is patterned within the same phonetic dimension as the one undergoing markedness reversal.

For example, [+acute, +continuant, +voiced] can be grouped with [+compact] either into one set, yielding /ž/ in Serbo-Croatian, or into two sets, yielding /zj/ in the same language. This possibility of a differential grouping is restricted e.g. by asymmetrical ordering according to which [±continuant] and [±voice] combine into sets only with those distinctive features which are unmarked for [±vocalic]. The asymmetrical ordering forms the paradigmatic context within which markedness is evaluated as relative to it in the sense of a dominating distinctive feature opposition dictating markedness reversal in another distinctive feature opposition with which it is symmetrically ordered. Symmetrical ordering as a rule equals phonetically patterning within the same phonetic dimension, but there are also less clear cases, such as that of [±vocalic] and [±consonantal] in the languages in which these distinctive feature oppositions are mutually exclusive in combination with a '+' specification of one of them (which then makes the '–' specification of the other one predictable). In those languages, [±vocalic] and [±consonantal] can be analysed as mutually symmetrically ordered, as this is not contradicted by the phonetic substance (but not clearly dictated by it either). An example of such a language is Serbo-Croatian, the distinctive feature matrices of which have been presented under (5) and (12) above. In Serbo-Croatian, [±vocalic] and [±consonantal] are symmetrically ordered, and [±continuant] and [±voice] are asymmetrically ordered with respect to [±vocalic]. This means that [±vocalic] is a dominating feature opposition triggering markedness reversal of [±consonantal], by which markedness of [±consonantal] is in the context of a distinctive specification for [±continuant] and/or [±voice] evaluated against the unmarked value of [±vocalic]. And in the context of the unmarked value [±vocalic], it is [+consonantal] which is unmarked, and [-consonantal], marked. The sequence of [+consonantal, -consonantal] is then 'unmarked, marked'. In such a case, either grouping of these two specifications into one set or into two distinctive feature sets, i.e. segments, is possible, and this is exactly what is found in various languages. Whereas Serbo-Croatian has an opposition between /ž/ and /zj/ such that they are capable of distinguishing words *ceteris paribus,* Dutch, for example, has in the given case only a sequence of two distinctive feature sets, i.e. segments, which phonologically equals /zj/, and is pronounced as [ž]. (The given sequence is also specified as [-compact, +compact], which – in the absence of asymmetrical ordering triggering markedness reversal – directly corresponds with 'unmarked, marked' and is, consequently, also liable to grouping either into one set or into two sets.)

In a comparable way, [±long] and [±rising] are in Serbo-Croatian asymmetrically ordered with [±consonantal], as they are only compatible with [-consonantal] segments and with those which are unspecified for *consonantal.* In other words, they are compatible only with segments which are unmarked for *consonantal.* In the context of the unmarked value of *consonantal* (or [±consonantal], I use these two graphical denotation ways interchangeably in order to refer to a distinctive feature opposition), it is [+vocalic] which is unmarked and [-vocalic] which is marked. The order [+vocalic, -vocalic] then equals the order 'unmarked, marked', which is characteristic of diphthongization in the sense of Andersen (1972), and within diphthongization liable to a differential grouping either into two segments or one, equalling phonologically either a sequence or a single distinctive segment. Thus segments which are unmarked for [±consonantal] in Serbo-Croatian can undergo diphthongization with respect to [±vocalic] such that the values of [±vocalic] are distributed in the order 'unmarked, marked', in the given case yielding [+vocalic, -vocalic]. This diphthongization as a phonetic process comes out clearly in the treatment of borrowings in which sonorants, which are unmarked for [±consonantal], appear as syllable nuclei and can as such be characterized by [±long] and [±rising]. The dominating distinctive feature opposition [±consonantal] triggers markedness reversal in [±vocalic] in the sense stated above, and enables diphthongization by which the values of [±vocalic] are distributed in the order [+vocalic, -vocalic]. This is why syllabic sonorants in borrowings can be pronounced as sequences of vowel + sonorant. They can, but need not necessarily, as diphthongization of syllabic sonorants is a matter of phonetic variation in Serbo-Croatian. Thus *ansamble* 'ensemble' can either be pronounced as [ansàmbl] or [ansàmbal], and *bicikl* 'bicycle' either as [bicìkl] or [bȉcikal] (the latter variant is usual in the southern and southwestern areas of Neoštokavian Serbo-Croatian).

Within the constraints imposed by markedness and asymmetrical ordering in Serbo-Croatian, grouping of distinctive features into sets called segments is distinctive indeed.

1.7.3. According to Bell and Hooper (1978: 8 etc.), the basic and available phonological evidence for syllables is found in the phonotactic distribution of segments, which depends on their sonority. Segments of a syllable are arranged in such a way that their sonority increases from the onset to the nuclear peak, and decreases thereafter. It is according to them possible to establish the following order of preference for occurrence as syllable peaks: stop – fricative – resonant (in my terminology, 'sonorant') – vowel.

The question to be asked now is, does this segment arrangement justify the syllable as a phonological level or not?

The answer to it is 'yes, it does', if sonority is at least partially independent of the distinctive features which constitute these segments and some general rule(s) of their possible linear arrangements. The answer to it is 'no, it does not', if the sonority arrangement is fully derivable from the distinctive features and rules for their linear arrangements on the one hand, and universal constraints on pronouncible sequences on the other.

Language-specific syllable structures and sonority scales as relating to them exist indeed as we have seen from the discussion of a different treatment of nasals with respect to liquids e.g. in English, Polish and Serbo-Croatian, presented in 1.2. above. Whereas nasals are less sonorous than liquids in English, they are more sonorous than liquids in Polish, and there is no fundamental difference between them in Serbo-Croatian. However, it cannot be stated on independent grounds that this is related to different distinctive feature specifications or their different evaluation, as indications as to the distinctive features involved were drawn exactly from this type of variation. So, the question relating to relative independence of the sonority arrangement must be considered integrally with respect to the entire scale. Is the position of a segment on the sonority scale derivable from the distinctive feature system of a given language or not?

Selkirk (1982) assumed the sonority scale to have fixed universal values, characterized by the following indexes: p, t, k (.5), b, d, g (1), f, θ (2), v, z, ð (3), s (4), m, n (5), l (6), r (7), i, u (8), e, o (9), a (10). According to Selkirk, there are dissimilarity requirements of the form 'position X in the onset/rhyme must be at least n points apart from adjacent position Y in the onset/

rhyme on the sonority scale'. Languages differ in the integer value of n.

Steriade (1982) criticized Selkirk's sonority scale with absolute values by showing that language-specific deviations from it occur as derivable from the distinctive features involved. Steriade proposed a universally fixed articulatory distinctive feature hierarchy as underlying language-specific sonority scales, the differences among them being due to utilization vs. nonutilization of distinctive features.

(39) Steriade's (1982: 98f.) sonority scales based on distinctive features:

Latin sonority scale

[−sonorant, −continuant, −coronal] : p, k, b, g
[−sonorant, −continuant, +coronal] : t, d
[−sonorant, +continuant, −coronal] : f
[−sonorant, +continuant, +coronal] : s
[+sonorant, −continuant, +nasal, −coronal] : m
[+sonorant, −continuant, +nasal, +coronal] : n
[+sonorant, +continuant, −nasal, +lateral] : l
[+sonorant, +continuant, −nasal, −lateral] : r.

Greek sonority scale

[−sonorant, −continuant, −voice] : p, t, k
[−sonorant, −continuant, +voice] : b, d, g
[−sonorant, +continuant, −voice] : s
[−sonorant, +continuant, +voice] : z
[+sonorant, −continuant, +nasal] : m, n
[+sonorant, +continuant, −nasal, +lateral] : l
[+sonorant, +continuant, −nasal, −lateral] : r.

An impossible sonority scale:

[−continuant, −sonorant, −coronal] : p, k, b, g
[−continuant, −sonorant, +coronal] : t, d
[−continuant, +sonorant, −coronal] : m
[−continuant, +sonorant, +coronal] : n
[+continuant, −sonorant, +coronal] : s
[+continuant, +sonorant, +coronal] : r, l.

(According to Chomsky and Halle (1968: 302), the feature [±sonorant] distinguishes vowels, glides, nasal consonants and liquids from stops, fricatives and affricates. Even though the usage of this feature may be possible for the given sonority scales, it can as well be replaced by [±vocalic] – which in Chomsky and Halle's approach distinguishes nasals, as [−vocalic], from liquids, as [+vocalic] – because nasals and liquids are systematically treated in a different way in these languages. For Serbo-Croatian, on the other hand, usage of [±sonorant] would be even fundamentally unsatisfactory, because the segments all considered to be [+sonorant] are treated in a different way in Serbo-Croatian: glides are there less sonorous than nasals and liquids, and this is exclusively due to the specification of the glides as [−vocalic], as I have shown in 1.1. above. In the further discussion of the sonority scales, I shall consequently propose a replacement of [±sonorant] by [±vocalic] as a generally valid one (also in principle for Serbo-Croatian, where nasals and liquids are unspecified for [±vocalic], as shown in 1.1. above). This replacement makes nasals [-vocalic, -continuant, +nasal], whereas liquids are (depending on the language for the first specification) [+vocalic, +continuant, -nasal]. In addition to these specifications, [±coronal] is relevant to their distinctive feature specification, and the sonority scale in Latin. The proposed replacement makes [±lateral] superfluous.)

How do the distinctive features shown to be relevant to the sonority scale relate to these distinctive features in the matrices of the given languages?

We can see in the scales that there is a fixed order of features, and that within it permutations from '-' to '+' can account for the increase of sonority. As to the '-' to '+' permutations, we can see that they are translatable into markedness in this sense that an unmarked specification is less sonorous than the corresponding marked one. If [±sonorant] is replaced by [±vocalic] in the way suggested above, then nasals appear to fit into that general pattern as well, as among the [-vocalic, -continuant] segments, those unmarked for nasality are less sonorous than those marked for it.

But what can the fixed order of features be related to? In the case of [±sonorant] – to be replaced by [±vocalic] – it is clear that its first position is directly related to its being the dominating distinctive feature opposition with respect to [±continuant], [±nasal], [±coronal], and [±voiced] in the respective matrices of Latin and Greek. But what can account for the consistently second position of [±continuant] in these matrices?

[±continuant] and [±nasal] can in principle be mutually asymmetrically ordered. If this is the case, dominance of the first one can account for its systematic preceding the second one in the permutations accounting for the sonority scale. It must be investigated for each language under consideration whether there is such a dominance relation between these two distinctive feature oppositions indeed. And the problem connected with it is that if in a language [+nasal] is always [-continuant], and [+continuant], [-nasal], there is no way to establish which one is dominating and which one is subordinate – and this question must be answerable in a clear way whenever an asymmetrical relation is established. At the same time, these two distinctive feature oppositions cannot be viewed as symmetrically ordered either, because they are not patterned within the same phonetic dimension. This is why I have assumed these distinctive feature oppositions to be mutually unordered in American English discussed in 1.4 above, on the basis of such specifications as stated by Chomsky and Halle (1968: 176f.). I have also assumed that these distinctive feature oppositions are mutually unordered in Serbo-Croatian, because all the sonorants there can be shown to be unspecified for [±continuant], as discussed in 1.1. above, and [±nasal] is distinctive only in the segments which are unspecified for [±continuant], whereas it is nondistinctive in those specified as [-continuant]. Only in Maori, discussed in 1.5.4., and in Hawai'ian and Samoan, discussed in 1.6.3., there is a clear case of asymmetry between [±continuant] and [±nasal], because the [-continuant] segments are there distinctively either [+nasal] or [-nasal] (and the [+continuant] ones predictably nonnasal), whereas both the [+nasal] and the [-nasal] segments can only be [-continuant]. In Maori, Hawai'ian and Samoan, [±continuant] is dominating and [±nasal] subordinate to it.

In a sonority scale, nasals are less sonorous than liquids if the former are [-vocalic] and the latter [+vocalic], or if [±nasal] is subordinate to [±continuant]. If neither of these conditions holds, then nasals are more sonorous than liquids.

How can it be that nasals in Polish are more sonorous than liquids, as established by Rubach (1977: 76)? Again, the answer can be formulated only if we examine the entire distinctive feature system. Then we can see that Polish differs from the other discussed languages by having nasal vowels as well. This means that in Polish, [±nasal] is unordered with respect to [±vocalic] and also [±continuant], and then the markedness rule by which an unmarked specification is less sonorous than the corresponding marked specification automatically makes liquids, as [-nasal], less sonorous than nasals, which are [+nasal].

We can conclude that sonority scales are fully derivable from the distinctive features of a language, asymmetrical patternings between them, and the general rule that given asymmetrical patterning, an unmarked specification is less sonorous than the corresponding marked one, and that this applies to the distinctive features in the order of their dominance: a distinctive feature which is dominating with respect to more other distinctive features in a given sound system will be more basic to sonority, too, and form a more basic division in it on the basis of the markedness rule formulated above, and less dominating features will then contribute further subdivisions by following the same markedness rule. It must only be further investigated whether the first basic feature to sonority is always [±vocalic], as I suppose it to be, indeed.

As related to sonority, syllable structure in the sense of (40) below is also fully analysable in the sense of distinctive features, asymmetrical patterning, and markedness involved.

(40) Syllable structure according to Kiparsky (1981: 249), following Hockett (1955):

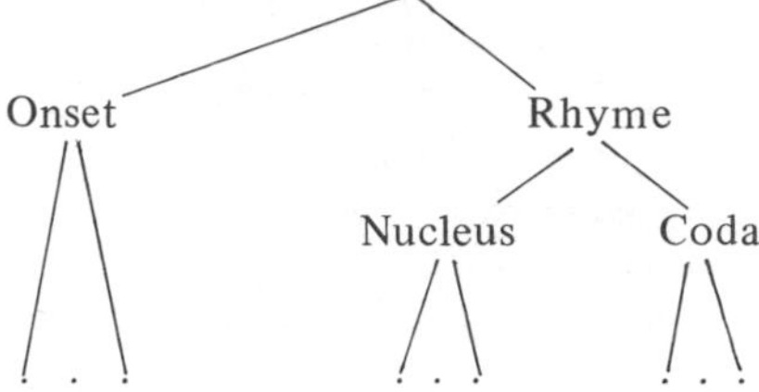

Whereas onsets are characterized by unmarked (i.e. '–' and predictable) specifications starting from the dominating distinctive feature(s), as compared with rhymes which are marked for them (i.e. characterized by '+' specifications), within the rhyme itself markedness reversal takes place due to the presence of distinctive feature oppositions which are subordinate to [±consonantal] and in the context of which – implying the unmarked value of [±consonantal] – [+vocalic] is unmarked and [–vocalic], marked.

Syllable structure thus appears to be characterized by the order 'unmarked, marked' of the dominating distinctive feature opposition [±vocalic] : whereas syllable onset is characterized by its unmarked value as compared with syllable rhyme, within the rhyme the nucleus is characterized by its unmarked value as compared with the coda, which is characterized by its marked value due to the markedness reversal which takes place within the rhyme, and which has also been discussed in 1.7.1. above. Thus Andersen's (1972) analysis of diphthongization as due to distribution of feature specifications in the order 'unmarked, marked' within a segment appears to fit into the general background of syllable structure, presumably forming a part of universal constraints on sequences.

The syllable is thus derivable from the distinctive feature patterning and markedness. It is restricted by morphological boundaries (in Dutch, for example, a consonant at the end of a prefix does not syllabify with the following stem-initial vowel) and by syntactic ones (in Kabardian, for example, an immediate constituent boundary prevents an otherwise automatic [ə] insertion even though both constituents contain two or more consonantal units; cf. Anderson (1978: 51) on Kuipers (1960)).

In addition to language-specific properties of syllable structure derivable from the corresponding language-specific asymmetrical orderings, languages also have specific contraints on linear sequences. For example, Japanese does not allow any (nonnasal) consonants in its rhymes, but does allow sequences of two identical vowels there (with the exception of the Kagoshima dialects, which allow only single phonological vowel segments in the rhymes). Serbo-Croatian, for example, does allow consonants in (the codas of) its syllable rhymes, but either does or does not allow vowel sequences in (the nuclei of) its rhymes, depending on the dialect (e.g. Čakavian and Slavonian Štokavian do allow them, as already discussed in 1.2 above, whereas Neoštokavian and the standard language which is based on it do not allow them). These constraints on allowable sequences are not fully derivable from the distinctive feature system and the possible distinctive feature sets, but are rather language-specific in the same way as e.g. grammatical constraints can be language-specific and idiosyncratic, for example, the question of whether a language expresses personal endings on the verb or not.

Apart from language-specific constraints on sequences, the syllable structure of a language is fully derivable from the asymmetrical patterning of its distinctive features and the universal markedness rule of feature distributions in the order 'unmarked, marked' between syllable onset and rhyme on the one hand, and within syllable rhyme on the other, and given markedness reversal there, between nucleus and coda. Given this derivability, there is not a separate level of the syllable. The syllable structure in fact follows from the nonlinear organization of the phonological system investigated in this study.

1.7.4. The foot is a unit of prosodic prominence. It is characterized by an alternation of weak and strong syllables, in either order, as connected with the segmental features of vowel duration and vowel quality, and the syllable structure in the sense of simple vs. complex rhymes, depending on the language under investigation.

In English, for example, the basic foot is bisyllabic, consisting of a strong and a weak syllable in that order, and monosyllabic feet can occur only at constituent boundaries. A monosyllabic foot can be either strong or weak, and consequently at the word level either accented (i.e. an 'accent foot') or unaccented. According to Selkirk (1980b: 572), it is generally the case that an open syllable containing a lax vowel may not be an accent foot on its own, whereas a syllable containing a tense vowel must always be either an accent foot on its own, or the strong syllable of a bisyllabic (i.e. 'binary') foot (the latter two possibilities are illustrated by the *Ti* and the *ro* of *Ticonderoga*). A closed syllable containing a lax vowel has a much freeer distribution. It may be a foot on its own, as with the first syllable of *Victrola* or the second syllable of *gymnast* (as well as the first), or it may be part of a bisyllabic foot, as with the second syllable of *modest* or of the foot *anec-* of *anecdote.*

However, a syllable containing a tense vowel is always either a monosyllabic accent foot or the strong syllable of a bisyllabic foot *only in the surface representation.* Selkirk (1980b: 590f.) discussed the vowel of the Latinate prefixes such as *de-* and *re-* and argued in favour of its being [+tense] in the underlying representation, even though it occurs in the weak position and is lax in the surface representation of the verbs containing such prefixes. She proposed to treat such cases by means of a Prefix Defooting transformation, accompanied by Vowel Detensing, which is restricted to such (zero suffix) verbs as compared with their corresponding nouns.

(41) Prefix Defooting transformation according to Selkirk (1980b):

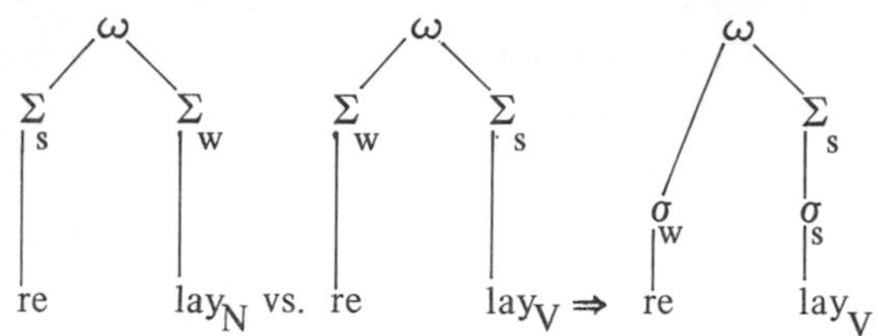

(where (ω) denotes the prosodic word, (Σ) denotes the foot, (σ) the syllable, (N) the noun, and (V) the verb).

Similar cases of morphologically conditioned change of the prosodic structure were discussed by Kiparsky (1983), who proposed to view the English affixes causing an accent shift on the stem as ordered at a different, higher, level of derivation than those not causing it. An example of the first type is found in the suffix *-al* in English, and of the second type in *-ize.*

(42) Foot assignment according to Kiparsky (1983):

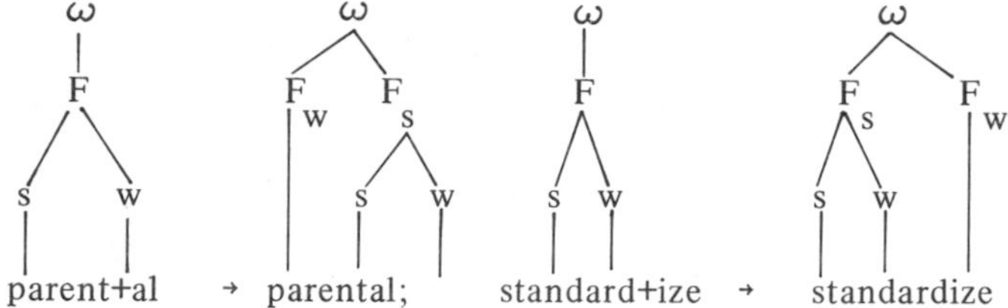

(Kiparsky denotes the syllable by means of (s) or (w) only, and the foot by means of (F).

It follows from the accounts of the English accent system mentioned above that in addition to a large amount of predictability given the *tense* vs. *lax* vowel specification, the syllable structure and the boundaries involved, the crucial points of the prosodic structure still have to be specified in the lexical representation. The lexical representation must contain information on whether the feet of a prosodic word are mutually arranged as *strong – weak* or *weak – strong* (cf. rélày_N vs. reláy_V, and àllỳ_N vs. allý_V, vs. Dùndée vs. níghtingàle, with (´) denoting so-called 'primary accent', and (`) denoting so-called 'secondary accent'). And not only that. In Selkirk's approach, the lexical representation must also contain information on whether the feet are monosyllabic or bisyllabic (cf. gýmnàst vs. módest).

Is the foot an independent prosodic level that must be encoded in the lexicon indeed, or is it derivable from accent specifications of lexical morphemes and their segmental specifications with any possible neutralizations due to combination of lexical with other lexical and/or grammatical morphemes?

As crucial to answering this question, let us examine Selkirk's statement that both *módest* and *gýmnàst* contain a lax vowel in the second, closed, syllable. It is the weak syllable of a bisyllabic foot in *módest,* and a monosyllabic foot in *gýmnàst.* Let us examine this statement by comparing *gýmnàst* with *reláy,* the latter, according to Selkirk, with an underlying tense vowel in the first syllable, because of its being tense in *rélày.* Why not then compare *gýmnàst* with *gỳmnásium,* the latter with a tense vowel in the second syllable? And now follow Jakobson's (1971, 2nd: 120) principle for morphophonological transcription (underlying Selkirk's and other generative approaches as well), by which *"if certain phonemic* [in my terminology, phonological; J.G.] *constituents of the given full-stem as compared with cognate forms appear in different alternants, we take as basic the alternant which appears in a position where the other alternant too would be admissible".* By this principle, we analyse the second syllable of the stem *gymnas–* as having a [+tense] vowel in the basic alternant, because it alone occurs under primary accent, the only position where both tense and lax vowels are phonologically permitted. As compared with the basic form, any other alternant can – on the basis of the methodology outlined in this study – be only characterized either by the same distinctive feature sign or by its omittance, not by any change of a distinctive specification. In the given alternation between *gýmnàst* and *gỳmnásium,* the latter form contains the basic vowel alternant in the second syllable, and the former form contains in the second syllable the alternant in which the distinctive feature sign [±tense] is omitted. Whenever a distinctive feature sign is omitted from a set, the realization of the given set within the phonetic dimension relating to the omitted feature sign equals phonetically the unmarked term of the given distinctive feature opposition as established on the basis of the distinctive feature matrix, as outlined in the section on markedness above. This general rule for realization of omitted signs as equalling the unmarked value of the given feature opposition, yields a phonetically lax vowel in *gýmnàst.* The crucial thing here is that it does not correspond phonologically with a [–tense] vowel, but rather with the absence of a sign for *tenseness* in that vowel.

The difference between the vowel of the second syllable of *módest* and that of the second syllable of *gýmnàst* can now be analysed in terms of the distinctive features involved: *módest* has a [−tense] vowel in its second syllable (which is the same in the corresponding noun, *módesty*), whereas *gýmnàst* has in its second syllable a vowel from which the sign for *tenseness* has been omitted, and it is realized as lax only due to the general implementation rule by which omitted signs are, in the absence of a conditioning context, implemented phonetically so as to equal the implementation (i.e. the form) of the unmarked term of the distinctive feature opposition in which they participate, which need not be the opposite of the implementation of the marked form, but may also equal phonetically only the absence of the given mark, and vary accordingly.

The prosodic difference between the second syllable of *módest* and that of *gýmnàst* can now be accounted for in terms of the relevant feature specifications, and a general rule of English by which a closed syllable containing a vowel which is unspecified for *tenseness* (i.e. from which the sign for either [+tense] or [−tense] has been omitted) forms a monosyllabic foot if occurring at a prosodic word boundary (which will be further defined in the next subsection).

In the approach I am proposing here, lexical representation contains maximal feature specifications in the sense of the rule stated above (which contains the condition that each maximally specified set of distinctive features must occur in at least one of the corresponding surface forms). In the various alternating forms, a distinctive feature sign may be omitted due to its predictability either in terms of the newly surrounding segments or in terms of the higher level phenomena connected with the derivation (such as accent alternation, which is caused by rules pertaining to the grammar). Implementation of the given distinctive feature set is in cases of sign omittance either governed by the context or by markedness as established independently of the given omittance.

Accent alternations in English are relatively restricted, and there is a large amount of predictability, to be captured in terms of the strong – weak alternation within bisyllabic feet, and a possibility of having monosyllabic feet at prosodic word boundaries. The only characteristic which is not simply computable is the position of the primary accent on stems and the capacity of affixes to affect it or not. This crucial point of the prosodic structure forms part of the lexical representation. All of the remaining regularities can be formulated in terms of a general rule on strong – weak or weak – strong phonetic alternations, which can due to its generality be kept out of the individual lexical representations.

The above statement is not restricted to English. Vogel and Scalise (1982) have shown that analysis of secondary accent in Italian does not necessitate reference to any feet assignment in the lexical (i.e. 'underlying' in their terminology) representation, but can rather be stated by means of general rules regulating the strong – weak alternations there, in addition to lexical marking of the main accent.

I conclude that the foot is fully derivable from the morphological and segmental specifications involved, and thus not a separate level in phonology, but only an additional rule on strong – weak or weak – strong alternations, which – within the segmental and morphological constraints imposed by the system – governs the phonetic implementation of a given language in a way general for that language.

1.7.5. The prosodic word has been defined by Selkirk (1980b: 570) as being constituted by a sequence of one or more feet or superfeet (a superfoot being a strong foot followed by a weak syllable in English, i.e. $\Sigma_s \overset{\Sigma}{\frown} \sigma_w$), joined in a right-branching constituent structure. Morphologically, the prosodic word in English is constituted by the simple nonbranching stem and any stem affixes. There is a distinction between cohering and noncohering affixes, and only the former form part of the prosodic word: the cohering affixes syllabify together with the stem, whereas the noncohering ones do not. In English, *-ic* is a cohering affix, and e.g. the prosodic word *rhythmic* is pronounced with a syllable-onset [m], whereas *-y* is an example of a noncohering affix, which means that it does not syllabify together with the preceding stem, and by definition also does not belong to the same prosodic word as the preceding stem. This is why e.g. *rhythmy* is pronounced with a syllable nucleus [m̩]: the prosodic word boundary directly following it and preceding *-y* prevents the former from becoming a syllable onset. (This is an example of a morphological boundary preventing syllabification, as mentioned in 1.7.3. above.)

Syllabification is consequently viewed as indicative of the domain of the prosodic word, within which prominence relations are operative. This is consistent with Selkirk's viewing the syllable as a prosodic level, characterized by the sonority hierarchy, which is viewed as a prosodic phenomenon.

I have shown in 1.7.3. above that the sonority hierarchy is entirely derivable from the distinctive features involved in the sets which constitute the syllable, and that the syllable can consequently be viewed as a phonological constraint on linear sequences, which can for each language be formulated by means of a general rule, and which is essentially constrained by the organization of the distinctive feature system of the given language. On the basis of these arguments, the syllable forms part of the phonological structure of a language and is indicative of it, whereas it is by necessity indicative of the prosodic structure only in so far as prosodic distinctive features are involved.

On the basis of the argumentation presented in 1.7.3., syllabification is indicative of the phonological word. And on the basis of the argumentation presented in 1.7.4., prominence relations are indicative of the prosodic word. Does the phonological word by necessity coincide with the prosodic word?

An example of a language in which the domain of prosodic phenomena need not coincide with that indicated by means of syllabification or by other phonological means, is found in Serbo-Croatian.

In Serbo-Croatian, the prosodic word is defined by its initial and final boundary (cf. Gvozdanović (1980a: 12 etc.)). Acoustically, the initial boundary of the prosodic word is characterized either by a high or a rising fundamental frequency, and the final boundary is characterized by a falling fundamental frequency in bi- and polysyllabic words, and by a nonfalling nonrising fundamental frequency in monosyllabic words. The rising fundamental frequency is an implementation of the rising tone, and the falling and nonrising nonfalling fundamental frequencies are an implementation of the nonrising tone. The high fundamental frequency, equalling perceptually the high pitch, indicates the beginning of the prosodic word in the absence of a word-initial rising tone. It shows us with certainty where the prosodic word begins.

And so we know with certainty that the initial prosodic word boundary can precede the boundary indicated by means of syllabification, as shown in (43) below, that it can coincide with the boundary indicated by means of syllabification, but follow the boundary indicated by means of voice assimilation phenomena, as shown in (44) below, or that it can coincide with all these boundaries, as shown in (45) below.

(43) The initial prosodic word boundary preceding the one indicated by means of syllabification in Serbo-Croatian:
nad ovcu 'above a/the sheep' is syllabified as [nȁd-ōv-cu], with a syllable-final [d];
(with (–) denoting a syllable boundary, (ˋ) the short falling tonal accent, and (ˋ) the short rising one).
od sad se 'from now on itself' is syllabified as [òt-sa-ce], with a syllable-final [t] at the end of the first syllable, but with its forming a [c] at the beginning of the third syllable, rather than staying a [t] at the end of the second syllable.
The prosodic word boundary begins on the first syllable, and the domain of syllabification on the second syllable.

(44) *od sad se* 'it is from now on that itself', with contrastive usage of either *od* or *sad,* is syllabified as [ot-sȁ-ce].
The prosodic word and the syllabification begin on the second syllable, but the domain of voice assimilation begins on the first syllable.

(45) *nadobudstvo* 'prosperity, lit. hope evokedness' is syllabified as [na-do-bùc-tvo].
The high pitch on the initial syllable shows that the prosodic word begins there, thus coinciding with the domain of the syllabification.

In Serbo-Croatian, the syllabification domain is given. It comprises the stem with any suffixes and enclitics (i.e. short forms of the auxiliaries, of the personal and reflexive pronouns, and the question particle *li,* which occur in the order: *li,* auxiliaries except *je,* personal, reflexive pronouns in the dative, genitive, accusative *se, je,* and follow the first constituent in the sentence), but excludes prefixes and proclitics (i.e. prepositions, the negative *ne,* and conjunctions *i* 'and', *a* 'and/but', and *no* 'but', which precede the first or any compatible constituent in the sentence, respectively).

The domain of consonant assimilation in Serbo-Croatian is also given. It comprises the stem with any suffixes and enclitics following it, and with any prefixes and proclitics preceding it.

Syllabification and consonant assimilation are phonological phenomena, characteristic of the phonological word, which are fully definable in terms of the grammatical structure involved. The phonological word is consequently not a separate level in Serbo-Croatian or in any language where it is definable in a comparable way.

The prosodic word, on the other hand, is not fully definable in terms of the grammatical structure involved. Whereas it always consists of a full stem with any affixes attached to it (which may be called together 'the morphological word') and any enclitics attached to it, it may but need not comprise the proclitics, as the speaker is free to use either a proclitic or the next following morphological word contrastively, and then he puts the prosodic word boundary between the proclitic and the next following morphological word, as in example (44) above.

The prosodic word in Serbo-Croatian neither equals the domain of syllabification (as illustrated by (43) above), nor that of consonant assimilation (as illustrated by (44) above). It is not fully definable in terms of the grammatical structure involved, although it is constrained by it in the way stated above.

The prosodic word is a prosodic level in Serbo-Croatian indeed, definable by its prosodic form. And what is its meaning?

In the cases in which the prosodic word is not simply derivable from the grammatical structure involved, there is contrast between what is expected on the basis of the frame of reference presented by the speaker as shared by himself and the adressee, and the information actually presented in the given sentence. If the adressee hears e.g. the example (44) mentioned above, with a high pitch on *sad* 'now', he will interpret it as: 'it is from now on, and not from some other point in time on'. And if he hears the high pitch on *od* 'from' as well, he will interpret it as: 'it is from now on, and not till now, or with reference to any other point in time'. This interpretation is entirely directed by the placement of the high or the rising pitch following the falling pitch as stated above. The given placement indicates the boundaries of the prosodic word. It can comprise the morphological word with the proclitics preceding it and enclitics following it – and be thus predictable from the grammatical structure and not contribute any new information, or it can deviate from this grammatical stretch by the placement of the prosodic word boundaries, which are en- and decoded as such whenever there is a falling pitch followed either by a high or a rising pitch. The interpretation of contrast is derived from this deviation. The meaning of the elements of the prosodic word (i.e. of the prosodic word boundaries) is comparable to the meaning of distinctive features, being 'mere otherness'. Whenever the given grammatical stretch denotes mere otherness due to its semantic features which are absent in the preceding grammatical stretch – as it does in the combination of a proclitic with the next following morphological word – and the prosodic word boundaries follow that stretch, the prosodic meaning of mere otherness does not contribute anything to the interpretation. Only when the prosodic word boundaries separate the proclitic from the next following morphological word, thus separating what semantically belongs together, then the meaning of the prosodic word boundaries, being mere otherness, comes into the picture and contributes to the interpretation. The interpretation always occurs against the background of the grammatical structure involved.

Here we have a difference between accent (or 'stress') which is given for lexical or grammatical morphemes, and prosodic word boundaries which are constrained by the grammatical structure, but are not fully derivable from it. Both types of prosodic phenomena are not segmental, but rather higher-level features (cf. also Ebeling (1968)). The difference between them is that the prosodic word – and the prosodic structure in general – is a language level of its own (cf. also Hattori's (1973) definition of the prosodic word as 'prosodeme'), whereas accent is part of the grammatical structure.

1.7.6. The phonological phrase is in all the proposed definitions fully derivable from the grammatical structure.

Against the background of Chomsky and Halle's (1968: 366f.) discussion of the boundaries which characterize syntactic clusters created around a major lexical item, Selkirk (1980b) offered the following definition of the phonological phrase:

(i) an item which is the specifier of a syntactic phrase joins with the head of the phrase;

(ii) an item belonging to a nonlexical category, such as determiner, preposition, complement, auxiliary verb, or conjunction, joins with its sister constituent.

Next to the nonlexical items which show up as clitics, the phonological phrase comprises also the phrase specifiers, and it is there that the distinction between the phonological word and the phonological phrase is to be found in a language, if any.

Nespor and Vogel (1980) made a distinction between the phonological phrase (φ) and the derived phonological phrase (φ') in order to distinguish between the obligatory and the optional domain of sandhi phenomena in Italian. This refers both to segmental phonological and prosodic phenomena, as will be shown in example (46) below. In Nespor and Vogel's view, the derived phonological phrase (φ') is due to restructuring as follows:

φ construction:

join into a φ any lexical head (X) with all items on its nonrecursive side with the maximal projection and with any other nonlexical items on the same side;

φ' restructuring:

a nonbranching φ which is the first complement of X on its recursive side loses its label and is joined to the φ containing X under a new node labeled φ'.

In Italian sandhi called *raddopiamento sintattico* 'syntactic doubling', a word-initial consonant is doubled following the final accent of the preceding word obligatorily within a φ, optionally within a φ', and not at all across φ's, as shown in (46).

(46) Italian sandhi (*raddopiamento sintattico*) according to Nespor and Vogel (1980):

'Luca will invite Daniele and Chiara will invite whoever she wants.'
((`) denotes word accent, and (:) denotes doubling, or lengthening.)

It is within the same domains that prosodic sandhi occurs in Toscanian Italian in this sense that if within a phonological phrase a word ends with an accented syllable, and the next following word begins with an accented syllable, than the former will be shifted backwards.

We can see that in Italian, the phonological phrase is fully definable in terms of the grammatical structure involved, and that the prosodic phrase (forming the domain of prominence phenomena as connected with accent) equals the phonological phrase.

The phonological phrase is not a separate level of language. It is a domain of phonological phenomena which is fully definable in terms of the grammatical structure, as stated above.

To my knowledge, no evidence has been presented so far for the prosodic phrase which would not equal the phonological phrase. If true, then everything stated about the phonological phrase applies *ceteris paribus* to the prosodic phrase.

1.7.7. Selkirk (1980b) defined also two higher prosodic levels: the intonation unit (I) and the utterance (U). The intonation unit is the domain over which an intonation contour is spread, and the utterance is the span between two pauses in connected speech.

These levels differ from the remaining ones defined by Selkirk by their being based on prosodic features indeed.

Can the intonation unit and the utterance be related to the grammatical structure involved? Nespor and Vogel (1983: 231f.) formulated the following correspondence rules:

I construction:

(i) any displaced syntactic constituents, parentheticals and nonrestrictive relative clauses obligatorily form at least one I;

(ii) starting with the first φ/φ' of a sentence, join as many φ/φ' as possible into an I until either a) the end of the maximal projection of an N (i.e. noun) is reached, or b) another $\overline{S}$ (i.e. clause) begins; once such an I is formed, proceed in the same way until the end of the main sentence is reached; join any remaining φ's at the end of a sentence into an I;

U construction:

join all I's in a root sentence (most generally the highest category of syntactic structure) into a U.

In spite of these correspondence rules, I and U are still not fully definable in terms of the syntactic structure, as can be concluded from Nespor and Vogel's formulation of I restructuring, which runs as follows:

I restructuring:

a. eliminate very short I's by joining them with adjacent I's;

b. eliminate very long I's by breaking them down into shorter I's.

The notion of 'very short' vs. 'very long' cannot be made explicit in terms of the syntactic structure, though. We can only assume that it depends on the speaker's evaluation of the frame of reference as shared by himself and the addressee, and his own choice of how to present it. This is compatible with Vogel's (forthcoming) assumption that U restructuring (as compared with U construction defined by Nespor and herself (1983)) takes place as well, and that it partly, though not fully, depends on the following factors.

U restructuring:

adjacent U's may be joined into a single U when a) they are produced by the same speaker, b) they are directed to the same addressee, and c) there is a *syntactic* relation (ellipsis, anaphora), or a *semantic* relation (*and, therefore, because*), or a *pragmatic* relation between the U's in question.

However, as long as the relevant linguistic factors are not fully known, the notion of restructuring is not applicable according to the methodology presented in this study, but it must first be investigated whether it is not another case of construction. And in order to answer this question, a full definition of construction is needed.

The presented definitions of I and U construction are based syntactically. And as observed by Nespor and Vogel already, they show that no full syntactic definition is possible. The additional factors mentioned as relevant to I and U restructuring may be relevant to I and U construction as well, but – again – only partly, not fully, determining it, as already mentioned by Vogel in connection with U restructuring.

Following the methodology presented in this study, the status of I and U as signs must be examined, which means that their form and the meaning connected with that form must be investigated for I and U separately and in connection with each other.

As to the form of I, its constituting elements have been established for Dutch by Cohen and 't Hart (1967) and a.o. Collier and 't Hart (1987). The established elements of form appeared to be applicable to other languages as well (cf. e.g. 't Hart (1982) and Keijsper (1983)), so we can hypothesize that they have general validity – which must further be tested, though.

(47) Elements of form constituting intonational units (following Collier and 't Hart (1978))

direction of pitch movement:	timing of pitch movement:
– rising pitch	– early in the accented syllable of the prosodic word
– rising pitch	– late in the accented syllable of the prosodic word, or following it
– falling pitch	– early in the accented syllable of the prosodic word
– falling pitch	– late in the accented syllable of the prosodic word, or following it.

The distinctive elements of form – call them 'distinctive features of intonation' – are consequently patterned within two phonetic dimensions: that of pitch movement (i.e. *rising* vs. *falling*) and that of timing (i.e. *early* vs. *late* in the accented syllable of the prosodic word, or in the prosodic word in general if there is no distinctive word accent; the notion of the prosodic word has been brought by myself into the definitions). These distinctive elements constitute together the intonation unit in the following way.

(48) Internal structuring of the distinctive features of intonation:
- rising pitch early in the accented syllable of the prosodic word: this is the first prosodic word of an intonation unit;
- rising pitch late in the accented syllable of the prosodic word or following it: the first prosodic word of an intonation unit will come next;
- falling pitch early in the accented syllable of the prosodic word: this is the last prosodic word of an intonation unit;
- falling pitch late in the accented syllable of the prosodic word or following it: the last prosodic word of an intonation unit will come next.

In addition to these distinctive features of intonation, there is also a gradually falling so-called declination line connecting the (rising and falling) distinctive features of one intonation unit. Depending on the language, there may also be three reference levels of pitch instead of the two basic ones between which the rising and falling pitch movements take place. And depending on the language, pitch levels may be conventionalized as the distinctive features of intonation instead.

The intonational contours with a late timing or a relatively limited extent can possibly be used by a language in order to express intonational subordination. This hypothesis about hierarchical structuring of intonation units – after being tested possibly leading to the conclusion that what is called 'uttterance' is just a superordinate intonation unit – must further be put to a test along the lines indicated by Martin's (1978) investigation of French intonation.

The distinctive features of intonation are signs in the same way as segmental distinctive features are. Only their at least partially unpredictable sequences – viewed as such against the background of the grammatical units covered by them – are language *forms* to which a meaning can be attached in a conventionalized way. (I shall return to this point in the next chapter, when I start discussing meaningful units of language.)

If viewed independently of the grammatical forms covered by them, then the distinctive features of intonation constitute intonation *units* which consist of a rising pitch, an optionally intervening high declination line, and a falling pitch. It is only due to their potential noncoincidence with grammatical units that they can constitute forms to which a meaning can be attached.

It is at the point of distinguishing between *intonation units*, as independent units of the prosodic structure, and *intonation forms*, as (parts of) intonation units which characterize grammatical units, that my approach differs from Keijsper's (1983), who does not explicitly distinguish them, and consequently does not analyse discontinuous rising and falling pitch contours (which are in my terminology *forms*) as elements of the entire intonation *units* in which they participate. In my approach, they are signs in the same way as other distinctive features are, and can be forms with a meaning other than 'mere otherness' only against the background of the grammatical structure they characterize.

The distinctive features of intonation resemble segmental ones in that they also constitute a unit only in combination with each other, not in isolation.

Any other assumed meaning of intonation equals its interpretation as derived from the grammatical structure covered by an intonation unit, the question of whether a grammatical unit coincides with the intonation unit covering it (and if not, this is interpreted as contrast in the way discussed in 1.7.5. above on the basis of prosodic words in Serbo-Croatian), the question of linear ordering of the distinctive features of intonation (e.g. a falling pitch followed by a rising pitch on the same prosodic word can be interpreted either as question or as amazement, depending on the language), or phonetic variation in the realization of the distinctive features of intonation as conventionalized in relation to other variational phenomena of a language.

1.7.8. We have seen in the preceding sections and subsections that there are two basic levels in phonology: the segmental one and the prosodic one. Both levels are characterized by distinctive features, the meaning of which is that of otherness, established whenever there is a possibility of choice.

Prosodic features are not *per se* relevant at a different level (as has been assumed by the autosegmental approach as formulated e.g. by Goldsmith (1976)), but can on the basis of the methodology presented here be analysed either as segmental or as intonational (including those defining the prosodic word as the minimal intonation unit). Intonational prosodic features are realized over parts of the grammatical structure – and this is the only level difference which can be established for prosodic features.

All language forms consist of linear sequences of partially internally ordered sets of distinctive features. Those linear sequences which are not (fully) derivable by means of general rules – are the distinctive forms of a language, to which a distinct meaning is attached. These combinations of form and meaning are signs at what may be called the meaningful level of language, consisting of a grammatical and a lexical part.

Whereas phonological signs are structured only in their form, grammatical and lexical signs can be hypothesized to be structured in their meaning as well.

This will be investigated in the next chapters.

2. Grammatical Variation and Change in Relation to the System

When considering signs at the meaningful level of language, we must keep in mind that they are based on a conventionalized association of form and meaning, as formulated by Saussure (1916: 158).

Distinctive forms of a language have been investigated in the preceding chapter, and shown to consist of unpredictable – or at least partially unpredictable – linear sequences of partially hierarchically structured sets of distinctive features. In addition to segmental distinctive features, prosodic distinctive features characterize forms and groups of forms in a language. Only in combination with each other do they constitute a chain of speech.

Prosodic features constitute intonation units, of which the prosodic word is the smallest one. We have seen in the preceding chapter that intonation units are constrained by the segmentally based forms of a language (as e.g. in Serbo-Croatian, any nonenclitical word can form a prosodic word, as illustrated by *od sad se* mentioned under (44) above, where *od* and *sad* can either form two separate prosodic words or a single one, but *se* – being an enclitic – always belongs to the same prosodic word as *sad* does; only the nonenclitical pendant of *se, sebe,* can form a prosodic word on its own). Constraints on intonation units in terms of segmentally based forms can be formulated by means of general rules for each language under investigation. Apart from these constraints, intonation units are unpredictable from segmentally based forms.

Given the fact that a chain of speech consists of simultaneously relevant segmental and prosodic sequences, they are by necessity evaluated in relation to each other. And it is in relation to segmentally based forms that prosodically based forms, constituting intonation units, are evaluated as unpredictable. Thus a chain of speech consisting of a sentence need not begin with a rising (or high) pitch, which – by virtue of its meaning of 'mere otherness' – denotes another, i.e. new, unit of information presented by the segmentally based forms. The beginning of a sentence may also begin with a falling pitch, or a low declination line. In the former case, the falling pitch will denote termination of the unit of information which has been opened preceding the sentence, and which was at the point of its opening new in comparison with the information presented by the speaker as already present in the frame of reference. In the latter case, the low declination line will denote absence of any new information expressed by means of the segmentally based forms which are covered by the low declination line, in comparison with the frame of reference as conceived of by the speaker. But if a sentence begins with a rising (or high) pitch early in the accented syllable of its first prosodic word (cf. 1.7.6. above), then the information contained in the forms starting from the given rising or high pitch until the falling pitch is presented as new in comparison with the frame of reference. The same holds if not the entire sentence, but only a part of it is covered by the rising or high pitch which is followed by a high declination line and/or a falling pitch in the same or following sentence.

(49) A schematized intonation unit (with the declination left out of the picture):

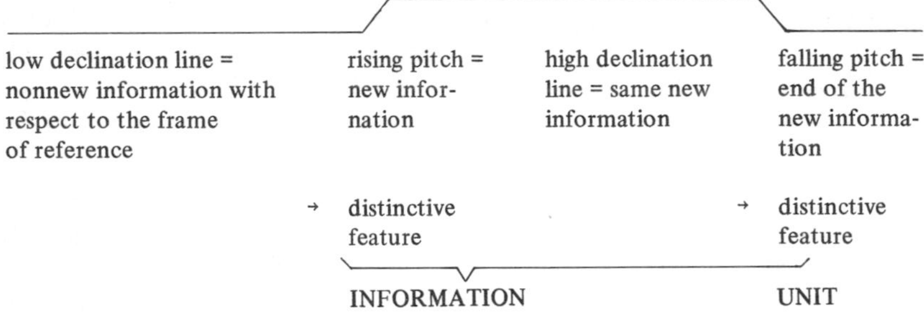

(50) Schematization of three intonation units (with the declination left out of the picture):

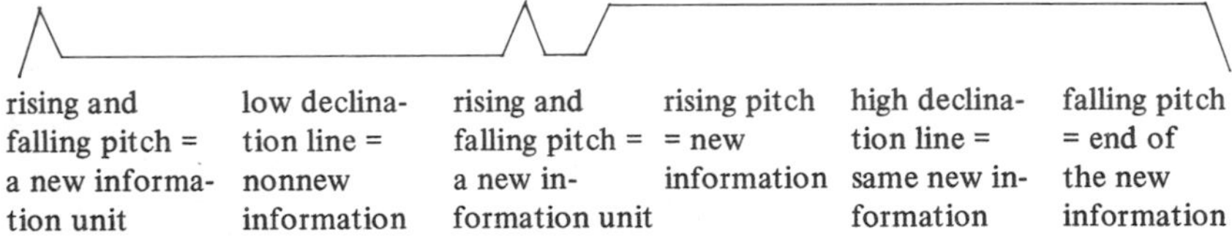

Timing of the rising and falling pitch contours with respect to the grammatical units covered by them is of crucial importance, as stated in 1.7.6. above. Thus a rising pitch early in the accented syllable shows that the given grammatical unit contains the beginning of a new information unit, whereas a rising pitch late in the accented syllable or following it shows that a grammatical unit containing the beginning of a new information unit will follow. Hence the usual interpretation of the latter as a question.

As I have stated in 1.7.6. already, there is a distinction between *intonation units,* which crucially consist of a pitch rise and a pitch fall and whose function is to group the information contained in the grammatical structure, and *intonation forms,* which consist of the distinctive feature(s) of intonation covering a single grammatical unit. Whereas the shape of the former is predictable, it is at least partially unpredictable which intonation feature(s) cover one grammatical unit. Hence possibility of languages to conventionalize a given intonation feature or a combination of intonation features with a linguistic meaning exclusively derived from the grouping property of the intonation unit as defined above. By this restriction, intonation forms differ from segmentally based forms and must be treated as belonging to a separate, prosodic level indeed, which only expresses grouping of the information expressed by segmental forms.

Other, segmentally based forms have a meaning of their own as expressing information which can be of two types: grammatical and lexical. Grammatical information consists of relational features which hold among the meaningful units of a chain of speech and are expressed by means of grammatical forms, and lexical information consists of features of relational and inherent information, which are expressed by means of lexical forms.

It can be hypothesized that both grammatical and lexical information are structured. If so, are they structured in a way which is in principle comparable to the structuring of the features of form established in the preceding chapter?

This chapter investigates structuring of grammatical features, and the next chapter, of lexical ones.

2.1. Case Development Against the Background of the Grammatical Features Involved

The system of grammatical cases offers an interesting test-case for the type of structure potentially involved in the grammatical features, because the hypothesis about the presence of a structure has been elaborated already by Jakobson (1936, 1971, 2nd).

(51) The common system of the Russian cases, assumed to have general validity (Jakobson (1971, 2nd: 66)):

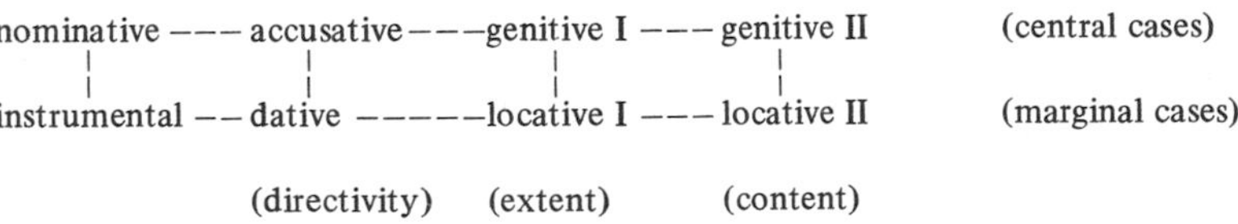

Jakobson thus analysed the common meanings of cases in terms of the following features: *central* vs. *marginal* (or *peripheral*), and in combination with these: *directivity* vs. *nondirectivity* (as a translation of Jakobson's *"Bezug"*), *extent* vs. *nonextent* (as a translation of Jakobson's *"Umfang"*), and *content* vs. *noncontent* (as a translation of Jakobson's *"Gestaltung"*).

(52) A schematic representation of the Russian case meanings (Jakobson (1971, 2nd: 66)):

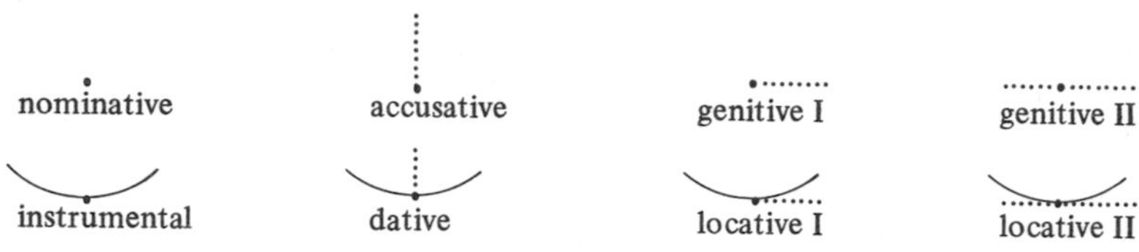

The oppositions among the Russian cases on the basis of the features of meaning involved are presented in (53). Jakobson conceived of them as binary, consisting of a marked and an unmarked term. In the schematic presentation, the marked term occurs either to the right or to the bottom of the unmarked one.

(53) The common system of oppositions among the Russian cases (Jakobson (1971, 2nd: 65)):

(nominative	~	accusative)	~	(genitive I	~	genitive II)
≀		≀		≀		≀
(instrumental	~	dative)	~	(locative I	~	locative II)

The given features of meaning are present in the marked term of the corresponding opposition, and absent in the unmarked term. This is why the nominative case, as unmarked for *marginal, directivity, extent,* and *content,* is used for naming a person, thing, or concept, irrespectively of any relational features of meaning.

Jakobson's analysis of the features of meaning which underlie the case system of Russian, has a more general applicability. For example, Ivić (1961: 41) derived from it the following characterization of the Serbo-Croatian case system.

(54) Analysis of the Serbo-Croatian case system, as derived from Jakobson's analysis of Russian (Ivić (1961: 41)):

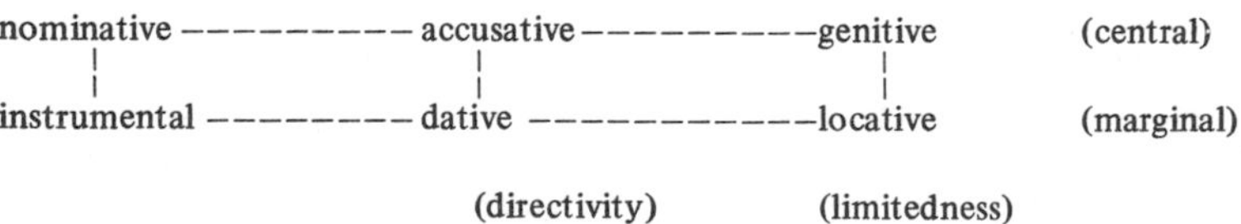

(Ivić defined limitedness as *"the presence of the idea of some limit set up for the phenomenon denoted by a case form"*, as an alternative to Jakobson's *"Umfang"*, translated by Ivić as *"quantifier"*, and rejected by her, because it would possibly include not only the genitive and the locative, but also the accusative.)

The features of meaning on which the case system is based are in principle comparable to the distinctive features of form discussed in the preceding chapter. They are e.g. comparable to the articulation place features in phonology. For these, as we have seen in 1.2. above, markedness need not hold in all cases. And if it does hold, then it is connected with asymmetrical ordering.

If we try to apply the notion of asymmetrical ordering to the case system presented above, we cannot establish any necessary ordering between the features which underlie the case system. If the features of meaning underlying the case system are comparable to the features of form indeed, then partial asymmetrical ordering must be observable among the features of the case system as well. At least, it can be hypothesized that partial asymmetrical ordering can be introduced in the course of the development. I shall investigate this matter by discussing the Serbo-Croatian case development from the 15. century on.

Until the 14. century, Serbo-Croatian had a case system which can be illustrated by the following paradigms (from Belić (1950: 10, 43, 58, 77)).

(55) Types of noun paradigms in Serbo-Croatian until the 14. century (from Belić (1950)); I give only one type for the masculine, neuter, feminine and consonant stems, leaving the distinction between palatal (or "laminal") and nonpalatal stems out of the consideration as well, as they do not contribute to the issue discussed here. The case names are abbreviated as follows: N = nominative, G = genitive, D = dative, A = accusative, V = vocative (i.e. a pendant of nominative used for calling), I = instrumental, and L = locative, in that order.

Singular

	masculine		neuter	feminine	consonant	(former -i)
N	*grad* 'city'	*sin* 'son'	*nebo* 'heaven'	*žena* 'woman'	*kost* 'bone'	(/ẹ/ = later /e/,
G	*grada*	**sinu*	*nenese*	*ženi*	*kosti*	/i/, or /ie/, depending on
D	*gradu*	**sinovi*	*nebesi*	*ženẹ*	*kosti*	the dialect; the starred forms
A	*grad*	*sin*	*nebo*	*ženu*	*kost*	are reconstructed.)
V	*grade*	*sinu*	*nebo*	*ženo*	*kosti*	
I	*gradom*	**sinəm*	*nebesəm*	*žen(oj)u*	*kostju*	
L	*gradẹ*	*sinu*	*nebese*	*ženẹ*	*kosti*	

Plural

	masculine			neuter	feminine	consonant (former -i)
N=V	*gradi*	*muži* 'men'	*sinove*	*nebesa*	*ženi*	*kosti*
G	*grad*	*muž*	*sinov*	*nebes*	*žen*	*kostī*
D	*gradom*	*mužem*	**sinəm*	*nebesəm*	*ženam*	*kostəm*
A	*gradi*	*muže*	*sini*	*nebesa*	*ženi*	*kosti*
I	*gradi*	*muži*	*sinmi*	*nebesi*	*ženami*	*kostmi*
L	*gradẹx*	*mužix*	*sinəx*	*nebesəx*	*ženax*	*kostəx*

(I mention the palatal stems only in the masculine plural, because it is only there that they partially deviate from the general pattern of desinential correspondences, which runs as follows:

Dual

	masculine		nuter	feminine	consonant	non-palatal	– palatal desinences
N=V=A	*grada*	**sini*	*nebesẹ*	*ženẹ*	*kosti*	o	e
G=L	*gradu*	*sinovu*	*nebesu*	*ženu*	**kostju*	e	u
D=I	*gradoma*	*sinma*	*nebesəma*	*ženama*	*kostma*	ẹ	i
						i	e.)

The following syncretism can be observed:

– N = V: singular neuter, plural all, dual all;
– N = A: singular masculine, neuter, consonant; plural masculine nonpalatal, neuter, feminine, consonant, dual all;
– N = I: plural masculine – but with accentual differences;
– G = L: singular consonant as illustrated by *sin*, dual all;
– G = L = D: singular consonant (former -i) – but with accentual differences;
– D = L: singular feminine, consonant (former -i) – but with accentual differences;
– D = I: dual all.

If we compare this list with Jakobson's analysis of case meanings presented above, we can see that syncretism systematically involves either a single feature of meaning or two or more transitively connected features of meaning (e.g. G = L = D, but no G = D without L or A involved). Given this restriction, it is possible to assume that the given feature (or transitively connected features) of meaning is (or are) neutralized in the way comparable to neutralization of phonological features discussed in the preceding chapter. Depending on the number, syncretism involves two central cases, or two marginal ones, or the two limited ones.

How can we know whether the meanings of these syncretized forms are distinguished or not?

Jakobson (1971, 2nd: 43) formulated the following answer to this question: syncretism of forms corresponds with nondistinction of meaning whenever the given case meanings are not distinguished in any gender or number.

But if they are distinguished in another gender or number? Jakobson assumed that then the difference in meaning persists in spite of identity in form.

I am stating here that the difference in meaning is dismissed between two cases if their form is identical and the meanings are originally distinguished by a single feature of meaning (such as e.g. *directivity* vs. *nondirectivity* in A = N). It cannot be shown to be dismissed if the meanings are originally distinguished by unconnected features (such as e.g. *directivity and marginality* in A and I). How can this statement be tested without circularity?

It can be tested by the following two predictions:

– syncretism involving unconnected features of meaning comes about either through sound change or through paradigmatic formal analogy, i.e. exclusively through formal development, whereas syncretism involving a single feature of meaning can come about either through formal development (then it is accidental) or through development of meaning (then it is systematic);
– syncretism involving a single feature equals its dismissal, thus introducing asymmetry into the system; asymmetry with the absence of a distinction attached to only one of the terms of another feature equals hierarchy; and hierarchy imposes constraints onto further development in this sense that a subordinate or unordered feature can change without consequences for the rest of the system, but the dominating feature affects its subordinate one(s).

A test case for the first prediction is found in syncretism between the accusative and the instrumental. It is found in Slavic plural masculine nonpalatal desinences already preceding the written period, and in singular feminine desinences in Slovenian in the later, attested period. The Slovenian cases fit into the Serbo-Croatian schema presented in (54). If we go back approximately to the 10. century, we find in the accusative singular feminine the desinence *-ǫ* (i.e. a nasal back round mid vowel), and in the instrumental, the desinence *-ǫjǫ*. The latter form developed in due course into *-ǫjǫ*, and through contraction into *-ǭ*, as shown by Rigler (1967). After the loss of tone, the two desinences merged. It was an independent development of the form indeed, and there is no reason to assume that it had consequences for the meaning.

A test case for the second prediction is lacking for Serbo-Croatian, because out of the syncretized forms, the D = L ones fall out of the consideration due to accentual differences, and N = I ones do not introduce a hierarchy into the system. What remains are the syncretized forms of the dual, exhibiting the hierarchy schematized in (56a) below. But the dual forms were getting out of usage starting from the 14. century, and are fully lost now. As their loss was not characterized by intervening mergers, the hypothesis about the constraining role of hierarchy cannot be tested by them.

(56a) Hierarchy between the features of case meanings involved in the Serbo-Croatian dual until the 14. century (as presented in (55) above):

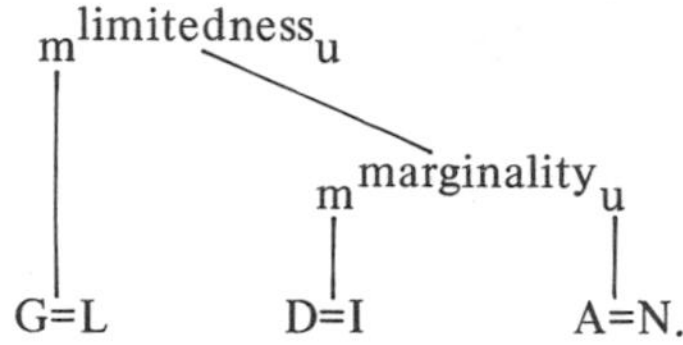

Hierarchy itself increases predictability in a system, and it is possible to hypothesize that syncretism which is triggered by the features of meaning in the sense of dismissing an opposition, will introduce hierarchy into the system. In order to test this hypothesis, let us examine the Serbo-Croatian case developments after the 14. century.

The following changes of the Serbo-Croatian noun desinences have taken place in the Štokavian dialect underlying the later standard language:

- loss of the dual in general, starting from the end of the 14. century;
- all masculine paradigms and all neuter ones merge, acquiring the desinences of the most frequent type, and the same desinence for the dative and the locative singular, but preserving the accentual difference;
- masculine nouns generalize in the accusative plural the (originally palatal) desinence *-e;*
- feminine nouns generalize the palatal desinences;
- feminine nouns generalize in the instrumental singular the desinence *-ōm,*
- all nouns develop a vocalic desinence in the genitive plural;
- all nouns in the plural develop syncretism of the instrumental, the dative, and the locative, with a common form resulting from a contamination of the instrumental and the dative forms (i.e. *-ima* for the masculine, neuter and consonant paradigms, and *-ama* for the feminine ones); the merger systematically affected the instrumental and the dative plural first (cf. Belić (1950: 102 etc.)), and only later the locative; a seeming exception is found in the merger of the instrumental and the locative in the language of some writers of the 17. century from the southern areas, which was, however, due to the loss of /x/ in the given areas (cf. Belić (1950: 108)), a purely formal phenomenon.

(In this survey, I do not mention phenomena which are of no relevance to distinguishing vs. nondistinguishing case desinences.)

The resulting case system in the plural exhibits the following hierarchy.

(56b) Hierarchy among the features of case meanings in the Serbo-Croatian plural, characterized by syncretism of the instrumental, the dative, and the locative:

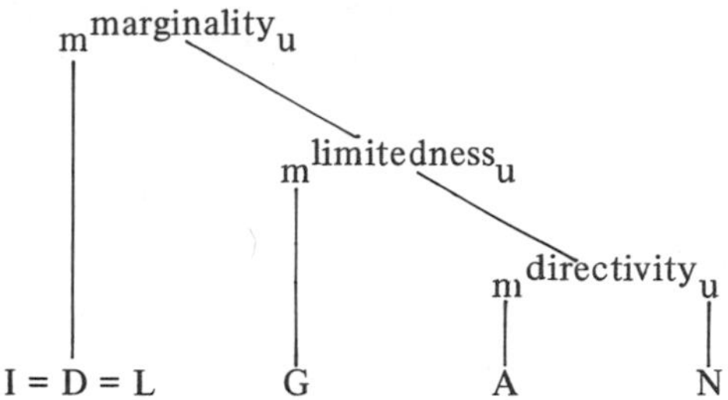

(feminine, neuter, and consonant nouns eliminate *directivity* as well by having N = A in the plural).

The way in which the given hierarchy came about, namely through merger of the dative and the instrumental plural first, shows that it was triggered by the features of meaning, such that *directivity* was eliminated first in the marginal cases, and *limitedness* followed afterwards. This stepwise elimination was constrained by the existing ordering (still a symmetrical one) among the features of meaning, as still reflected by the nonmarginal cases. And the side at which this elimination took place was governed by markedness in the sense of the presence of the mark for *marginality,* as opposed to its absence.

An additional indication in support of this reconstruction can be found in the formal indication of the results of elimination: the form of I = D is also that of contamination. And the locative plural joined later, not leaving traces of contamination in the form any more.

In a comparable way, the dative singular equals the locative singular in the absence of (lexically bound) accentual differences, and it is there that the original desinence of the dative is found, not that of the locative. Against the background of markedness as outlined here, we can conclude that the form of the unmarked term of the feature of meaning is attached to the result of the neutralization in cases of full syncretism.

We can see that even implementation of the results of feature dismissal occurs in parallel ways in phonology on the one hand, and grammar on the other: it either equals the form which is otherwise attached to the unmarked term of the operative opposition, or it equals a contamination – or an intermediate form – of the forms attached to the two terms of the operative opposition.

Finally, let me mention that the observed Slavic regularities are not language-idiosyncratic. Sonderegger (1979: 250 etc.) discussed development of the case system in Germanic, and showed that the instrumental plural had merged with the dative plural in the development of Old Germanic already, followed by the same development in the singular from Old High German to Middle High German. This was followed by a merger of the accusative and the nominative first in the plural and then in the singular from Old High German to Middle High German, and then by an additional merger of the genitive plural with the (already merged) nominative and accusative plural in the development from Middle High German to New High German.

(57) Development of the case system in the nouns from Old Germanic to New High German (Sonderegger (1979: 250)):

	Old Germanic	Old High German	Middle High German	New High German
singular	nominative	nominative/ (accusative)	nominative/ accusative	nominative/ accusative
	vocative			
	genitive	genitive	genitive	genitive
	dative	dative	dative	dative
	accusative	accusative	(accusative)	(accusative)
	instrumental	(instrumental)		
plural	nominative	nominative/ accusative	nominative/ accusative	nominative/ accusative
	genitive	genitive	genitive	
	dative	dative	dative	dative
	accusative			

In New High German, the dative is the only case marked for marginality, whereas those unmarked for it are either marked for limitedness (i.e. the genitive) or unmarked for it (i.e. the nominative = the accusative).

We can now conclude in a more general way that the features of grammatical case meanings are relevant as dimensions indeed, and patterned according to the same principles, including hierarchy, as the phonological features are.

2.2. Syncretism in Verb Endings Against the Background of the Grammatical Features Involved

2.2.1. We have seen in the preceding section that grammatical features can participate in asymmetrical orderings and that it is only there that markedness becomes overt.

As long as there is no asymmetrical ordering involved, there is strictly speaking no logical ground for viewing one term of a meaningful-feature opposition as containing a mark and the opposite term as not containing it, because logically, either term is the negation of the opposite one (as to the latter point, consider also Hjelmslev (1935), (1961, 2nd)). Languages show that this is the case even if it would not seem to us to be the case. For example, the *singular* vs. *plural* opposition, patterned within the conceptual dimension of numbers, may either be viewed as based on the mark 'one' (by which *singular* is marked), or 'several' (by which *plural* is marked). Only if a language distinguishes *dual* next to *singular* and *plural,* there is asymmetrical patterning involved, and it seems to be unequivocally of the following type:

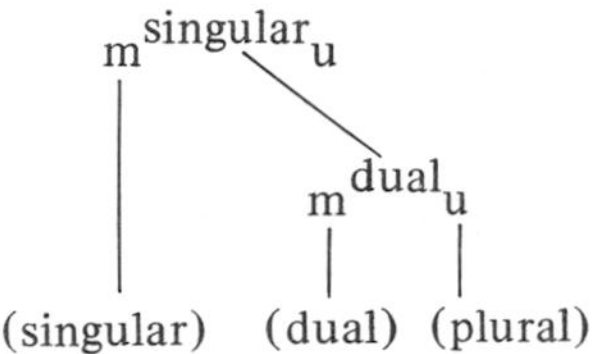

In other words, such a partitioning is logically conceived of as 'one' vs. ('two' vs. 'more than two').

But how can we know that this is the case indeed, without making the reasoning circular? In other words, how can we know that in the given case, and only in the given case, it is the singular which is the dominating meaningful-feature opposition, and the plural is patterned as one of the partitions of the number dimension which are unmarked for *singular* (i.e. [u singular]) and subordinate with respect to it?

We can know it only if the relation between the singular and the plural in a language changes when the dual is abandoned – and this change is observable on independent grounds. Any other type of evidence is strictly speaking circular.

An example of a language which had the *singular – dual – plural* opposition and subsequently abandoned the dual is found in Russian, and in other Slavic languages. But Russian is interesting in this respect because it gives independent evidence of a change in the relation between the singular and the plural *after* the abandonment of the dual, which took place between the 11. and the 13. century (cf. Borkovskij and Kuznecov (1963: 203 etc.)). What kind of change? A change of markedness, becoming overt through asymmetrical patterning. An asymmetrical patterning with gender, but with number as the dominating feature opposition, thus showing its markedness relation.

Whereas Old Russian distinguished gender both in the singular and the plural of its impersonal pronouns, adjectives and participles, the oldest attestations of a full loss of this distinction in the plural are found in the second half of the 14. century (cf. Borkovskij and Kuznecov (1963: 249)). The given loss was a final stage of the development which set in at the end of the 11. and in the 12. century, by which occasional merger of the masculine and the feminine gender – which had identical desinences in the accusative plural anyhow – could occur in the nominative plural as well. The remaining cases had the same desinences throughout anyhow, also for the neuter gender. However, the neuter gender remained distinct until the second half of the fourteenth century, and joined only afterwards. The final form appeared to be based on the original form for the masculine and feminine plural.

What is of interest to us here is that gender became nondistinctive in the plural, whereas it remained distinctive in the singular. What we now find in Russian is the following asymmetrical ordering:

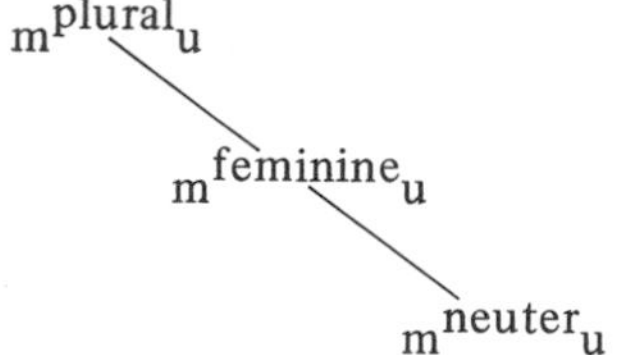

In this ordering, it is the plural which is marked, whereas the singular is unmarked. And it follows from the hypothesis about grammatical markedness as connected with asymmetry, and from the general approach by which ordering in language excludes ambiguity (possibly leading to two different solutions for a single case), that this kind of patterning is incompatible with the patterning of *singular* vs. *dual* vs. *plural,* by which it is the singular which is marked, not the plural.

The neuter gender could consequently merge with the masculine and feminine in the plural only (thus introducing asymmetry, which is not yet introduced if only the masculine and the feminine merge) after the full loss of the dual, not while the dual was still present in the language. As long as the dual was still present, it was responsible for the asymmetry by which the singular was marked – and this asymmetry could apparently not be contradicted by another asymmetry in the same system by which the plural was marked.

The merger between the masculine and the feminine plural, dated three centuries earlier than that of the neuter with the merged masculine and feminine, was a different process indeed. It was based on the form – as established by Borkovskij and Kuznecov (1963: 249) – and it is due to its origin in the form, not the meaning, that it could crosscut the hierarchy of meaning by which the masculine should merge with the neuter first, not the feminine. And it is due to the same reason that further elimination of gender in the plural – which had its origin in the meaning – did not follow so that it could be viewed as a part of the same process. Rather, it followed only later, when the patterning of the features of meaning in that language made it possible. And this was the case when the dual was eliminated, thus eliminating asymmetry by which the singular was marked, not the plural. After the elimination of this asymmetry, either the singular or the plural could be patterned by the language as marked, and it was only then that the process based on meaning, leading to the evaluation of the meaning of the plural as marked, could set in.

We can conclude that in the features of meaning, markedness within a feature opposition is directly related to asymmetrical patterning, and thus derivable from it in the unique way.

2.2.2. The next step is to test for the features of meaning the hypothesis that feature omittance is constrained by the asymmetrical ordering involved. This hypothesis appeared to stand the test for the phonological features, as shown in the preceding chapter. Can it stand the test for the features of meaning as well?

I shall now test this hypothesis on the basis of syncretism in verb endings in Bantawa Rai, a Tibeto-Burman (Kiranti) language spoken in East Nepal, with its main centre in Bhojpur (from where it spread due to migrations further to the east and to the south). Further linguistic characterization of Kiranti languages will be presented in the next chapter.

Bantawa – like other Kiranti languages in East Nepal – is a so-called complex pronominalizing language. This means that original pronominal elements referring to the first and the second argument of the predication are morphologized in the verb desinences if the verb is transitive, and only referring to the first argument if it is intransitive. (The terminology of 'argument' and 'predication' is derived from Dik (1978).)

The complex pronominalizing languages are consistently verb-final. The pronominalization in the verb desinence is not sufficient for expressing the first two arguments of the predication, though, but at least the first argument must be overtly expressed preceding the verb as well. If the verb is transitive, and both its arguments are expressed preceding the verb, then the first argument gets what is usually called the ergative marker *-a*. In my material, the ergative marker is obligatory only if the first argument does not precede the second one in the overt expression preceding the verb. It is only there that the ergative marker is a distinctive means of disambiguation indeed. In any other case in my material, the ergative marker *-a* may optionally be added to the expression means of the first argument of the predication.

The necessity of overtly expressing the arguments as well shows that their expression on the verb is not fully unambiguous. There is a considerable amount of syncretism, indeed. Let us investigate regularities underlying it, if any.

The Bantawa verb is not characterized by gender. It is only characterized by person – the first, second, or third – and by number – the singular, the dual, and the plural. In the first persons of the dual and the plural, the distinction between so-called 'inclusive' and 'exclusive' is relevant. 'Inclusive' denotes that the addressee is included in the meaning of 'we' (either dual or plural), whereas 'exclusive' denotes that the addressee is excluded from the meaning of 'we' (either dual or plural).

As to the time dimension, there is only the distinction between *past* and *nonpast,* and the latter can refer either to the present or the future.

In terms of asymmetrical patterning, we can see that there is only a single case where hierarchy is found: in the number distinctions. They exhibit asymmetry of the following type:

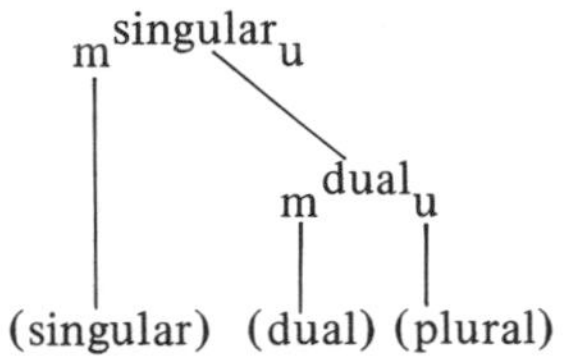

m singular u

m dual u

(singular) (dual) (plural)

This hierarchy can be expected to impose constraints on variation, including syncretism in verb endings. In order to test this, I shall now present my materials on the Wana dialect of Bantawa from South Bhojpur, as spoken by Ash Bahadur Rai, aged 67, now living in Ilam in the outer eastern district of Nepal, to where he has migrated 50 years ago.

(58) Complex pronominalization in the verb endings of Bantawa Rai (Wana dialect from South Bhojpur); the positive paradigm: nonpast/past *dhaťma* 'to beat':

1st argument	2nd argument 1 sg: ŋka	2 sg: khana	3 sg: moko	1 du-incl.: ŋkaci	1 du-excl.: ŋkacia	2 du khanaci	3 du: mokohuaŋ	1 pl-incl.: ŋkań	1 pl-excl.: ŋkańka	2 pl: khananiń	3 pl: mokoci
1 sg: ŋka		dhaṭna ḍhaṭna	dhaṭṭuŋ ḍhaṭṭuŋ			dhaṭnaci dhaṭnaci	dhaṭṭuŋcuŋ dhaṭṭuŋcuŋ			ḍhaṭnaniń ḍhaṭnaniń	ḍhaṭṭuŋcuŋ ḍhaṭṭuŋcuŋ
2 sg: khana	tʉḍhaťŋa tʉḍhaṭṭaŋ		tʉḍhaṭṭu tʉḍhaṭṭu		tʉḍhaṭnicia tʉḍhaṭnicia		tʉḍhaṭṭuci tʉḍhaṭṭuci		tʉḍhaṭnicia tʉḍhaṭnicia		tʉḍhaṭṭuci tʉḍhaṭṭuci
3 sg: moko	ḍhaťŋa ʉdhaṭṭaŋ	tʉḍhať tʉḍhaṭṭa	ḍhaṭṭu ḍhaṭṭu	ʉḍhaṭci ʉḍhaṭṭaci	ʉḍhaṭcia ʉḍhaṭṭacia	tʉḍhaṭci tʉḍhaṭṭaci	ḍhaṭṭuci ḍhaṭṭuci	ʉḍhaṭṭiń ʉḍhaṭṭiń	ʉḍhaṭṭińka ʉḍhaṭṭińka	tʉḍhaṭṭiń tʉḍhaṭṭaniń	ḍhaṭṭuci ḍhaṭṭuci
1 du-incl. ŋkaci			ḍhaṭcu ḍhaṭṭacu				ḍhaṭcucuń ḍhaṭṭacucuń				ḍhaṭcucuń ḍhaṭṭacucuń
1 du-excl. ŋkacia		ḍhaṭni ḍhaṭni	ḍhaṭcua ḍhaṭṭacua			ḍhaṭnicia ḍhaṭnicia	ḍhaṭcucuńka ḍhaṭṭacuńka			ḍhaṭnicia ḍhaṭnicia	ḍhaṭcucuńka ḍhaṭṭacuńka
2 du: khanaci	tʉḍhaťŋacʉŋ tʉḍhaṭṭaŋcʉŋ		tʉḍhaṭcu tʉḍhaṭṭacu		tʉḍhaṭnicia tʉḍhaṭnicia		tʉḍhaṭcucuń tʉḍhaṭṭacuń		tʉḍhaṭnicia tʉḍhaṭnicia		tʉḍhaṭcucuń tʉḍhaṭṭacuń
3 du: moko hʉaŋ	ḍhaṭŋacʉŋ ʉḍhaṭṭaŋcʉŋ	mʉḍhať mʉḍhaṭṭa	ʉḍhaṭcu ʉḍhaṭṭacu	ʉḍhaṭci ʉḍhaṭṭaci	ʉḍhaṭcia ʉḍhaṭṭacia	tʉḍhaṭci tʉḍhaṭṭaci	ʉḍhaṭcucum ʉḍhaṭṭacum	ʉḍhaṭṭiń mʉḍhaṭṭiń	ʉḍhaṭṭińka mʉḍhaṭṭińka	mʉḍhaṭṭiń mʉḍhaṭṭaniń	ʉḍhaṭcucuń ʉḍhaṭṭacuń
1 pl.-incl. ŋkań			ḍhaṭṭʉm ḍhaṭṭʉm				ḍhaṭṭʉmcʉm ḍhaṭṭʉmcʉm				ḍhaṭṭʉmcʉm ḍhaṭṭʉmcʉm
1 pl.-excl. ŋkańka		ḍhaṭnicia ḍhaṭnicia	ḍhaṭṭʉmka ḍhaṭṭʉmka			ḍhaṭnicia ḍhaṭnicia	ḍhaṭṭʉmcʉmka ḍhaṭṭʉmcʉmka			ḍhaṭnicia ḍhaṭnicia	ḍhaṭṭʉmcʉmka ḍhaṭṭʉmcʉmka
2 pl: khananiń	tʉḍhaťŋanʉŋ tʉḍhaṭṭaŋnʉŋ		tʉḍhaṭṭʉm tʉḍhaṭṭanʉm		tʉḍhaṭnicia tʉḍhaṭnicia		tʉḍhaṭṭʉmcʉm tʉḍhaṭṭanʉmcʉm		tʉḍhaṭnicia tʉḍhaṭnicia		tʉḍhaṭṭʉmcʉm tʉḍhaṭṭanʉmcʉm
3 pl: mokoci	mʉḍhaťŋa mʉḍhaṭṭaŋ	mʉḍhať mʉḍhaṭṭa	ʉḍhať ʉḍhaṭṭa	mʉḍhaṭci mʉḍhaṭṭaci	mʉḍhaṭcia mʉḍhaṭṭacia	mʉḍhaṭci mʉḍhaṭṭaci	mʉḍhaṭṭuci mʉḍhaṭṭuci	mʉḍhaṭṭiń mʉḍhaṭṭiń	mʉḍhaṭṭińka mʉḍhaṭṭińka	mʉḍhaṭṭiń mʉḍhaṭṭiń	mʉḍhaṭṭuci mʉḍhaṭṭuci

(A dot under a consonant denotes that it is retroflex; [ť] is a palatal variant of /t/, and [ń], of /n/, occurring syllable–finally, unless followed by a retroflex or a dental (including the nasal) stop; [ŋ] denotes the velar nasal, and [ʉ] an unround back vowel.)

As a general fact about the system, we can see that if the referents of the first and the second argument form partially overlapping sets, there is no conventionalized form for that in the language. There is thus no form in order to express that the first argument is in the first person singular and the second argument in the first person dual or plural, that the first argument is in the second person and the second argument in the inclusive first person dual or plural, or in the second person dual or plural, that the first argument is in the first person dual or plural inclusive and the second argument is in the first or second person singular, the first person dual or plural exclusive, or the second person dual or plural, that the first argument is in the first person dual or plural exclusive and the second argument is in the first person singular, or the first person dual or plural inclusive, or that the first argument is in the second person dual or plural and the second argument is in the second person singular or the first person dual or plural inclusive. All these are partially overlapping sets, because participants in a speech situation are deictically uniquely determined. There are no comparable restrictions for the third person, as it can be deictically different.

As to the identity in person between the first and the second argument, it is expressed by means of reflexive forms for the first and the second person, and also the third one if deictically identical. I have left them out of the schema, because they are built on the basis of a different formal procedure (e.g. the first person dual inclusive has the reflexive form *ḍhat-paḍhat́muaci* for both tenses, etc.), and in the grammar they are presumably treated in terms of derived predicates, because their semantic characteristics differ from those of basic predications such as those for which the schema has been worked out.

We can see that the desinences are only partially directly derivable from the pronouns which have presumably historically served as the basis for those desinences. In addition to the desinences, there are also prefixes *tu-*, *u-*, and *mu-*. They do not simply represent a grammatical dimension either. The following distributional regularities can be observed:

	first argument	–	second argument
tu-:	2 sg, du or pl	–	any;
	3 sg	–	2 sg, du or pl;
	3 du	–	2 du;
u-:	3 sg	–	1 sg (past), 1 du-incl., 1 du-excl., 1 pl-incl., 1 pl-excl. (past and nonpast);
	3 du	–	1 sg (past), 3 sg, 1 du-incl., 1 du-excl., 3 du, 1 pl-incl. (nonpast), 1 pl-excl. (nonpast), 3 pl;
	3 pl	–	3 sg (past and nonpast);
mu-:	3 du	–	2 sg, 1 pl-incl. (past), 1 pl-excl. (past), 2 pl;
	3 pl	–	all except 3 sg.

Even though these prefixes do not simply represent any of the grammatical dimensions involved, their distribution is not random either, but rather constrained by number, gender and tense, as can be seen above. They disambiguate potentially identical forms only in a limited number of cases, to be observed in the dual and plural.

There are many cases of syncretism between past and nonpast on the one hand, and numbers on the other.

Tense syncretism occurs in the following cases:

	first argument	–	second argument
past=nonpast	1 sg	–	any;
	2 sg	–	3 sg, 1 du-excl., 3 du, 1 pl-excl., 3 pl;
	3 sg	–	3 sg, 3 du, 1 pl-incl., 1 pl-excl., 3 pl;
	1 du-excl.	–	2 sg, 2 du, 2 pl;
	2 du	–	1 du-excl., 1 pl-excl.;
	1 pl-incl.	–	any;
	1 pl-excl.	–	any;
	2 pl	–	1 du-excl., 1 pl-excl.;
	3 pl	–	3 du, 1 pl-incl., 1 pl-excl., 2 pl, 3 pl.

Syncretism in number and person of the first argument:

identity in the first argument	–	second argument
3 du = 3 pl	–	2 sg;
2 sg = 2 du = 2 pl	–	1 du-excl.;
1 du-excl. = 1 pl-excl.	–	2 du;
2 sg = 2 du = 2 pl	–	1 pl-excl.;
1 du-excl. = 1 pl-excl.	–	2 pl.

Syncretism in number and person of the second argument:

first argument	–	identity in the second argument
any	–	3 du = 3 pl;
2 sg	–	1 du-excl. = 1 pl-excl.;
1 du-excl.	–	2 du = 2 pl;
2 du	–	1 du-excl. = 1 pl-excl.;
1 pl-excl.	–	2 du = 2 pl;
2 pl	–	1 du-excl. = 1 pl-excl.

What do we see? That there is only syncretism in number, along the dimensions of the various persons involved. The tables presented above show surprisingly that there is never syncretism in person, along the dimensions of the numbers involved.

In order to investigate whether syncretism in the verb endings in Bantawa from South Bhojpur is an idiosyncratic phenomenon, let us compare it with the other main Bantawa dialect, namely that from North Bhojpur.

As a representative of Bantawa from North Bhojpur, I take the system used by Tika Ram Rai, aged 35, from Chhinamakhu, in the western part of North Bhojpur.

(59) Complex pronominalization in the verb endings of Bantawa Rai (North Bhojpur); the positive paradigm: nonpast/past of *ḍhaṭma* 'to beat':

1st argument	2nd argument 1 sg: ʉŋka	2 sg: khana	3 sg: moko	1 du-incl.: ʉŋkaci	1 du-excl.: ʉŋkaca	2 du: khanaci	3 du: mocihʉapok	1 pl-incl.: ʉŋkanci	1 pl-excl.: ʉŋkanka	2 pl: khananci	3 pl: moci
1 sg: ʉŋka		ḍhaṭna ḍhaṭna	ḍhaṭṭuŋ ḍhaṭṭuŋ			ḍhaṭnaci ḍhaṭnaci	ḍhaṭṭuŋcʉŋ ḍhaṭṭuŋcʉŋ			ḍhaṭnanin ḍhaṭnanin	ḍhaṭṭuŋcʉŋ ḍhaṭṭuŋcʉŋ
2 sg: khana	ḍhaṭŋa ḍhaṭṭaŋ		ḍhaṭṭu ḍhaṭṭu		ḍhaṭnici dhatnici		ḍhaṭṭuci ḍhaṭṭuci		ḍhaṭnici ḍhaṭnici		ḍhaṭṭuci ḍhaṭṭuci
3 sg: moko	ḍhaṭŋa ḍhaṭṭaŋ	ḍhaṭ ḍhaṭṭa	ḍhaṭṭu ḍhaṭṭu	ḍhaṭci ḍhaṭṭaci	ḍhaṭca ḍhaṭṭaca	ḍhaṭci ḍhaṭṭaci	ḍhaṭṭuci ḍhaṭṭuci	ḍhaṭṭin ḍhaṭṭin	ḍhaṭṭinka ḍhaṭṭinka	ḍhaṭṭin ḍhaṭṭanin	ḍhaṭṭuci ḍhaṭṭuci
1 du-incl. ʉŋkaci			ḍhaṭcu ḍhaṭṭacu				ḍhaṭcu ḍhaṭṭacu				ḍhaṭcu ḍhaṭṭacu
1 du-excl. ʉŋkaca		ḍhaṭni ḍhaṭni	ḍhaṭca ḍhaṭṭaca			ḍhaṭni ḍhaṭni	ḍhaṭca ḍhaṭṭaca			ḍhaṭni ḍhaṭni	ḍhaṭca ḍhaṭṭaca
2 du: khanaci	ḍhaṭŋacʉŋ ḍhaṭṭaŋcʉŋ		ḍhaṭcu ḍhaṭṭacu		ḍhaṭnici ḍhaṭnici		ḍhaṭcu ḍhaṭṭacu		ḍhaṭnici ḍhaṭnici		ḍhaṭcu ḍhaṭṭacu
3 du: moci hʉapok	ḍhaṭŋacʉŋ ḍhaṭṭaŋcʉŋ	ḍhaṭ ḍhaṭṭa	ḍhaṭcu ḍhaṭṭacu	ḍhaṭci ḍhaṭṭaci	ḍhaṭca ḍhaṭṭaca	ḍhaṭci ḍhaṭṭaci	ḍhaṭṭuci ḍhaṭṭuci	ḍhaṭṭin ḍhaṭṭin	ḍhaṭṭinka ḍhaṭṭinka	ḍhaṭṭin ḍhaṭṭin	ḍhaṭṭuci ḍhaṭṭuci
1 pl-incl. ʉŋkanci			ḍhaṭṭum ḍhaṭṭum				ḍhaṭṭumcʉm ḍhaṭṭumcʉm				ḍhaṭṭumcʉm ḍhaṭṭumcʉm
1 pl-excl. ʉŋkanka		ḍhaṭni ḍhaṭni	ḍhaṭṭumka ḍhaṭṭumka			ḍhaṭni ḍhaṭni	ḍhaṭṭumcʉmka ḍhaṭṭumcʉmka			ḍhaṭni ḍhaṭni	ḍhaṭṭumcʉmka ḍhaṭṭumcʉmka
2 pl: khananci	ḍhaṭŋanʉŋ ḍhaṭṭaŋnʉŋ		ḍhaṭṭum ḍhaṭṭum		ḍhaṭnici ḍhaṭnici		ḍhaṭṭumcʉm ḍhaṭṭumcʉm		ḍhaṭnici ḍhaṭnici		ḍhaṭṭumcʉm ḍhaṭṭumcʉm
3 pl: moci	ḍhaṭŋa ḍhaṭṭaŋ	ḍhaṭ ḍhaṭṭa	ḍhaṭ ḍhaṭṭa	ḍhaṭci ḍhaṭṭaci	ḍhaṭca ḍhaṭṭaca	ḍhaṭci ḍhaṭṭaci	ḍhaṭṭuci ḍhaṭṭuci	ḍhaṭṭin ḍhaṭṭin	ḍhaṭṭinka ḍhaṭṭinka	ḍhaṭṭin ḍhaṭṭin	ḍhaṭṭuci ḍhaṭṭuci

(A dot under a consonant denotes that it is retroflex; there are no palatal variants of /t/ and /n/ in Bantawa of North Bhojpur; [ŋ] denotes the velar nasal, and [ʉ] a back unround vowel which is in Bantawa of North Bhojpur high, whereas in South Bhojpur it may vary between high and mid. In North Bhojpur, the velar nasal cannot be a syllable nucleus, whereas it can in South Bhojpur.)

The Chhinamakhu dialect, as Bantawa from North Bhojpur in general, does not have any prefixes in the verb paradigm, and it is interesting to see whether due to the lack of prefixes only the forms which are in the Wana dialect disambiguated through them fall together in Chhinamakhu, or that there are also other morphological differences involved.

Tense syncretism occurs in the following cases:

	first argument	–	second argument
past=nonpast	1 sg	–	any;
	2 sg	–	3 sg, 1 du-excl., 3 du, 1 pl-excl., 3 pl;
	3 sg	–	3 sg, 3 du, 1 pl-incl., 1 pl-excl., 3 pl;
	1 du-excl.	–	2 sg, 2 du, 2 pl;
	2 du	–	1 du-excl., 1 pl-excl.;
	3 du	–	3 du, 1 pl-incl., 1 pl-excl., 2 pl, 3 pl;
	1 pl-incl.	–	any;
	1 pl-excl.	–	any;
	2 pl	–	3 sg, 1 du-excl., 3 du, 1 pl-excl., 3 pl;
	3 pl	–	3 du, 1 pl-incl., 1 pl-excl., 2 pl, 3 pl.

Syncretism in number and person of the first argument:

identity in the first argument	–	second argument
2 sg = 3 sg = 3 pl	–	1 sg;
2 du = 3 du	–	1 sg;
3 sg = 3 du = 3 pl	–	2 sg;
1 du-excl. = 1 pl-excl.	–	2 sg;
2 sg = 3 sg	–	3 sg;
1 du-incl. = 2 du = 3 du	–	3 sg;
1 pl-incl. = 2 pl	–	3 sg;
3 sg = 3 du = 3 pl	–	1 du-incl.;
3 sg = 3 du = 3 pl	–	1 du-excl.;
2 sg = 2 du = 2 pl	–	1 du-excl.,
3 sg = 3 du = 3 pl	–	2 du;
1 du-excl. = 1 pl-excl.	–	2 du;
2 sg = 3 sg = 3 du = 3 pl	–	3 du;
1 du-incl. = 2 du	–	3 du;
1 pl-incl. = 2 pl	–	3 du;
3 sg = 3 du = 3 pl	–	1 pl-incl.;
2 sg = 2 du = 2 pl	–	1 pl-excl.;
3 sg = 3 du = 3 pl	–	1 pl-excl.;
1 du-excl. = 1 pl-excl.	–	2 pl;
3 sg (nonpast) = 3 du = 3 pl	–	2 pl;
2 sg = 2 du = 2 pl	–	3 pl;
1 du-incl. = 2 du	–	3 pl;
1 pl-incl. = 2 pl	–	3 pl.

Syncretism in number and person of the second argument:

first argument	–	identity in the second argument
any	–	3 du = 3 pl;
2 sg	–	1 du-excl. = 1 pl-excl.;
3 sg	–	1 du-incl. = 2 du;

1 du-incl.	– 3 sg = 3 du = 3 pl;
1 du-excl.	– 3 sg = 3 du = 3 pl;
2 du	– 3 sg = 3 du = 3 pl;
2 du	– 1 du-excl. = 1 pl-excl.;
3 du	– 1 du-incl. = 2 du;
3 du	– 1 pl-incl. = 2 pl;
1 pl-excl.	– 2 sg = 2 du = 2 pl;
2 pl	– 1 du-excl. = 1 pl-excl.;
3 pl	– 2 sg = 3 sg;
3 pl	– 1 du-incl. = 2 du;
3 pl	– 1 pl-incl. = 2 pl.

We can observe considerably more syncretism in the latter system than in the former one, more than due to the absence of the prefixes in the latter system. The origin of this difference is not at issue in this study – it may be either geographical or sociolinguistic, including the generation difference between the former, older speaker, and the latter, younger one – but only the observable systematic constraints are at issue within the scope of this investigation.

As to the systematic constraints, we can observe that Bantawa from South Bhojpur has syncretism in number only, whereas Bantawa from North Bhojpur has syncretism in number and person, but always with either the number or the person kept constant, or with an intersection of these two dimensions such as 2 sg = 3 sg = 3 du = 3 pl.

The treatment of number in Bantawa from North Bhojpur differs from that of person: whereas number can fully undergo syncretism (as in 2sg = 2 du = 2 pl, or 3 sg = 3 du = 3 pl), person undergoes it only with the dual inclusive. Otherwise, there is either syncretism between the first person dual or plural inclusive and the corresponding second person dual or plural, or between the second and the third person singular or dual, respectively. This shows that syncretism in person occurs along two dimensions: that involving the first and the second person, and that involving the second and the third person, and that it is related to the number marked in addition to the person which one of these dimensions of person will be involved. Syncretism in person is consequently constrained, and in a complex way. So let us examine it in detail.

The dimensions involved in distinguishing the first person from the second one and from the third one can be tentatively formulated as follows: *X outside of the speaker* vs. *X involving the speaker*, and *X outside of the speech situation* vs. *X involving the speech situation.* These two feature oppositions can in principle be asymmetrically ordered in either way, with the corresponding markedness reversal. Which of the two possible orderings does Bantawa have?

Depending on the number involved, Bantawa has both types of asymmetrical ordering. In combination with the singular, the dimension which concentrates on the speaker is dominating, whereas in combination with the dual and the plural, the dimension which concentrates on the speech situation is dominating as shown in (60).

(60) Asymmetrical ordering between the feature oppositions of person, in relation to number in Chhinamakhu Bantawa from North Bhojpur:

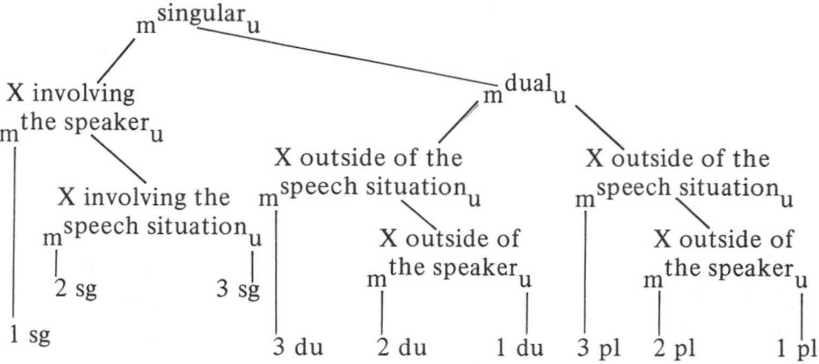

The distinction between *inclusive* and *exclusive* becomes understandable, too, given the feature hierarchy in the dual and the plural: *inclusive* equals 'the speaker and X outside of the speaker, but not outside of the speech situation', and *exclusive* equals 'the speaker and X outside of the speech situation', thus making reference to person features of a different level. It is not accidental, then, that only the first person dual and plural inclusive, which makes reference to 'X outside of the speaker, but not outside of the speech situation', undergoes syncretism with the second person dual or plural, respectively. This equals elimination of a subordinate feature opposition, within which no reference is being made to the dominating feature opposition.

It is in the same way not accidental that the second and the third person singular undergo syncretism. This equals elimination of a subordinate feature opposition, too. But I am not able to say why there is syncretism between the third person singular and the third person plural of the first argument in combination with the first person singular of the second argument, as it does not follow the rule of eliminating hierarchy in a stepwise way. This syncretism is not motivated by the patterning of the features of meaning involved.

Finally, let me state that person is context-sensitive to number on the grounds of meaning, but that there is no asymmetrical patterning involved between these two pairs of distinctive feature oppositions. Viewing the constellation from the perspective of the features of person, we get (61). Note that from that perspective, the asymmetrical ordering which holds for the features of person in the context of the unmarked value(s) of number appears to be the general one.

(61) Asymmetrical ordering between the feature oppositions of person, and between those of number, viewed from the perspective of person, in Chhinamakhu Bantawa from North Bhojpur:

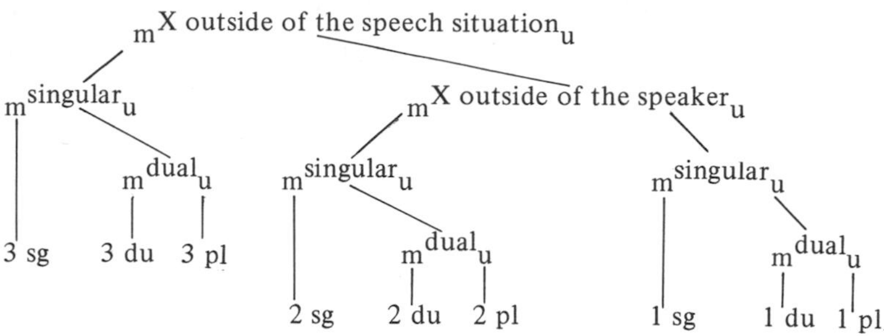

Whereas person and number in Bantawa are not mutually asymmetrically ordered – they only always cooccur, hence the context-sensitiveness – there are languages which do have asymmetrical ordering there. An example of such a language is Dutch, which has full person syncretism in the plural, but its distinction in the singular e.g. *ik werk* 'I work', *jij werkt* 'you work', *jij/zij/het werkt* 'he/she/it works', *wij werken* 'we work', *jullie werken* 'you work', *zij werken* 'they work'). In Dutch, number is dominating and person subordinate, and number is rendered as [m plural] vs. [u plural], not as [m singular] vs. [u singular] as in Bantawa. This is shown by the attested asymmetry.

Somebody could ask: 'but isn't it circular, deriving asymmetrical ordering from the observed language data, and then using it in order to account for the same data?'. The answer to it is: 'no, it is not circular, because the notion of asymmetry and markedness as attached to it is restrictive in the way which goes beyond the observed data'. Namely, it is predicted that markedness of the plural occurs only in languages which have no dual. And this is supported by the Dutch data indeed.

The investigated syncretism in the verb endings of Bantawa – as well as that of Dutch mentioned above – gives independent evidence of the grammatical features involved (as they define the dimensions along which syncretism occurs), and of their partial asymmetrical ordering (as it imposes constraints on syncretism, without fully determining it).

Grammatical features are consequently patterned on the basis of the same principles as phonological features are. And only the principles have been hypothesized to be universal without being rejected, not the extent of their relevance in a language or the direction of their application.

3. Lexical Variation and Change in Relation to the System

We have seen in the first chapter of this study that the distinctive forms of a language consist of linear sequences of partially asymmetrically ordered sets of distinctive features, and that feature ordering imposes constraints on variation by which a change of a dominating feature opposition has consequences for its subordinate one(s), whereas a change of a subordinate or an unordered feature opposition need not have consequences for the remaining feature oppositions.

And we have seen in the second chapter of this study that the meaning of grammatical language signs (called 'morphemes') can be analysed in terms of partially asymmetrically ordered pairs of feature oppositions as well, imposing constraints on variation. Also, asymmetrical ordering appeared to be the only system-internal condition under which markedness comes into the picture. At the level of meaning, there is either an assertion of a characteristic or its negation, and it is not *a priori* given which characteristic of the appropriate referent (in the sense of Ebeling (1978)) will be patterned by a language as an assertion of a characteristic, and which one as its negation. Hence even both possibilities of patterning can occur within one language as dependent on the feature context, as attested for the features of person in Bantawa from North Bhojpur, discussed in 2.2. above.

The next step is to extend the hypothesis about ordering as imposing constraints on variation onto lexical morphemes.

The area of the lexicon which shows regularities of patterning in the most clear-cut way are the numerals. So let us investigate numeral variation and change with respect to the features of meaning involved, and the forms attached to them.

For an optimal investigation of numeral variation, a well-documented area is needed, if possible characterized by contact phenomena of different numeral systems. Such an area appears to exist in Nepal, where Tibeto-Burman languages are changing at a fast rate due to Indo-Aryan influences, especially that of the official language Nepali, which is spoken everywhere in the country.

For East Nepal, we have access to the intricate language variation data by now, thanks to the Linguistic Survey of Nepal, financed by the German Research Council and guided by W. Winter, assisted by A.K. Weidert and G. Hansson from the German side, and S. Subba and formerly also R. Yadav from the Nepalese side. The data have been collected by a group of trained Nepalese students, who have filled out language questionnaires in the *panchayats* of the three outer eastern zones of Nepal, Mechi, Kosi and Sagarmatha.

The collected data enable us more insight especially into the Kiranti group of Tibeto-Burman. They have given me the necessary background for carrying out my research on numeral change.

3.1 The Kiranti Group of Tibeto-Burman Languages in East Nepal and Contact Phenomena with Indo-Aryan

The first extensive source for Tibeto-Burman in Nepal is Grierson's (1909) Linguistic Survey of India. It distinguishes Himalayan as a separate subgroup of Tibeto-Burman and further subdivides the Himalayan languages into 'nonpronominalized' and 'complex pronominalized' (the latter with pronominal suffixes added to the verb in order to indicate the first two arguments of the predication, as we have seen on the basis of the Bantawa examples discussed in the preceding chapter). Of the complex pronominalized Himalayan languages, the eastern subgroup is of interest to us here. Grierson listed among them: Dhimal, Thāmi, Limbu, Yākhā, Khambu, Bahing, Rai, Vayu/Hayu, and the following Khambu dialects (as he called them): Bālāi, Sāngpāng, Lōhōrōng, Lāmbichhōng, Waling, Chhintāng, Rungchhēnbūng, Dūngmāli, Rōdōng, Nāchherēng, Kūlung, Thūlung, Chouraśya, Khāling, and Dūmi. (And among the nonpronominalized he listed: Gurung, Murmi (i.e. Tamang), Sunwar, Magarī, Newarī, Pahari, Lepcha/Rong, and Tŏtŏ.) The presented list was not a result of linguistic classification, but rather of the native names of the language varieties presented to the investigator. For some of them, he presented a word list, remarks on the morphology and syntax, and a text.

Out of the later classifications on the basis of additional data, let me mention Shafer (1966), who classified the East Himalayan section of Tibeto-Burman as follows.

(62) Shafer's (1966) classification of East Himalayan (or 'Himalayish') languages:

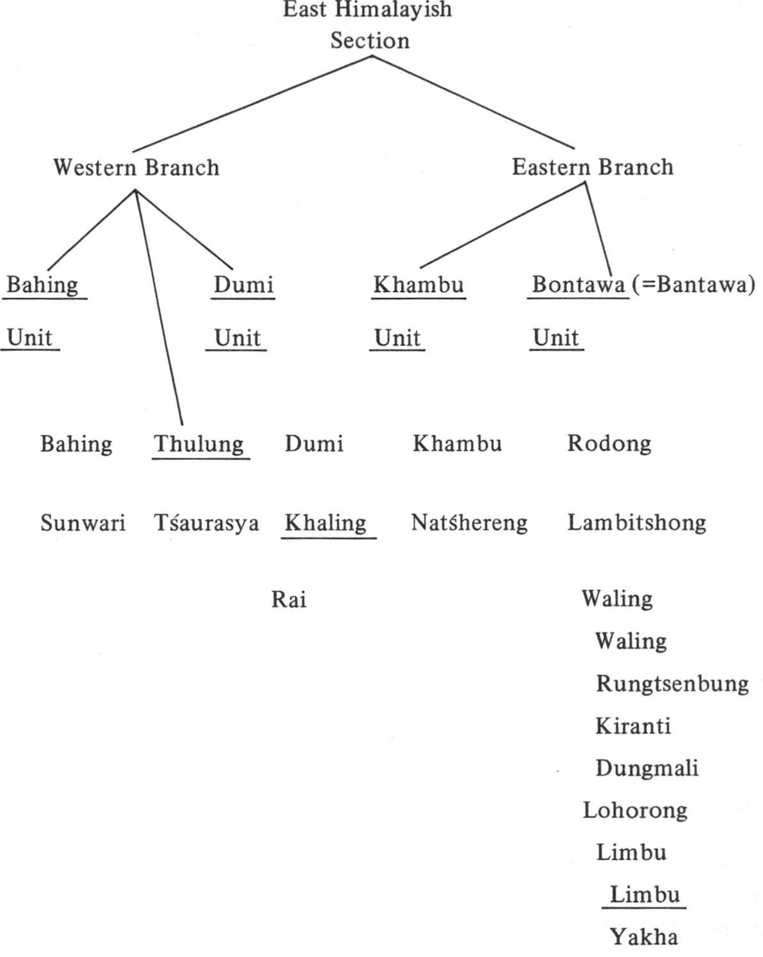

(Language varieties considered to determine the type are underlined. Note that Shafer transcribes as *tś* for what Grierson used *ch.*)

In Shafer's classification, Sunwari is correctly treated as belonging to this, complex pronominalized, group, and Khambu appears to be just one variety of the eastern branch.

Finally, Benedict (1972) distinguished Kiranti as the main language group of what he called the Bahing-Vayu nucleus.

(63) Bahing-Vayu (Kiranti) after Benedict (1972):

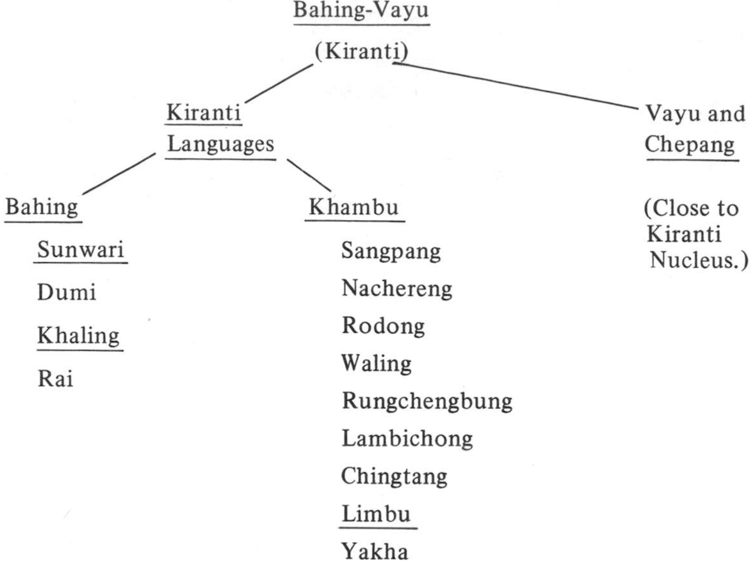

A fundamental revision of the proposed list of the Kiranti languages, which all belong to the complex pronominalized group of Tibeto-Burman languages spoken in East Nepal, has become possible and necessary since the Linguistic Survey of Nepal has systematically collected lexical and grammatical data (phonological ones being a part of their form) for the entire eastern zones, which have brought to our knowledge some earlier unknown languages, and showed extinction of some others. But the main result is a new grouping of the Kiranti languages into Rai on the one hand, and Limbu on the other. This appears to be related to the ethnological classification of the peoples of East Nepal as classified by Bista (1980), but not fully predictable by it: Sunwari (or 'Sunwar') can on ethnological, but not on linguistic grounds be separated from the Kiranti nucleus. The main characteristic of the Kiranti nucleus is its complex pronominalization, and this is found in Sunwar as well. In some other respects it is relatively (but not exceptionally) conservative as compared with the Kiranti nucleus: it still preserves the original Tibeto-Burman word order 'noun, determiner', which has either been lost or is not any more the only possibility within the Kiranti nucleus; its remnants are still found, though, e.g. in Limbu.

As to further classification within the Kiranti group, grammatical morphemes appear to provide a better discriminating basis than the lexicon, which is either conservative (in the sense of largely spread Tibeto-Burman variants) or borrowed from Indo-Aryan (cf. also Winter, forthcoming). Phonological phenomena, on the other hand, either represent areally bound isoglosses, or local subdivisions which are smaller than the ones indicated by the grammar. An example of an areally bound isogloss can be found in the preservation of the *high* vs. *low* tone in northwestern Rai languages, with remnants of it in Bantawa from North Bhojpur (in minimal pairs, and opposed verb classes), but not from South Bhojpur. This isogloss binds Sunwar with the Rai languages. Another areally bound isogloss is found in the syllable-final palatalization of /t/ and /n/ unless followed by a homorganic dental or a retroflex stop, which is found in Bantawa from South Bhojpur and in the other two neighbouring central Rai languages, Chamling and Puma (illustrations of it can be found in the complex pronominalized verb forms of Bantawa from South Bhojpur presented in 2.2. above).

On the basis of the attested grammatical morphemes, the following tentative list of the Kiranti languages can be proposed on the basis of their geographical distribution as attested by the Linguistic Survey of Nepal, with additional classificatory remarks forwarded to me by A.K. Weidert, and following W. Winter's and G. Hansson's proposal to include Sunwar, Hayu and Thami into the Kiranti, but not the Rai group.

(64) Kiranti Tibeto-Burman languages spoken in East Nepal:

<u>Northwestern Rai:</u> <u>Northeastern Rai:</u>
Khaling Yamphe
Thulung Kulung Mewahang
Dumi Lohorong
Sangpang Koi Limbu

<u>Western Rai:</u> <u>Eastern Rai:</u>
Sunwar Bahing <u>Central and</u> Yakkha
Hayu Ombule <u>Southern Rai:</u> Athpare
Thami Chamling
Puma Bantawa

The presented list includes a tentative classification of the attested language varieties of languages for which the name of the variety with the widest distribution has been chosen as the language name. With minor changes (e.g. concerning the status of Puma), this tentative list follows Weidert's classificatory remarks, according to which the remaining language varieties can be seen as closely related to the aforementioned more widely spread ones as follows:

- Amchoke, Arthare, Chhintange, Dilpali, Khesange and Wahitpang to Bantawa;
- Chourase and Jerunge to Ombule;
- Deosali to Thulung;
- Kharmile to Sangpang;
- Yakkhaba to Yamphe and Yakkha (cf. also the next chapter), and
- Rokhung presumably to Bahing (a full record is still missing).

Only after a comprehensive evaluation of the data collected for the Linguistic Survey of Nepal, and additional indepth studies, will a full classification of the Kiranti language varieties be possible.

I shall report in this chapter on one structural aspect of various Kiranti languages and its change under Indo-Aryan influence. Out of the two aspects of language structure most influenced by Indo-Aryan, namely numerals and adjectives, I shall highlight on the numerals, because they exhibit not only replacement by the Indo-Aryan forms and word order change from postposition to preposition (as both adjectives and numerals do), but also other regularities which are indicative of the organization of their meaning and the relation between meaning and form.

3.2. Numerals in Kiranti Languages and Their Change

3.2.1. Numerals in Kiranti languages are changing and decaying, and the corresponding Nepali numerals are being taken over. The process of decay reveals some system-internal regularities, though, which can be established only after a systematic investigation of the picture presented by the data collected for the Linguistic Survey of Nepal. The picture is even more complicated due to migrations to the east and southeast, which took place during the past two centuries, and can be traced back for this century through the older generation (as illustrated by the Bantawa speaker mentioned in 2.2. above, who had migrated from South Bhojpur to Ilam fifty years ago).

I shall now present exemplificatory data from the Linguistic Survey of Nepal, beased on the original distribution of the language varieties, not the localities in which some of them are found now, after the migrations. For each language, I mention the *panchayat* and the district in East Nepal in which it has been attested. All of the districts (e.g. Okhaldunga etc.) can be found on the map of the Nepal Eastern Development Region which comes from Winter (1984).

(65) Preserved Tibeto-Burman numerals in Rai languages (data collected for the Linguistic Survey of Nepal and preserved at the Linguistics Department, University of Kiel):

Western Rai:

	Bahing	Bahing	Chourase	Chourase
	Moli, Okhaldunga	Biguṭar, Okhaldunga	Chhintang, Dhankuṭa	Simle, Tehrathum
1	kong	kong	kolo	kwalo
2	niksi	niksi	–	nimpha
3	sam	sam	–	summakha
4	lɛ	lɛ	–	–
5	ngɔ	ruka	–	kollabremci
6	rukhu	cani	–	–
7	cʉni	kodhim	–	–
8	ja	–	–	–
9	gu	–	–	–
10	kudum	–	–	nimphalabremci
20	–	–	–	–
100	–	–	–	–

Northwestern Rai:

	Dumi	Dumi	Kulung	Kulung	Kulung
	Saptesor, Khoṭang	Kubhinde, Khoṭang	Gudel, Solukhumbu	Bung, Solukhumbu	Pawoi, Solukhumbu
1	tʉkpo	tɔkpu	ibum	ibum	ibim
2	sakpo	sɔkpu	nicci	nicci	nicci
3	sukpo	bhlɔkpu	supci	supci	sukli
4	bhalukpo	rɔkpu	lici	lici	likci
5	tumpo	–	ngaci	ngaci	tupci
6	dumpo	–	tupci	tupci	tikci
7	sɔmpo	–	–	retci	–
8	ɔmpo	–	retci	–	–
9	rekpo	–	nuci	–	–
10	–	–	bɔci	–	–
20	–	–	–	–	–
100	–	–	–	–	–

Northeastern Rai:

	Mewahang	Yakkhaba	Yakkhaba
	Tamku, Sankhuwasabha	Makalu, Sankhuwasabha	Paṭibhara, Sankhuwasabha
1	ekku	ikko	ikko
2	hicci	nicci	nicci
3	sumji	sumji	sumji
4	–	riji	riji
5	ihuk	ngaji	ngaji
6	–	cukji	–
7	–	yetci	–
8	–	ɔkci	–
9	–	nɔkci	–
10	hukhu	ippong	–
20	–	–	–
100	–	–	–

Central and Southern Rai:

	Bantawa	Bantawa	Bantawa	Bantawa
	Annapurna, Bhojpur	Chhinamakhu, Bhojpur	Dhunge Sarang, Panchthar	Durdimba Panchthar
1	ʉkṭai	ʉkṭak/ʉkpok	ʉkṭa	ʉkbok
2	hʉapok	hʉapok	husaṭ	husaṭ
3	sumkapok	sumkapok	sumka	sumka
4	reṭkapok	–	caroṭa (=Nepali)	–
5	–	–	–	ʉkchuk
6	–	–	–	–
7	–	–	–	–
8	–	reṭkapok	reṭka	reṭkabok
9	–	–	–	–
10	–	–	–	hʉachuk
20	–	–	–	–
100	–	–	–	bhung

	Bantawa	Eastern Rai Yakkha	Translation of the
	Raniṭar Panchthar	Jitpur, Dhankuta	Yakkha examples:
1	ʉkṭa	kolok	'1'
2	hʉaṭa	hitci	'2'
3	sumkaṭ	sumci	'3'
4	reṭkaṭaṭ	sumcibi usongbi kolok	'3 + 1'
5	ʉkchuk	muktapi	'hand'
6	bhankachuk	muktapi usongbi kolok	'hand + 1'
7	bhanhʉchuk	muktapi usongbi hitci	'hand + 2'
8	bhansumchuk	muktapi usongbi sumci	'hand + 3'
9	bhanreṭchuk	mukcurukbi kolok hongbi	'hands – 1'
10	hʉachuk	muktapi hita	'hand 2' (= 2 hands)
20	retkachuk	langcurukmukcuruk	'legs hands'
100	ʉtopchuk/ukbhung	—	

(Everywhere in the transcription, *c* = [ts], and *j* = [dz]; *y* = [j], *ng* = the velar nasal [ŋ], a dot underneath denotes retroflexion, aspiration is represented by means of a following *h*, ʉ is an unround back vowel, and ɛ and ɔ are open mid vowels. The transcription is phonological as far as possible on the basis of the collected data, except for *c* and *j*, which are phonologically sequences.)

We can see in several language varieties a new form for 'five', based on the language-specific form for 'hand' (i.e. in Chourase: /la/ = 'hand' and /brem/ = 'finger'; in Mewahang /huk/ = 'hand', in Bantawa /chuk/ = 'hand', and in Yakkha /mukta/ = 'hand'). These forms can be used in sentences only in Bantawa. The remaining languages replace the forms for 'five' based on 'hand' (and for 'ten' on 'two hands' etc.) by the corresponding Nepali forms. Also the Kulung shifted forms in Bung and Pawoi cannot be used in sentences, which shows that their meaning has not been changed. The corresponding Nepali forms are used instead of these, and all of the lacking forms.

Only a small part of the observable variation in the extent of numeral preservation can be ascribed to areal phenomena:

- preservation of the form for '1' only is found in Western Rai;
- preservation of the numeral forms up to '10' is found in Northern and Western Rai, and in northern and western areas in general;
- preservation of the numeral forms up to '3' is found in all the areas, but predominantly in Central and Southern Rai, and in central and southern areas in general;

– a new form for 'five' based on 'hand' and further derivations from it (i.e. 'two hands' for 'ten' etc.) is found in eastern areas; the fact that this phenomenon is only bound to the area, and not to the Rai language originally spoken in the area, shows that it can be dated after the beginning of the migrations to the east, which took place during the past two centuries.

The fact that the first three numeral forms are preserved in all the areas except for Western Rai shows that the numeral preservation in the lexicon is related to the numbers relevant to the grammar of the language: except for Western Rai, all of the remaining Rai languages have three numbers in the grammar (i.e. the singular, the dual and the plural). Only Western Rai exhibits loss of the dual, and only these languages exhibit loss of the original numeral form for 'two' and/or 'three'.

The established geographical distribution in the numeral preservation appears to be reflected by the migrated language varieties as well. For example, Dumi, which is originally a Northern Rai language, preserves occasionally the original numeral forms up to 'ten' in Khoṭang, whereas in outer southeastern areas the Dumis count up to 'six' or 'five' only, and in the southern district Morang only up to 'three'.

However, the geographic distribution cannot account for all of the variation. Languages appear to have a specific 'cut-off' point for the numeral loss, at least at an intermediate stage, and this is a general phenomenon in Tibeto-Burman undergoing Indo-Aryan influence, not one restricted to the Rai languages. A cut-off point can be recognized by the preservation of the original numeral forms up to a certain point, and their loss above that point without any observable downward shift. It can be illustrated by the Yakkhaba examples from Sankhuwasabha mentioned above, where the counting goes up to 'ten', or – at the next stage – up to 'five', without any downward shift. Outside of the Rai languages, Tamang (belonging to the Tamang-Gurung-Thakali Nucleus of Tibeto-Burman, originally spoken in Central Nepal) has a cut-off point at 'twenty' and afterwards, at the next stage, at 'ten'. Or Magar, originally spoken in the northern and central areas of Nepal, and due to migrations also in the South and East, has a cut-off point at 'five'. These data have also become available through the Linguistic Survey of Nepal – which gives a picture of all of the languages attested in East Nepal – be it originally or due to migrations – but I shall not concentrate on them, as they are much better known than the Rai (or Kiranti in general) Nucleus so far (cf. also the bibliography presented by Hale (1973)).

How to recognize the cut-off point independently of the question of whether the preserved forms are attached to their original meanings, or that the preserved forms are shifted downwards in comparison with their original meanings (as e.g. in Bahing of Biguṭar, or in Dumi of Kubhinde)? In other words, how to recognize whether the cut-off point is related functionally to the original association of form and meaning in a given language indeed?

A test case is provided by numeral usage in sentences. The questionnaires of the Linguistic Survey of Nepal contained several sentences of the type 'I see five black stones'. And it appeared that the forms which were linearly shifted down (such as presumably the form for '6' onto '5' in Bahing of Biguṭar, Okhaldunga) were not actively used in numeral constructions in sentences, but rather replaced by the corresponding Nepali forms.

I view as the cut-off point in numeral change and decay the highest numeral which is actively used in numeral constructions in a language.

An interesting case in this respect is presented by Dumi from Kubhinde, Khoṭang, where a merger of the original forms for '2' and '3' occurred, the original form for '4' was linearly shifted down onto '3', and the (apparent) original form for '9' was shifted onto '4'. These forms appear to be used in numeral constructions in sentences, which shows that a reinterpretation has taken place there. The merger of the forms for '2' and '3' is presumably due to a phonological change of redistributing the back vowels as nondiffuse in closed syllables and diffuse in open ones; there is no reason to assume that it was a change based on the meaning, and also not that it was due to a linear shifting down. The linear downward shift of the original form for '4' onto '3' was presumably motivated by the regularity mentioned above by which language systems which have three numbers in the grammar tend to preserve the first three original numeral forms in the lexicon as well. This was consequently not a mere linear shift, but one motivated by the system. And finally, the downward shift of the original form for '9' onto '4' was by no means a linear one. It can be understood only against the background of the meaning of '9' as '5+4': the shift from '9' onto '4' then equals a change of meaning which can be formulated as 'diminishing by five'. I call such a shift 'conceptual': motivated by a (presumed) change of the conceptual unit from 'ten' to 'five', a corresponding shift of forms occurred, yielding new numeral signs – and this is why such forms in Dumi of Kubhinde are used actively in numeral constructions.

Other cases of conceptual downward shift are found in Bantawa of Annapurna, Bhojpur, and in Bantawa of Raniṭar, Panchthar, where the original form for '8' can be assumed to be shifted onto '4', which equals conceptually 'diminishing by one half'. (No wonder, again, that this conceptual shift occurs above the first three numerals, which are apparently related to the three numbers in the grammar.)

As far as the questionnaires of the Linguistic Survey of Nepal go, it is possible to conclude that there is a fundamental difference between simply linearly shifted forms in counting, which are not actively used in numeral constructions, and conceptually shifted forms, which are actively used indeed, so that they can be viewed as underlying a new sign formation in the numerals of the given language.

The next problem is that of how to evaluate the new forms for '5', based on the language-specific words for 'hand', as attested in Chourase of Simle, Mewahang of Tamku, Bantawa of Durdimba and Raniṭar, and Yakkha of Dhankuṭa mentioned above. Here again the same criterion appears to be applicable: only the forms which are actively used in numeral constructions can be considered to be due to a reinterpretation. An inspection of the questionnaires shows that the Chourase, Mewahang and Yakkha numerals are not actively used above '3', but rather replaced by the corresponding Nepali forms. In these language systems, no proof of a reinterpretation can be found, even though this reinterpretation – in terms of a system based on '5' instead of '10' – belongs to one of the language possibilities. A proof of such a reinterpretation is found only in Bantawa, where the new numeral forms, based on '5' as expressed by means of the form for 'hand', are actively used in numeral constructions indeed. A further proof of this reinterpretation is presented by the Raniṭar Bantawa numeral forms above that for '5', which are derived from the new form for '5', and actively used as such.

Comparative evidence shows that the forms for '5' based on 'hand' are due to an innovation. And the fact that whenever the new form for '5' is found, the form for '10' is derived from it, shows that this innovation can be analysed as reinterpretation – or reanalysis – in terms of a quinary system.

More general Tibeto-Burman evidence, as presented by Benedict (1972: 93f.), points to a general decimal basis, but with traces of a quinary basis according to Benedict to be found in the form for '7' which can be etymologized as *s-nis (i.e. '5+2' = '7'). (Benedict assumed also that the Tibeto-Burman numeral system had included a vigesimal basis as well, along with the distinctive root *m-. Its attestations in the Tibeto-Burman languages of East Nepal are based on a different root, as will be seen below.)

On the basis of the attested forms, and on the basis of the geographical restriction to the eastern-most districts, the quinary numeral systems found in the Kiranti languages can be analysed as due to a language change which took place after the migrations to the east, and is thus presumably not older than the last century.

The numerals attested by the questionnaires filled out for the Linguistic Survey of Nepal thus lead to the following hypotheses about numeral decay in Kiranti and other Tibeto-Burman languages of East Nepal:

– the process of numeral decay is at each stage characterized by a language-specific cut-off point, defined by the highest numeral which is actively used in numeral constructions;

– the cut-off point is related to the conceptual basis of the numeral system.

3.2.2. In addition to these inductively-deductively based hypotheses, also purely deductive ones can be formulated on the basis of the theory-inherent assumption that the various parts of the language system are organized according to the same principle by which there is partial ordering, and in so far as present, ordering imposes constraints on variation and change. On the basis of this assumption, and taking into account the characteristics of the numeral systems which have been established in the preceding chapter, the following additional hypotheses about numerals can be advanced.

A. It is hypothesized that cardinal numerals impose an upper limit on the occurrence of other numerals in the systems: a language does not have more ordinal numerals than cardinal ones; it also does not have more distributive or multiplicative numerals than cardinal ones.

B. It is hypothesized that ordinal numerals, reflecting ordering in space, will be related to ordering in time as expressed by multiplicative numerals such as 'once', 'twice' etc. and to lexicalized time expressions such as 'yesterday', 'tomorrow' etc. It is hypothesized that the number of lexicalized ordinal numerals (if there are any not directly derivable from the corresponding cardinal ones) will impose the upper boundary on the number of lexicalized expressions referring to ordering in time.

If a language distinguishes between a single verb action and a repeated one by means of lexicalized forms, it can be hypothesized that the number of these forms will not exceed the number of lexicalized expressions for temporal ordering in that language.

C. As to the expression form of numeral constructions, it is hypothesized that in the generally observed word order change from noun + determiner (to be reconstructed as the original one on the basis of comparative Tibeto-Burman evidence) into determiner + noun, ordinal numerals will undergo this change earlier than the corresponding cardinal ones. It is also hypothesized that in the first stage of this change, the number of positions preceding the noun is restricted to two if there is a possessive determiner involved, and to one otherwise. (This because in Tibetan and in Burmese languages which are more archaic in this respect, a possessive determiner precedes its noun, whereas all of the remaining ones follow in the order from the most specific to the most general one.)

In order to investigate numeral variation as a part of the lexicon and thus indicative of it, I went to Nepal and designed a numeral questionnaire with the help of A.K. Weidert, the field supervisor of the Linguistic Survey of Nepal, and for the Nepali equivalents of the English numeral constructions with the help of D.B. Ingwaba, a guiding Nepalese field-worker in the project.

The questionnaire concentrated on the following aspects:
- cardinal numerals,
- ordinal numerals,
- distributive numerals ('one each' etc.),
- multiplicative numerals ('once' etc.),
- cardinal numeral + noun of the following types: human, nonhuman animate, inanimate, body parts,
- ordinal numeral + noun of the same types,
- distributive numeral + noun of the same types,
- cardinal numeral + noun + possessive pronoun,
- ordinal numeral + noun + possessive pronoun,
- distributive numeral + noun + possessive pronoun,
- multiplicative numeral + noun + possessive pronoun,
- cardinal numeral + adjective + noun,
- ordinal numeral + adjective + noun,
- cardinal numeral + adjective + noun + possessive pronoun,
- ordinal numeral + adjective + noun + possessive pronoun,
- cardinal numeral + adjective (implied noun),
- ordinal numeral + adjective (implied noun),
- cardinal numeral + adjective + possessive pronoun,
- ordinal numeral + adjective + possessive pronoun,
- cardinal numeral + adjective + adjective + noun (in order to compare adjective stacking with numeral stacking),
- distributive numeral + cardinal numeral + adjective + possessive pronoun,
- distributive numeral + cardinal numeral + adjective + noun + possessive pronoun,
- temporal ordering of the type 'yesterday', 'today', 'tomorrow' etc.,
- multiplication of the verb object (of the type 'I shall beat him two beatings'), and
- difference in distributive numerals of the type 'each of your two houses' vs. 'your two houses each'.

The data were collected through work with native informants in Kaṭhmandu and in East Nepal, representing the following Kiranti languages: Sunwar (Western Kiranti), Kulung (Northwestern Kiranti Rai), Lohorong (Northeastern Kiranti Rai), Yakkhaba (related to Yamphe in Northeastern Kiranti Rai and to Yakkha in Eastern Kiranti Rai), Bantawa (Central and Southern Kiranti Rai), Athpare (Eastern Kiranti Rai), and Limbu (Eastern Kiranti).

I shall now present the data for each language, and then discuss them against the hypotheses advanced above.

SUNWAR

Informant: Nar Bahadur Jyatisha, male aged 20, born in panchayat Dura Gaon, village Saat Gaon, district Ramechap, zone Janakpur; he has spent

18 years at his birthplace, and the years afterwards in Kaṭhmandu; he is unmarried, the native language of both his parents' is Sunwar. The questionnaire has been filled out by D. Bieri.

Notes on the notation: (ˈ) denotes the distinctive high tone on the (stem) syllable nucleus following that mark; long vowels are analysed as double; a double vowel (i.e. a sequence of two identical vowels) which is followed by /n/ in the same syllable is pronounced as nasalized, and followed by /k/ as glottalized; /ng/ is pronounced as [ŋ], /ts/ as [c], and /dz/ as [j] (the notation as /ts/ and /dz/, which is phonologically justifiable for Sunwar, differs from the indistinguishable notation as /c/ and /j/ used for the examples cited from the questionnaires of the Linguistic Survey of Nepal, as data for further analysis were lacking). This notation is phonological, in accordance with Bieri and Schulze's (1971) analytical remarks on Sunwar. Phonetic phenomena such as devoicing of the word-final vowel except in words which form an intonation unit expressing a new information unit, have not been indicated in the transcription.

Cardinal numerals:

1 /kaa/
2 /ˈniikši/
3 /saan/
4 /lee/
5 /ngoon/
6 /ruku/
7 /tsəni/
8 /tsəsi/
9 /yaan/
10 /gow/
20 /khal kaa/
100 –

Out of these numeral forms, only the first three ones are actively used. The higher ones are replaced by the corresponding Nepali forms.

Ordinal numerals:

the first = /ngoiti/ (i.e. 'the front one')
the second = /noole/ (i.e. the back one')
the third – etc.

Distributive numerals:

one each = /kaa kaa/
two each = /ni ˈniikši/
three each = /saan saan/; Nepali forms for higher numerals.

Multiplicative numerals:

once = /kaale/
twice = /ˈniikši khep/
three times = /saan khep/; Nepali forms for higher numerals;
only = /la/

both = /'nimpha/.

Cardinal numeral + noun:

– human, type 'one woman' = /'miišmur kaa/
'two women' = /'miišmur 'niikši/
'three women' = /'miišmur saan/
above three: Nepali forms, including the classifier desinence for human beings /-dzənə/, and word order: numeral + noun;

– nonhuman animate, type 'one goat' = /kyarš kaa/
'two goats' = /kyarš 'niikši/
'three goats' = /kyarš saan/ etc. Nepali;

– inanimate, type 'one stone' = /phullu kaa/
'two stones' = /phullu 'niikši/
'three stones' = /phullu saan/ etc. Nepali;
inanimate, type 'one fire' = /mii kaa/
'two fires' = /mii 'niikši/
'three fires' = /mii saan/ etc. Nepali;

– body parts, type 'one hand' = /gui kaa/
'two hands' = /gui 'niikši/
'three hands' = /gui saan/ etc. Nepali.

Only in combination with Nepali numerals can a noun be followed by the plural desinence /-puki/.

Ordinal numeral + noun:

– all the types follow the pattern of 'the first woman' = /ngoiti miišmur/.

Distributive numeral + noun:

– all the types follow the pattern of 'one woman each' = /miišmur kaa kaa/, and with Nepali numeral forms the pattern of 'hundred women each' = /səi kaa miišmurpuki/.

Cardinal numeral + noun + possessive pronoun:

– The possessive pronouns are: 'my' = /aan ke/, 'your' = /i ke/, 'his=her=its'= /meko ke/ 'our' = /go ain ke/, 'your, plural' = /ge in ke/, 'their' = /mekopuki an ke/;

– all the types follow the pattern of 'my two goats' = /aan ke kyarš 'niikši/, and with Nepali numerals the pattern of 'your five rings' = /i ke pantsota aunthipuki/, with the numeral (and the Nepali desinence *-ota*) preceding the noun, which occurs in the plural.

Ordinal numeral + noun + possessive pronoun:

– all the types follow the pattern of 'my second goat' = /aan ke noole nga kyarš/ (lit. 'my back me goat').

Distributive numeral + noun + possessive pronoun:

– all the types follow the pattern of 'each of your boys' = /i ke alpuki kaa kaa pa/ (lit. 'your boys one by one').

Multiplicative numeral + noun + possessive pronoun:

– all the types follow the pattern of 'my only goat' = /ann ke kyarš kaa la/.

Cardinal numeral + adjective + noun:

– all the types follow the pattern of 'one beautiful woman' = /daršo 'miišmur kaa/.

Ordinal numeral + adjective + noun:

– all the types follow the pattern of 'the first beautiful woman' = /daršo 'miišmurpukimi ngoiti nga/ (lit. 'beautiful women-of front me', i.e. 'of the beautiful women the front one to me').

Cardinal numeral + adjective + noun + possessive pronoun:

– all the types follow the pattern of 'my two beautiful girls' = /aan ke daršo miišal 'niikši/ (lit. 'my beautiful girl two').

Ordinal numeral + adjective + noun + possessive pronoun:

– the same type as that of ordinal numeral + adjective + noun, with the possessive pronoun preposed.

Cardinal numeral + adjective (implied noun):

– all the types follow the pattern of 'two black ones' = /kyer 'niikši/.

Ordinal numeral + adjective (implied noun):

– all the types follow the pattern of 'the second white one' = /noole nga bušse/ (lit. 'back (to) me white').

Cardinal numeral + adjective + possessive pronoun:

– all the types follow the pattern of 'my two black ones' = /aan ke kyer 'niikši/.

Ordinal numeral + adjective + possessive pronoun:

– all the types follow the pattern of 'your second white one' = /i ke noole nga bušse/.

Cardinal numeral + adjective + adjective + noun:

– all the types follow the pattern of 'two little black stones' = /kyer aihts phullu 'niikši/.

Distributive numeral + cardinal numeral + adjective + noun + possessive pronoun:

– all the types follow the pattern of 'each of my three big houses' = /aan ke theeb khiin saan pa/.

Distributive numeral + cardinal numeral + adjective + possessive pronoun:

– all the types follow the pattern of 'each of my two black ones' = /aan ke kyer 'niikši kaa kaa pa/.

Temporal ordering:

– more lexicalized forms for the past than for the future, i.e. 'today' = /mulaakti/, 'yesterday' = /sinaati/, 'the day before yesterday' = /sabernaati/, 'two days before yesterday' = /gabernaati/; 'tomorrow' = /diisa/, 'the day after tomorrow' = /nitnaati/, 'two days after tomorrow' = /saanbunaati/, 'three days after tomorrow' = /lebunaati/; in the latter examples, 'today' is the starting point for counting forwards.

Multiplication of the verb object is expressed either by means of a multiplicative numeral (i.e. 'once', 'twice' etc.), or by means of a cardinal numeral, of the type 'I jump one jumping' = /go khep kaa preeknu/ (lit. 'I time one jump').

The informant does not differentiate between 'each of your two houses' and 'your two houses each', or any of the comparable expressions.

KULUNG

Informant: Gyenwar Sing Rai, male aged 60, born in panchayat Makalu, village Hollu, district Sankhuwasabha, zone Koshi; he has spent 47 years at his birthplace, and the years afterwards in panchayat Pancakanya, village Boksiṭar, district Dharan, zone Koshi; he is married, both his parents' and wife's native language is Kulung. The questionnaire has been filled out by myself.

There are no special notes on the notation. The informant has remnants of tone in minimal pairs only, e.g. he consistently pronounces /pim/ 'to give' with a low tone, as distinguished from /'pim/ 'to say', with a high tone. I have not been able to establish any such consistent differences in the numeral system.

As to the affricates in Kulung, there is a clear distinction between [tc] (e.g. in [retci] 'eight') and [cc] (e.g. in [nicci] 'two'), both in pronunciation and alternation. As the observed difference cannot be ascribed to morpheme boundaries, I assume that in Kulung [c] and [j] are single distinctive segments, not analysable as /ts/ and /dz/, respectively.

Cardinal numerals:
1 /ibhim/
2 /nicci/
3 /supci/
4 /lici/
5 /ngaci/
6 /tukci/
7 /bhoci/
8 /retci/
9 /noci/
10 /ikpong/
20 /ngipong/
30 /sukpong/
40 /likpong/
50 /ngakpong/
60 /tukpong/
70 /bhocipong/
80 /retpong/
90 /nocipong/
100 /ikbu/.

(Note partial irregularities in numeral derivation. I am mentioning them only here, as this is my only Rai attestation of the numerals '30' – '90', which have been lost elsewhere.).

Ordinal numerals:
the first = /laspako/ = 'the front one', used as /omilaspako/ = 'their front one'
the second = /mhampiko/ = 'the middle one', used as /omimhampiko/ = 'their middle one'

the third = /dospiko/ = 'the back one', used as /omidospiko/ = 'their back one'
the fourth – etc.

Distributive numerals:

one each = /iibhim/ vs. /iikpo/ for [+human]
two each = /ninicci/, vs. /ningippo/ for [+human]
three each = /sumsupci/, vs. /sumsuppo/ for [+human].

Multiplicative numerals:

once = /ikchem/
twice = /ngischem/
three times =/ /sukchem/
only = /matta/
both = /ngippo/.

Cardinal numeral + noun:

– human, type 'one woman' = /ippo nimcha/
'two women' = /ngippo nimcha(ci)/
'three women' = /suppo nimchaci/;
– nonhuman animate, type 'one goat' = /ibhim chara/
'two goats' = /nicci chara(ci)/
'three goats'= /supci characi/;
– inanimate, type 'one fire' = /ibhim lung/
'two stones' = /nicci lung(ci)/
'three stones'= /supci lung(ci)/;
– inanimate, type 'one fire' = /ibhim mi/
'two fires' = /nicci mi/
'three fires' = /supci mi/;
– body parts, type 'one hand' = /ibhim hu/
'two hands' = /nicci hu/
'three hands' = /supci hu/.

Ordinal numeral + noun:

– all the types follow the pattern of 'the first woman' = /omilaspako nimcha/.

Distributive numeral + noun:

– all the types follow the pattern of 'one woman each' = /iikpo nimcha/ (vs. /iibhim/ etc. for [-human]).

Cardinal numeral + noun + possessive pronoun:

– the possessive pronouns are: 'my' = /o-/, 'your /am-/, 'his=her=its' = /m-/, 'our' = /im-/, 'your plural' = /amnim-/, 'their' = /omi-/;
– except for body parts, all the other types follow the pattern of 'my two goats', for which the informant has two possibilities /ochara nicci/ or /nicci ochara/ (the latter possibility does not equal 'two of my goats', for which the plural desinence /-ci/ is obligatory, i.e. /nicci ocharaci/); body parts must always be preceded by a possessive pronoun according to the pattern of e.g. 'your two hands' = /amnicci amhu/ (lit. 'your-two your-hand').

Ordinal numeral + noun + possessive pronoun:

– all the types follow the pattern of 'my second goat' = /omimhampiko ochara/ (lit. 'their-middle my-goat').

Distributive numeral + noun + possessive pronoun:

– all the types follow the pattern of 'each of your boys' = /amikpoikpo wachacha/ (lit. 'your-one-one boy').

Multiplicative numeral + noun + possessive pronoun:

– all the types follow the pattern of 'my only goat' = /ibhim matta ochara/
'my both goats' = /nicci ochara/.

Cardinal numeral + adjective + noun:

– all the types follow the pattern of 'one beautiful woman' = /ibhim ngallop nimcha/, on the understanding that [+human] has the forms /ngippo/, /suppo/, /lippo/ etc. for 'two', 'three', 'four' etc., whereas the remaining types have the forms of cardinal numerals given at the beginning.

Ordinal numeral + adjective + noun:

– all the types follow the pattern of 'the first beautiful woman' = /omilaspako ngallop nimcha/ (lit. 'their-front beautiful woman').

Cardinal numeral + adjective + noun + possessive pronoun:

– all the types follow the pattern of 'my two beautiful girls' = /ongippo ngallop solome/ (vs. /onicci/ etc. for [–human] according to the general pattern as above);

Ordinal numeral + adjective + noun + possessive pronoun:

– the same pattern as that of ordinal numeral + adjective + noun, with the possessive pronoun preposed, and repeated preceding a noun denoting a body part.

Cardinal numeral + adjective (implied noun):

– all the types follow the pattern of 'two black ones' = /nicci gugurpa/, on the understanding that this cannot be an utterance by itself in Kulung, but either a verb or any deictic element must be added; depending on the deixis, either the forms for [+human] or for [–human] are used.

Ordinal numeral + adjective (implied noun):

– all the types follow the pattern of 'the second white one' = /omimhampiko omlop/, with the same remark as for cardinal numeral + adjective (cf. above).

Cardinal numeral + adjective + possessive pronoun:

– all the types follow the pattern of 'my two black ones' = /onicci gugurpa/, with the same remarks as above.

Ordinal numeral + adjective + possessive pronoun:

– all the types follow the pattern of 'your second white one' = /ammi omimhampiko omlop/, with the same remark as above.

Cardinal numeral + adjective + adjective + noun:

– all the types follow the pattern of 'two little black stones' = /nicci cima gugurpa lung/ but the informant tends to reproduce only the adjective which is the most near to the noun.

Distributive numeral + cardinal numeral + adjective + noun + possessive pronoun:

– all the types follow the pattern of 'each of my three big houses' = /osupci dhep khim iibhim/ (lit. 'my-three big house each').

Distributive numeral + cardinal numeral + adjective + possessive pronoun:

- all the types follow the pattern of 'each of my two black ones' = /onicci gugurpa iibhim/ with a necessary deictic addition, as stated above.

Temporal ordering:

- more lexicalized forms for the future than for the past, i.e. 'today' = /ese/, 'yesterday' = /espa/, 'the day before yesterday' = /keska/, 'two days before yesterday' = /inika/, 'three days before yesterday' = /keceka/, 'four days before yesterday' = /neceka/; 'tomorrow' = /sela/, 'the day after tomorrow' = /chindi/, 'two days after tomorrow' = /dokthum/, 'three days after tomorrow' = /khethum/, 'four days after tomorrow' = /watthum/, 'five days after tomorrow' = /kecheka/, 'six days after tomorrow' = /necheka/.

Multiplication of the verb object may be expressed by means of a multiplicative numeral, or a cardinal one. There is neither a lexicalized nor a grammaticalized way of expressing it.

The informant does not differentiate between 'each of your two houses' and 'your two houses each', or any of the comparable expressions.

LOHORONG

Informant: Chandraman Rai, male aged 51, born in panchayat Kolbung, village Ponorigaun, district Ilam, zone Mechi; he has spent his whole life at his birthplace; he is married, his both parents' and wife's native language is Lohorong. The questionnaire has been filled out by D.B. Ingwaba.

There are no special notes on the notation. The material does not allow a solution as to the phonological status of *c* and *j*. Provisionally, I assume that they are single distinctive segments. Two vowels always form two syllable nuclei (as e.g. in /bombae/ below).

Cardinal numerals:

1 /ṭhikko/
2 /ngicci/
3 /sumci/
4 /ricci/
5 /ngaci/
6 –
7 –
8 –
9 –
10 –
20 –
100 –

Above 'five', the Nepali numeral forms are used instead.

Ordinal numerals:

the first = /bombae/ (i.e. 'the front one')
the second = /rumbae/ (i.e. the middle one')

the third = /ṭhengbae/ (i.e. 'the back one')
the fourth = – etc.

Distributive numerals:

one each = /ṭhikko ṭhikko/
two each = /ngicci ngicci/
three each = /sumci sumci/.

Multiplicative numerals:

once = /ṭhikḍhek/
twice = /ngiḍhek/
three times = /sumḍhek/
only = /reno/
both = /ngiccino/

Cardinal numeral + noun:

– human, type 'one woman' = /ṭhikko bengmusa/
'two women' = /ngicci bengmusaci/
'three women' = /sumci bengmusaci/;
– nonhuman animate, type 'one goat' = /ṭhikko jaspa/
'two goats' = /ngicci jaspaci/
'three goats' = /sumci jaspaci/;
– inanimate, type 'one stone' = /ṭhikko rungoa/
'two stones' = /ngicci rungoaci/
'three stones' = /sumci rungoaci/;
– inanimate, type 'one fire' = /ṭhikko mi/
'two fires' = /ngici mici/
'three fires' = /sumci mici/;
– body parts, type 'one hand' = /ṭhikko huk/
'two hands' = /ngicci hukci/
'three hands' = /sumci hukci/.

Ordinal numeral + noun:

– all the types follow the pattern of 'the first woman' = /bombae bengmusa/.

Distributive numeral + noun:

– all the types follow the pattern of 'one woman each' = /ṭhikko ṭhikko bengmusa/.

Cardinal numeral + noun + possessive pronoun:

– the possessive pronouns are: 'my' = /gangmi/, 'your' = /ommi/, 'his' = /akkomi/, 'our' = /ganingmi/, 'your, plural' = /omnimi/, 'their' = /akhacimi/,
– all the types follow the pattern of 'my two goats' = /gangmi ngicci jaspaci/.

Ordinal numeral + noun + possessive pronoun:

– all the types follow the pattern of 'my second goat' = /gangmi rumbae jaspa/.

Distributive numeral + noun + possessive pronoun:

– all the types follow the pattern of 'each of your boys' = /ommi ṭhikko ṭhikko bichaci/ (lit. 'your one (by) one boys').

Multiplicative numeral + noun + possessive pronoun:

– all the types follow the pattern of
'my only goat' = /gangmi ṭhikko reno jaspa/
'my both goats' = /gangmi ngiccino jaspaci/.

Cardinal numeral + adjective + noun:
- all the types follow the pattern of 'one beautiful woman' = /ṭhikko komnue bengmusa/.

Ordinal numeral + adjective + noun:
- all the types follow the pattern of 'the first beautiful woman' = /bombae komnue bengmusa/.

Cardinal numeral + adjective + noun + possessive pronoun:
- all the types follow the pattern of 'my two beautiful girls' = /gangmi ngicci komnukme rangmici/.

Ordinal numeral + adjective + noun + possessive pronoun:
- the same type as that of ordinal numeral + adjective + noun, with the possessive pronoun preposed.

Cardinal numeral + adjective (implied noun);
- all the types follow the pattern of 'two black ones' = /ngicci makhikpaci/ (i.e. with the adjective in the plural).

Ordinal numeral + adjective (implied noun):
- all the types follow the pattern of 'the second white one' = /rumbae makhike/.

Cardinal numeral + adjective + possessive pronoun:
- all the types follow the pattern of 'my two black ones' = /gangmi ngicci makhikpaci/.

Ordinal numeral + adjective + possessive pronoun:
- all the types follow the pattern of 'your second white one' = /ommi rumbae phitrija/.

Cardinal numeral + adjective + adjective + noun:
- all the types follow the pattern of 'two little black stones' = /ngicci miele makhike rungoaci/.

Distributive numeral + cardinal numeral + adjective + noun + possessive pronoun:
- all the types follow the pattern of 'each of my three big houses' = /gangmi ṭhikko ṭhikkonung sumci bee khimci/.

Distributive numeral + cardinal numeral + adjective + possessive pronoun:
- all the types follow the pattern of 'each of my two black ones' = /gangmi ṭhikko ṭhikkonung makhikpaci/

Temporal ordering:
- as many lexicalized forms for the past as for the future, i.e. 'today' = /ai/, 'yesterday' = /asen/, 'the day before yesterday' = /simre/, 'two days before yesterday' = /khomren/, 'three days before yesterday' = –; 'tomorrow' = /wahenḍa/, 'the day after tomorrow' = /sinḍa/, 'two days after tomorrow' = /khonḍa/.

Multiplication of the verb object is expressed by means of a cardinal numeral and the verbal noun, in addition to the verb desinence, of course, of the type elaborated for Bantawa in 2.2. above. All the Lohorong types follow the pattern of:

'I dreamt one dream' = /ge ṭhikko semang khaksung/ (lit. 'I one dream dreamt-it')

'I dreamt two dreams' = /ge ngicci semang khaksucing/ (lit. 'I two dreams dreamt-them, dual')

The Lohorong informant does differentiate between 'each of your two houses' and 'your two houses each', used in sentences 'please, show me each of your two houses' = /hene, ga ṭhikko ṭhikkonung ommi ngiccino khimci khangmete/ (lit. 'please, (to) me one by one your two houses show') vs. 'please, show me your two houses each' = /hene, ga ommi ngiccino khimci ṭhikko ṭhikkonung khangmete/ (lit. 'please, (to) me your two houses one by one show'). It is conceivable that the impossibility of other informants to produce this distinction spontaneously is not a matter of their language structure.

YAKKHABA

Informant: Lal Bahadur Rai, male aged 50, born in panchayat Ankhibhuin, village Omruwa, district Sankhuwasabha, zone Koshi; he has spent 25 years at his birthplace, 24 years in Nagaland in India, and the past year in panchayat Dharan, village Amarhat, district Sunsari, zone Koshi; he is married, his both parents' and wife's native language is Yakkhaba. The questionnaire has been filled out by myself.

Notes on the notation: in view of the fact that in the reduplicated distributive numeral 'two each' we get [hichicci] and not [hithicci], I assume that [hicci] cannot equal [hitci] = /hittsi/, but rather that it is /hicci/, and that – in other words – the affricates *c* and *j* are single distinctive segments /c/ and /j/.

Yakkhaba differs from the other Kiranti languages discussed above in that it has the glottal stop /ˀ/ as a distinctive segment, which cannot be ascribed to any other distinctive segment in the language (i.e. it is not a variant of a syllable-final /k/, as in Sunwar). Presence of glottal stop, and absence of tone, binds Yakkhaba as a representative of the northeastern and eastern branch of the Rai languages with Limbu, which is geographically neighbouring to it further to the east. This areal phenomenon is opposed to presence of tone and absence of glottal stop (as a distinctive segment not ascribable to any other distinctive segment) in northwestern Rai, thus pointing to a possible mutual causal relationship between glottal stop and tone (elaborated for other Tibeto-Burman languages by Weidert (1979)).

Cardinal numerals:

1 /eko/
2 /hicci/
3 /sumci/
4 –

5 –
6 –
7 –
8 –
9 –
10 –
20 –
100 –

Above 'three', the Nepali forms are used instead.

Ordinal numerals:

the first = /aghina/ (i.e. 'the front one')
the second = /ulumbetna/ (i.e. 'the middle one')
the third = /heksangna/ (i.e. 'the back one')
the fourth = – etc.

Distributive numerals:

one each = /ekeko/
two each = /hichicci/
three each = /sumci sumci/; Nepali forms for higher numerals.

Multiplicative numerals:

once = /imaʔ/
twice = /hipmaʔ/
three times = /summaʔ/
only = /ekose/
both = /hippangse/.

Cardinal numeral + noun:

– human, type 'one woman' = /eko mecha/
'two women' = /hippang mechaci/
'three women' = /sumbang mechaci/
above three: Nepali forms, including the classifier desinence for human beings /-jana/;
– nonhuman animate, type 'one goat' = /eko mendhak/
'two goats' = /hicci mendhakci/
'three goats' = /sumci mendhakci/ etc. Nepali;
– inanimate, type 'one stone' = /eko lunghwak/
'two stones' = /hicci lunghwakci/
'three stones' = /sumci lunghwakci/ etc. Nepali;
– inanimate, type 'one fire' = /eko mi/
'two fires' = /hicci mici/
'three fires' = /sumci mici/ etc. Nepali;
– body parts, type 'one hand' = /eko muk/
'two hands' = /hicci mukci/
'three hands' = /sumci mukci/ etc. Nepali.

Ordinal numeral + noun:

– all the types follow the pattern of 'the first woman' = /aghina mecha/.

Distributive numeral + noun:

– all the types follow the pattern of 'one woman each' = /ekeko mechaci/ (with the corresponding differences between the forms for [+human] and [-human]).

Cardinal numeral + noun + possessive pronoun:

- the possessive pronouns are: 'my' = /akka/, 'your' = /ngga/, 'his=her-its' = /nningga/, 'our' = /akkaci/, 'your; plural' = /nggaci/, 'their' = /nninggaci/;
- all the types follow the pattern of 'my two goats' = /akka hicci mendakci/ (and, of course, /hippang/ for [+ human], which is valid throughout).

Ordinal numeral + noun + possessive pronoun:

- all the types follow the pattern of 'my second goat' = /akka ulumbetna mendak/.

Distributive numeral + noun + possessive pronoun:

- all the types follow the pattern of 'each of your boys' = /ngga ekeko wemphaci/ (lit. 'your one (by) one boys').

Multiplicative numeral + noun + possessive pronoun:

- all the types follow the pattern of 'my only goat' = /akka eko sena mendak/ (lit. 'my one only goat').

Cardinal numeral + adjective + noun:

- all the types follow the pattern of 'one beautiful woman' = /eko ucunna mecha/ (with the distinction in form between [+human] and [-human] as stated above).

Ordinal numeral + adjective + noun:

- all the types follow the pattern of 'the first beautiful woman' = /aghina ucunna mecha/.

Cardinal numeral + adjective + noun + possessive pronoun:

- all the types follow the pattern of 'my two beautiful girls' = /akko hippang ucunna mechaci/ (vs. /hicci/ etc. for nonhuman as stated above).

Ordinal numeral + adjective + noun + possessive pronoun:

- the same type as that of ordinal numeral + adjective + noun, with the possessive pronoun preposed.

Cardinal numeral + adjective (implied noun):

- all the types follow the pattern of 'two black ones' = /hicci makhruhaci/ (if nonhuman is referred to, otherwise /hippang makhruhaci/).

Ordinal numeral + adjective (implied noun):

- all the types follow the pattern of 'the second white one' = /ulumbetna phuna/.

Cardinal numeral + adjective + possessive pronoun:

- all the types follow the pattern of 'my two black ones' = /akka hicci makhruhaci/ (with the distinction in form between [+human] and [-human] as stated above).

Ordinal numeral + adjective + possessive pronoun:

- all the types follow the pattern of 'your second white one' = /ngga ulumbetna phuna/.

Cardinal numeral + adjective + adjective + noun:

- all the types follow the pattern of 'two little black stones' = /hicci mimiha makhruha lunghwakci/ (with the distinction in form between [+human] and [-human] as stated above).

Distributive numeral + cardinal numeral + adjective + noun + possessive pronoun:

– all the types follow the pattern of 'each of my three big houses' = /akka ekeko mamaha sumci phangci/ (lit. 'my one (by) one big three houses').

Distributive numeral + cardinal numeral + adjective + possessive pronoun:

– all the types follow the pattern of 'each of my two black ones' = /akka ekeko hicci makhruhaci/ (with the distinction in form between [+human] and [-human] as stated above).

Temporal ordering:

– more lexicalized forms for the future than for the past, i.e. 'today' = /hen/, 'yesterday' = /asening/, 'the day before yesterday' = /anchotning/, 'two days before yesterday' = /akhoʔplening/; 'tomorrow' = /wendek/, 'the day after tomorrow' = /ucumphak/, 'two days after romorrow' = /okomphak/, 'three days after tomorrow' = /olemphak/, 'four days after tomorrow' = /colemphak/.

Multiplication of the verb object is expressed by means of multiplicative numerals (i.e. 'once', 'twice' etc.).

The informant does differentiate between 'show me each of your two houses' = /ngga ka ekeko hicci phangci sopmettang/ (lit. 'your (to) me one (by) one two houses show') and 'show me your two houses each' = /ngga ka hicci phangci ekeko sopmettang/ (lit. 'your (to) me two houses one (by) one show').

BANTAWA

Informant: Man Prasad Rai, male aged 64, born in panchayat Raniṭar, village Danḍagaon, district Panchthar, zone Mechi; he has spent his whole life at his birthplace; he is married, his father's native language is Bantawa, his mother's and his wife's, Chamling. The questionnaire has been filled out by A.K. Weidert and A. Gurung.

There are no special notes on the notation. As to the language, it cannot be considered to be influenced by Chamling, as the numerals characteristic of this system do not occur there, and in general, it is Chamling which is among the Rai languages influenced by Bantawa and not *vice versa.*

Cardinal numerals:

1 /ʉkṭa/
2 /hʉsaṭ/
3 /sumkaṭaṭ/
4 /reṭkaṭaṭ/
5 /ʉkchuk/
6 /ʉkchuk ʉkṭa/
7 /ʉkchuk hʉsaṭ/
8 /reṭkaṭaṭ/
9 (forgotten; another informant: /ʉkchuk-reṭkaṭaṭ/)
10 /hʉachuk/

15 /sumkachuk/
20 /cuppabhung/ (i.e. 'small hundred')
100 /ʉkbhung/
200 /hʉabhung/
300 /sumkabhung/
400 /reṭkabhung/
500 /ʉkchukbhung/
1000 /ʉghakma/ (another informant: /toppabhung/, i.e. 'big hundred').

These are the numeral forms known by the informant.

Ordinal numerals:

the first = /ʉbuḍha/ (i.e. 'the front one', but cf. also ordinal numeral + noun below)
the second = /hʉsaṭḍaḍha/
the third = /sumkaṭaḍaḍha/
the fourth = /reṭkaṭaḍaḍha/.

Distributive numerals:

one each = /ʉkṭa ʉkṭa/
two each = /hʉsaṭ hʉsaṭ/
three each = /sumka sumkaṭaṭ/
four each = /reṭka reṭkaṭaṭ/.

Multiplicative numerals:

once = /ʉkḍu/
twice = /hʉaḍu/
three times =/sumkaḍu/, etc.
only = /ʉkṭeṭ matte/
both = /hʉsaṭnga/.

Cardinal numeral + noun:

– human, type 'one girl' = /ʉkṭeṭ chekuma/
'two girls' = /hʉsaṭ chekuma/
'three girls' = /sumkaṭaṭ chekuma/ or /sumkaoṭa chekuma/, but
'five girls' = /ʉkchuk chekumaci/ (with the plural desinence /-ci/);

– nonhuman, type 'one goat' = /ʉkṭeṭ chenggara/
'two goats' = /hʉaṭaṭ chenggara/
'three goats' = /sumkaṭaṭ chenggara/ or /sumkaoṭa chenggara/
'five goats' = /ʉkchuk chenggara/;

– inanimate, type 'one stone' = /ʉkṭeṭ chelungma/
'two stones' = /hʉaṭaṭ chelungma/
'three stones'= /sumkaṭaṭ chelungma/;

– inanimate, type 'one fire' = /ʉkṭeṭ mi/
'two fires' = /hʉaṭaṭ mi/
'three fires' = /sumkaṭaṭ mi/;

– body parts, type 'one hand' = /ʉkṭeṭ ʉkchuk/
'two hands' = /hʉachuk/
'three hands' = /sumkachuk/.

Ordinal numeral + noun:

– there is a difference between [+human] and [−human] as follows:
type 'the first wife' = /ʉbuḍhao ʉtayama/ (lit. 'his-front his-wife')
'the second wife' = /ʉdengmao ʉtayama/ (lit. 'his-back his-wife'),
vs.
type 'the first goat' = /ʉbusio ʉchenggara/
'the second goat' = /hʉaḍuo chenggara/ (I have no means of establishing whether /hʉaḍuo ʉchenggara/ would be correct).

The remaining types follow that of 'the second goat', on the understanding that a noun denoting property must be preceded by a prefix of a personal pronoun.

Distributive numeral + noun:

– there are two types: [+human] occurs in the plural with 'two each' etc., whereas [−human] always keeps the singular, i.e. 'two girls each' = /hʉsaṭ hʉsaṭ chekumaci/ vs. the other types according to the pattern of 'two goats each' = /hʉsaṭ hʉsaṭ chenggara/.

Cardinal numeral + noun + possessive pronoun:

– the possessive pronouns are: 'my' = /ngko/, 'your' = /amko/, 'his=her=its' = /amnuo/, 'our' = /anka/, 'your, plural' = /khananin/, 'their' = /amnuoda/;
– all the types follow the pattern of 'my two goats' = /ngko hʉaṭaṭ chenggara/.

Ordinal numeral + noun + possessive pronoun:

– all the types follow the pattern of 'my second goat' = /ngko hʉaḍuo chenggara/.

Distributive numeral + noun + possessive pronoun:

– nouns denoting [+human] or a body part are followed by the plural desinence /−ci/, whereas the remaining ones remain in the singular according to the following patterns:
'each of your boys' = /amko ʉkṭeṭ ʉkṭeṭ chaci/ vs. 'each of his houses' /amnuo ʉkṭeṭ ʉkṭeṭ cikhim/. (N.B. As distinguished from other Bantawa dialects, and from other Rai languages, this Bantawa dialect is characterized by nominal prefixes, which are a.o. responsible for /cikhim/ here and /khim/ elsewhere for 'house'.)

Multiplicative numeral + noun + possessive pronoun:

– all the types follow the pattern of 'my only goat' = /ngko ʉkṭeṭ matte chenggara/ (with the difference between 'both my goats' = /ngko hʉaṭaṭ chenggaraci/ vs. 'my two goats' = /ngko hʉaṭaṭ chenggara/).

Cardinal numeral + adjective + noun:

– all the types follow the pattern of 'one beautiful girl' = /ʉkṭeṭ ḍemkhannuo chekuma/.

Ordinal numeral + adjective + noun:

– the same two types as with ordinal numeral + noun, with the adjective bewteen the ordinal numeral and the noun, e.g. 'the first beautiful girl' = /ʉbuḍhao ngayʉnghangma chekuma/ vs. e.g. 'the fourth black stone' = /reṭkaḍuo makyango chelungma/ (N.B. Due to a morpheme boundary between /makyang/ and /−o/, the /ng/ is pronounced as a syllable-final [ŋ].)

Cardinal numeral + adjective + noun + possessive pronoun:

– all the types have the noun in the plural with 'two' or more, according to the pattern of 'his three big houses' = /amnuo sumkaoṭa dhiwang cikhimci/.

Ordinal numeral + adjective + noun + possessive pronoun:

– the same type as that of ordinal numeral + adjective + noun, with the possessive pronoun preposed.

Cardinal numeral + adjective (implied noun):

– all the types follow the pattern of 'two black ones' = /hʉaṭaṭ makyango/.

Ordinal numeral + adjective (implied noun):

– all the types follow the pattern of 'the second white one' = /hʉaḍuo omyango/ (with the same pronunciation of /ng/ as in /makyango/, by the way).

Cardinal numeral + adjective + possessive pronoun:

– all the types follow the pattern of 'my two black ones' = /ngko hʉaṭaṭ makyango/.

Ordinal numeral + adjective + possessive pronoun:

– all the types follow the pattern of 'your second white one' = /amko hʉaḍuo omyango/ (but if reference is made to [+human], then /amko ʉdengmao omyango/, of course).

Cardinal numeral + adjective + adjective + noun:

– all the types follow the pattern of 'two little black stones' = /hʉsaṭ cuko makyango chelungma/.

Distributive numeral + cardinal numeral + adjective + noun + possessive pronoun:

– all the types follow the pattern of 'each of my three big houses' = /ngko ʉkṭeṭ ʉkṭeṭ sumkaoṭa dhiwang cikhimci/.

Distributive numeral + cardinal numeral + adjective + possessive pronoun:

– all the types follow the pattern of 'each of my two black ones' = /ngko ʉkṭeṭ ʉkṭeṭ hʉaṭaṭ makyango/ (or: /ngko ʉkṭeṭ ʉkṭeṭ hʉsaṭ makyango/).

Temporal ordering:

– there are as many lexicalized forms for the past as for the future, i.e. 'today' = /ai/, 'yesterday' = /akhomang/, 'the day before yesterday' = /achosa/, 'two days before yesterday' = /achʉ/; 'tomorrow' = /mangkolen/, 'the day after tomorrow' = /chinto/, 'two days after tomorrow' = /suinya-kolen/.

Multiplication of the verb object is expressed either by means of a multiplicative numeral (i.e. 'once', 'twice' etc.), or by means of e.g. /hʉakhep/ = 'twice' (lit. 'two time').

The informant does not differentiate between 'each of your two houses' and 'your two houses each'; in order to express some difference, he adds in the latter case preceding /cikhim/ = 'house(s)' /tʉmnuo/ = 'made (by you)'.

ATHPARE

Informant: Phouda Singh Limbu, male aged 36, born in panchayat Dhankuṭa, district Dhankuṭa, zone Koshi; he has spent his whole life at his birthplace; he is married, his father's native language is Limbu, and his mother's and wife's, Athpare.

Notes on the notation: [c] and [j] are phonologically sequences /ts/ and /dz/. I have not observed any voice assimilation in consonants.

Cardinal numerals:

1 /ṭhik/
2 /ippok/
3 /sumbok/
4 –
5 –
6 –
7 –
8 –
9 –
10 –
20 –
100 –

The informant uses only the Nepali forms for ordinal numerals.

Distributive numerals:

one each = /ṭhiṭhibbang/ for [+human] and /ṭhik ṭhik/ for [-human]
two each = /iippong/ for [+ human] and /ippok ippok/ for [-human]
three each = /sumsumbong/ for [+human] and /sumbok sumbok/ for [-human].

Multiplicative numerals:

– Nepali forms, except for 'only' = /ṭhibbang eḍok/ for [+human] and /ṭhik eḍok/ for [-human], and 'both' = /ippang/ for [+human] and /ippok/ for [-human].

Cardinal numeral + noun:

– human, type 'one woman' = /ṭhibbang mendzema/
'two women' = /ippang mendzematsi/
'three women' = /sumbang mendzematsi/
– nonhuman animate, type 'one goat' = /ṭhik meḍuba/
'two goats' = /ippok meḍubatsi/
'three goats' = /sumbok meḍubatsi/;
– inanimate, type 'one stone' = /ṭhik linggokwa/
'two stones' = /ippok linggokwatsi/
'three stones' = /sumbok linggokwatsi/;
– inanimate, type 'one fire' = /ṭhik mi/
'two fires' = /ippok mitsi/
'three fires' = /sumbok mitsi/;
– body parts, type 'one hand' = /ṭhik muk/
'two hands' = /ippok muktsi/
'three hands' = /sumbok muktsi/.

Ordinal numeral + noun: Nepali forms.

Distributive numeral + noun:

– [+human] follows the pattern of 'one woman each' = /ṭhiṭhibbong mendzematsi/, and [–human] follows the pattern of 'one goat each' = /ṭhik ṭhik meḍubatsi/.

Cardinal numeral + noun + possessive pronoun:

– the possessive pronouns are: 'my' = /angana/, 'your' = /khannana/, 'his=her =its' = /unnana/, and the same corresponding forms for the plural;
– with the distinction between human and nonhuman kept in mind, all the types follow the pattern of 'my two goats' = /angana ippok meḍubatsi/.

Ordinal numeral + noun + possessive pronoun: Nepali forms for the ordinal numeral.

Distributive numeral + noun + possessive pronoun:

– all the types follow the pattern of 'each of your boys' = /khannana ṭhiṭhibbong pitshatsi/.

Multiplicative numeral + noun + possessive pronoun:

– with the distinction between human and nonhuman kept in mind, all the types follow the pattern of 'my only goat' = /angana ṭhik eḍok meḍuba/.

Cardinal numeral + adjective + noun:

– with the distinction between human and nonhuman kept in mind, all the types follow the pattern of 'one beautiful woman' = /ṭhibbong utsetnuna mendzema/.

Ordinal numeral + adjective + noun: Nepali forms for the ordinal numeral.

Cardinal numeral + adjective + noun + possessive pronoun:

– with the distinction between human and nonhuman kept in mind, all the types follow the pattern of 'my two beautiful girls' = /angana ippang utsetnuna kaipmatsi/.

Ordinal numeral + adjective + noun + possessive pronoun: Nepali forms for the ordinal numeral.

Cardinal numeral + adjective (implied noun):

– with the distinction between human and nonhuman kept in mind, all the types follow the pattern of 'two black ones' = /ippang makna/ (i.e. without the plural desinence /–tsi/).

Ordinal numeral + adjective (implied noun): Nepali forms for the ordinal numeral.

Cardinal numeral + adjective + possessive pronoun:

– all the types follow the pattern of 'my two black ones' = /angana ippok makna/ (with the distinction between human and nonhuman kept in mind).

Ordinal numeral + adjective + possessive pronoun: Nepali forms for the ordinal numeral.

Cardinal numeral + adjective + adjective + noun:

– with the distinction between human and nonhuman kept in mind, all the types follow the pattern of 'two little black stones' = /ippok naṭiwna makna linggokwatsi/.

Distributive numeral + cardinal numeral + adjective + possessive pronoun:

- all the types follow the pattern of 'each of my three big houses' = /angana thik thik nungtsa sumbokrok ṭhega pangtsi/ (lit. 'my one by one three-of big houses).

Distributive numeral + cardinal numeral + adjective + possessive pronoun:

- all the types follow the pattern of 'each of my two black ones' = /angana ṭhik ṭhik nungtsa ippokrok makna/ (lit. 'my one by one two-of black'), with the distinction between human and nonhuman kept in mind.

Temporal ordering:

- there are as many lexicalized forms for the past as for the future, i.e. 'today' = /hatle/, 'yesterday' = /asen/, 'the day before yesterday' = /achumbu/; 'tomorrow' = /hanḍeng/, 'the day after tomorrow' = /chinḍeng/.

Multiplication of the verb object is expressed by means of Nepali borrowings for multiplicative numerals.

The informant does not differentiate between 'each of your two houses' and 'your two houses each', or any of the comparable expressions.

LIMBU

Informant: Dilli Bikram Ingwaba, male aged 34, born in panchayat Phidim, district Panchthar, zone Koshi; he is unmarried, the native language of his both parents' is Limbu; he has spent 18 years at his birthplace, 6 years in Dharan, and the years afterwards in Kaṭhmandu. The questionnaire has been filled out by myself.

Notes on the notation: Limbu has the glottal stop /ʔ/ as a distinctive segment (cf. e.g. /hiptusi/ = 'he beat them two, past' vs. /hiptusiʔ/ 'he beats them two, nonpast' in the informant's dialect of Limbu); it is distinctive in the syllable coda if the nucleus contains a short vowel, and predictable in absolute syllable onset preceding a short vowel, and on syllable-final voiceless stops. Given this distributional regularity of the glottal stop as a distinctive segment, I assume that the long vowels in Limbu are phonologically sequences indeed, which follows from the absence of an opposition between [V̄] and [VV] in that language, but within the restricted scope of the numeral (and verb) investigation I have done one cannot strictly speaking be sure to have mastered the language phonology sufficiently. Given the fact that both the decisive criterion and the additional distributional check of it point in the same direction, I write the long vowels in Limbu as sequences. As distinguished from the other Kiranti languages presented above, Limbu has a phonological distinction between the close mid vowels /ẹ/ and /ọ/ and their open counterparts /e/ and /o/. Within the scope of my material, there is no opposition between [c] and [ts] on the one hand, and between [j] and [dz] on the other within a morpheme, so I analyse the Limbu affricates as phonological sequences.

Cardinal numerals:

1	/thik/, /lotthik/, /lottsha/
2	/netsshi/
3	/sumsi/
4	/liisi/
5	/ngaasi/, /naasi/
6	/tuksi/
7	/nuusi/
8	/phangsi/
9	/iboong/
10	/thiboong/
11	/thikthik/
12	/thiknet/
13	/thiksum/
14	/thiklii/ etc.
20	/niboong/
21	/niboongang thik/
22	/niboongang nettshi/ etc.
30	/sumboong/
40	/liboong/
50	/ngaboong/, /naboong/
60	–
70	–
80	–
90	–
100	/kapthik/, /kugapthik/.

Ordinal numerals:

the first = /togang/ (i.e. 'the front one')
the second = /kulummoˀ ban/ (i.e. 'the middle one').

Distributive numerals:

one each = /thik thik/, /lottsha lottsha/, /lolottsha/
two each = /nenettshi/
three each = /sumsumsi/
four each = /liliisi/
five each = – etc.

Multiplicative numerals:

once = /thitleng/
twice = /nenettshileng/
three times = /sumleng/
four times = /lileng/
only = /-lok/ (preceded by the same form as in the other multiplicative numerals /-leng/)
both = /nepphang/ for [+animate] and /nepmang/ for [-animate].

Cardinal numeral + noun:

– human, type 'one woman' = /lottsha mentshya/, /lotthik mentshya/, /thik mentshya/

'two women' = /nettshi mentshya/
'three women' = /sumsi mentshya/;

– /lottsha/, /lotthik/ and /thik/ can be used invariably in all the examples;
– in all the examples – here and to follow – the numeral can either precede or follow the noun, so I shall not repeat it for each case;

– nonhuman animate, type 'one goat' = /lottsha meendak/
'two goats' = /nettshi meendak/
'three goats' = /sumsi meendak/;

– inanimate, type 'one stone' = /lottsha lung/
'two stones' = /nettshi lung/
'three stones' = /sumsi lung/;

– inanimate, type 'one fire' = /lottsha mii/
'two fires' = /nettshi mii/
'three fires' = /sumsi mii/;

– body parts, type 'one hand' = /lottsha huk/
'two hands' = /nettshi huk/
'three hands' = /sumsi huk/.

It is noteworthy that Limbu allows for both word orders: the numeral can either precede or follow the noun with a pragmatic difference which can be paraphrased as either e.g. 'two stones' or 'as to stones, there are two of them'.

I have presented here the numeral constructions in their absolute form. Within a sentence, the end of a phrase denoting two entities is characterized by /-siˀ/ following a stop and /-tsiˀ/ elsewhere, and the end of a phrase denoting three or more entities by /-haˀ/, which occurs at the end of the last word in the phrase, irrespectively of its word class (i.e., it can follow the noun, the adjective, or any numeral, but not the possessive pronoun, according to the rule which will be formulated in connection with possessive pronouns below).

Ordinal numeral + noun:

– all the types follow the pattern of 'the first woman' = /togangma mentshya/ (lit. 'front-in woman/girl'); the spacial correlates of the ordinal numerals always precede the noun.

Distributive numeral + noun:

– all the types follow the pattern of 'one woman each' = /lotottsha mentshya/, /lottsha lottsha mentshya/, or /thik thik mentshya/, with either order between the numeral and the noun.

Cardinal numeral + noun + possessive pronoun:

– the possessive pronouns are: 'my' = /a-/, 'your' = /ke-/, 'his=her=its' = /ku-/, 'our' = /aniˀ/, 'your' = /khiniˀ/, 'their' = /huntshiˀ/; note that the possessive pronouns for the singular are prefixes, whereas those for the plural are morphological words; the former ones always precede the noun, whereas the latter ones can occur freely with the only restriction that they cannot follow the noun, but must either directly or indirectly precede it (with any possible intervening and/or preceding other elements of the noun phrase); the pattern can be illustrated by 'their eight baskets' = /huntshiˀ phangsi pokwahaˀ/, or /phangsi huntshiˀ pokwahaˀ/, or /huntshiˀ pokwa phangsihaˀ/.

Ordinal numeral + noun + possessive pronoun:

- all the types follow the pattern of 'my second goat' = /kulummoˀban ameendak/ (lit. 'his-middle-absolutive my-goat').

Distributive numeral + noun + possessive pronoun:

- all the types follow the pattern of 'each of your boys' = /lolottsha ked-hangbentshiˀ/; note that in the absence of a cardinal numeral, /-tshiˀ/ is the dual desinence following a stop, and /-siˀ/ elsewhere (the given example consequently equals 'each of your two boys'; with more than two, /-haˀ/ is added).

Multiplicative numeral + noun + possessive pronoun:

- all the types follow the pattern of 'my only goat' = /lotthiklok ameendak/, /lottshalok ameendak/, or /thiklok ameendak/, in any order.

Cardinal numeral + adjective + noun:

- all the types follow the pattern of 'one beautiful woman' = /lottsha nuuma mentshya/, /lotthik nuuma mentshya/, or /thik nuuma mentshya/, in any order.

Ordinal numeral + adjective + noun:

- all the types follow the pattern of 'the first beautiful woman' = /togangma nuuma mentshiin/ (the informant produces spontaneously only this word order).

Cardinal numeral + adjective + noun + possessive pronoun:

- the same pattern as with cardinal numeral + noun + possessive pronoun, with the same remarks valid as above.

Ordinal numeral + adjective + noun + possessive pronoun:

- the same pattern as that of ordinal numeral + noun + possessive pronoun, with both the ordinal numeral and the possessive pronoun necessarily preceding the noun.

Cardinal numeral + adjective (implied noun):

- all the types follow the pattern of 'two black ones' =/nettshi makloˀ-banhaˀ/ (apparently, the /-tsiˀ/ (or /-siˀ/, respectively) desinence does not occur here following 'two').

Ordinal numeral + adjective (implied noun):

- all the types follow the pattern of 'the second white one' = /kulummoˀ-ban kebhoraban/.

Cardinal numeral + adjective + possessive pronoun:

- all the types follow the pattern of 'my two black ones' = /nettshi amakloˀ-banhaˀ/.

Ordinal numeral + adjective + possessive pronoun:

- all the types follow the pattern of 'your second white one' = /kulummoˀ-ban kebhoraban/ (lit. 'his middle-absolutive your-white').

Cardinal numeral + adjective + adjective + noun:

- all the types follow the pattern of 'two little black stones' = /nettshi cuukpa makloˀban lunghaˀ/, in any order, and with /-haˀ/ at the end.

Distributive numeral + cardinal numeral + adjective + noun + possessive pronoun:

– all the types follow the pattern of 'each of my three big houses' = /thik thik sumsi yomba ahimhaʔ/, in any order.

Distributive numeral + cardinal numeral + adjective + possessive pronoun:

– all the types follow the pattern of 'each of my two black ones' = /thik thik nettshi amakloʔbanhaʔ/, in any order.

Temporal ordering:

– there are as many lexicalized forms for the past as for the future, i.e. 'today' = /ain/, 'yesterday' = /mipmaʔ/, 'the day before yesterday' = /sinyaan/, 'two days before yesterday' = /thonjaan/; 'tomorrow' = /taandik/, 'the day after tomorrow' = /atshindan/, 'two days after tomorrow' = /akhendan/.

Multiplication of the verb object is expressed by means of cardinal numeral + verbal noun.

The informant does not differentiate between 'each of your two houses' and 'your two houses each', or any of the comparable expressions.

At the end of this geographically based survey of numerals and numeral constructions in Kiranti languages, some general remarks must be made in addition.

The numerals and numeral constructions were asked in Nepali. Only spontaneously produced answers were recorded.

Male informants had a significantly better performance than female ones. In the Tibeto-Burman communities of East Nepal, language is considered to be a property, and it is owned by the man. (Hence in Raniṭar in Panchthar, people showed their fear from linguistic work by saying: "first they will steal our language, and then they will kill us".) Women exhibit more language decay than men do, without using any women's language. The latter phenomenon is absent in Tibeto-Burman communities as much as social class languages are.

As a general linguistic peculiarity of the investigated languages, let me mention the absence of any word accent. There is only a prosodic word boundary, implemented by means of an initial high pitch, and additional language-specific characteristics, such as e.g. lengthening of the word-final syllable in Bantawa from Chhinamakhu in North Bhojpur.

I shall not go into the grammatical details of the investigated numeral constructions here, but only relate them to the hypotheses formulated at the beginning of this section.

Hypothesis A:

This hypothesis remains unrefuted. Ordinal, distributive and multiplicative numerals never allow for more distinctions than the cardinal ones do, indeed. In fact, ordinal numerals are everywhere except for Bantawa of Raniṭar restricted to spatial denotations which either include only 'front' vs. ('middle' or) 'back', or 'front' vs. 'middle' vs. 'back'. These spatial denotations are translatable into one or two distinctive features of meaning, respectively.

Hypothesis B:

The hypothesis that ordinal numerals impose the upper boundary on the number of distinctions observable in temporal relations must be rejected, though. Languages which have replaced ordinal numerals by spatial denotations can have more temporal denotations than spatial ones. But the data provide the basis for a new hypothesis, namely that there is a basic distinction between lexicalized denotations on the one hand, and those derived in the form and the meaning associated with it on the other. The latter appear to be constrained indeed – as can be illustrated by the Sunwar examples mentioned above – whereas the former are not constrained in any linguistically relevant way – as can be illustrated by Kulung in comparison with other Kiranti languages (where differences may possibly be due to cultural phenomena, or simply to memory limitations). The derived temporal denotations appear to follow the bipartition in time between past and nonpast which is characteristic of the Kiranti verb. And the derived temporal denotations consist in fact of syntagmatically ordered forms and syntagmatically and paradigmatically ordered meanings associated with them (the latter in the sense of a determinandum and a determinatum, with an asymmetrical implication between them).

The new hypothesis states that the syntagmatically and/or paradigmatically ordered lexical signs (including features and feature units of meaning) are constrained by the same principles as the grammatical ones are, whereas the unordered signs are in themselves unconstrained. If unrefuted on the basis of larger material, this will lead to a further extension of the theory proposed here along the same basic lines.

Hypothesis C:

This hypothesis remains unrefuted. Sunwar provides the only test case for it and shows that the number of positions preceding the noun is restricted indeed in the way hypothesized above (namely to two positions if there is a possessive pronoun involved, and otherwise to one), and that *ceteris paribus* a spatial denotation used as the ordinal numeral precedes the noun whereas the cardinal numeral follows it. Spatial denotations used as ordinal numerals behave in this respect like adjectives indeed, but if there is an adjective and a spatial denotation used as a numeral, then the order is adjective + noun + ordinal numeral, as illustrated by the Sunwar examples above. However, as soon as a Nepali numeral form is used, the restricted number of positions is abandoned and the order numeral + adjective + noun appears to be the usual one. This shows that the word order change may be ascribed to Nepali influence indeed, and that the restricted number of positions preceding the noun (and an unrestricted one following it, which is the original case) is only characteristic of the first stage of the word order change, as a preservative trait of the original situation.

Distributive and multiplicative numerals are derived from the cardinal ones and follow the same placement rules, leaving the hypothesis unrefuted.

3.3. Numerals in Other Tibeto-Burman Languages

In order to place the Kiranti data against a more general Tibeto-Burman background, I have collected the same data for representatives of other Tibeto-Burman languages. As to main Tibeto-Burman groups, let me give the chart of Sino-Tibetan groups presented by Benedict (1972: 6).

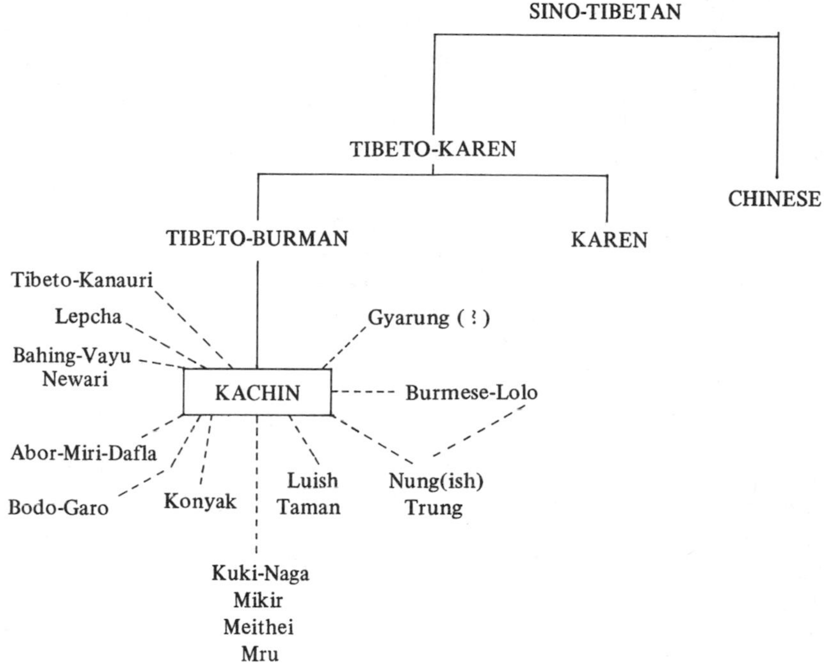

I shall not go into the details of this chart now. The reader will be able to place Bahing within the Kiranti Rai group, Vayu (or Hayu) within the Kiranti group, and view Newari as separate, though in some respects related to it (as mentioned by Benedict already), but classification of Tibeto-Burman languages is not at issue at the moment, only the relative placement of the languages I have taken for further numeral investigation. And these languages are: Karen and Kachin because of their crucial placement, and additional representatives of the main geographically and linguistically divided groups, namely Tibetan, Tamang – as a representative of nonpronominalizing Himalayan languages, Ashö Chin – as a representative of the Chin nucleus, related to Kuki, and Burmese. I am thankful to A.K. Weidert for providing me with the necessary linguistic information about the investigated systems.

The same hypotheses about the numeral system have been investigated, and the same sets of data collected. The hypotheses can be briefly repeated as follows:

A: cardinal numerals impose the upper limit on the ordinal ones:

B: (revised on the basis of the preceding section): ordered temporal designations follow the same division as the relevant temporal distinctions in the grammar do;

C: if there is a restricted number of determiner positions preceding the noun, then either only possessive pronouns or possessive pronouns and ordinal numerals precede whereas cardinal ones follow *ceteris paribus.*

I shall present the data in two separate sections, 3.3.1. for the languages spoken in Nepal and thus potentially influenced by Nepali (i.e. Tibetan and Tamang), and 3.3.2. for the languages spoken in Burma and thus not exposed to any comparable influence (i.e. Karen, Kachin, Ashö Chin and Burmese).

3.3.1. Numerals in Lhasa Tibetan and Tamang as Spoken in Nepal

LHASA TIBETAN

Informant: Tsetan Chonjore, male aged 31, born in Shigatse, Tibet; he has spent 11 years at his birthplace, 14 years in Darjeeling in India, and the years since 1978 in Kaṭhmandu in Nepal; he is married, his both parents' and wife's native language is Lhasa Tibetan. The questionnaire has been filled out by myself.

Notes on the notation: following the conventions used e.g. by Chang and Shefts (1964), (_) denotes the low tone and (¯) the high tone; tone is a distinctive feature of vowels, the velar nasal /ŋ/ and the labial nasal /m/. Long vowels are phonologically sequences, and nasalized vowels, sequences of oral vowel + dental nasal. In the former, either vowel can be characterized by either tone, on the understanding that the sequence high + low is phonetically implemented as high + falling, and the sequence low + high as low + falling. The remaining two possibilities, i.e. low + low and high + high, are implemented as such. The same tone possibilities are found in sequences oral vowel + velar nasal, and oral vowel + labial nasal. (I therefore assume that [ŋ] = /ŋ/, ≠ /ng/.)

Following the notation used in this study, /e/ denotes a low (i.e. open) vowel, and /ẹ/, its high (i.e. close) counterpart, and so do /o/ and /ọ/, respectively. In addition to these, Lhasa Tibetan has /i/ on the front side and /u/ on the back one, and a set of central vowels: /a/ as the low one, /ö/ as the mid nonback round one, and /ü/ as the high nonback round one.

Lhasa Tibetan has progressive voice assimilation in the consonants, which I indicate by means of capitals. [c] = /tŚ/ and [ɟ] = /dŚ/.

Lhasa Tibetan has a fully elaborated numeral system in all its subcomponents, including fraction designations, which are absent in the remaining languages of Nepal except for the designation for 'one half', so I have not taken them into consideration in this study.

The Lhasa Tibetan numerals cited here are thus exemplificatory of the fully elaborated system.

Cardinal numerals:

1 /tŚīq/
2 /ńīī/
3 /sūm̄/
4 /śi̱/
5 /ŋā/
6 /thu̱q/
7 /dǖǖn/
8 /ke̱ē/
9 /qu̱/
10 /cū/
20 /ńi̱śū/
100 /ka̱/.

Ordinal numerals:

the first = /tha̱nqō/
the second = /ńīīpā/
the third = /sūm̄pā/
the fourth = /śi̱pā/ etc.

Distributive numerals:

one each = /tŚīq tŚīq/, /re̱ re̱/
two each = /ńīī ńīī/, /ńīī re̱/
three each = /sūm̄ sūm̄/, /sūm̄ re̱/ etc.

Multiplicative numerals:

once = /the̱ŋ tŚīq/ (i.e. present tense class + 'one'), /kȫp tŚīq/ ('one time'), /tǖǖ tŚīq/ ('once upon a time').

twice = /th<u>e</u>ŋ ńīī/
three times = /th<u>e</u>ŋ sūm̄/ etc.
only = /tŚīqPō/
both = /ńīīkā/

Cardinal numeral + noun:

– there is no differentiation of types; all of them follow the pattern of
'one goat' = /r<u>a</u> tŚīq/
'two goats' = /r<u>a</u> ńīī/
'three goats' = /r<u>a</u> sūm̄/ etc.

Ordinal numeral + noun:

– the general pattern is exemplified by 'the first goat' = /r<u>a</u> th<u>a</u>nqō/
'the second goat' = /r<u>a</u> ńīīpā/
'the third goat' = /r<u>a</u> sūm̄pā/.

Distributive numeral + noun:

– the general pattern is exemplified by 'one goat each' = /r<u>a</u> tŚīq tŚīq/ etc.

Cardinal numeral + noun + possessive pronoun:

– the possessive pronouns are: 'my' = /ŋ<u>ee</u>/, 'your' = /khẹ̄rāān qhī/, 'his=her=its' = /qhọ̄ọ̄n qhī/, 'our' = /ŋ<u>a</u>ntShō/, 'your, plural' = /khẹ̄rāān qhī/, 'their' = /qhōtShō/;
– the general pattern is exemplified by 'my two goats' = /ŋ<u>ee</u> r<u>a</u> ńīī/.

Ordinal numeral + noun + possessive pronoun:

– the general pattern is exemplified by 'my second goat' = /ŋ<u>ee</u> r<u>a</u> ńīīpā/.

Distributive numeral + noun + possessive pronoun:

– the general pattern is exemplified by 'each of your boys' = /khẹ̄rāān qhī b<u>u</u> tŚīq tŚīq l<u>a</u>/.

Multiplicative numeral + noun + possessive pronoun:

– the general pattern is exemplified by 'my only goat' = /ŋ<u>ee</u> r<u>a</u> tŚīqPō/; note that this necessitates an addition of a demonstrative pronoun such as /d<u>i</u>/ 'this' at the end in order to make a phrase.

Cardinal numeral + adjective + noun:

– the general pattern is exemplified by 'one beautiful girl' = /ph<u>o</u>mō dŚ<u>ee</u>qō tŚīq/.

Cardinal numeral + adjective + noun + possessive pronoun:

– the general pattern is exemplified by 'my two beautiful girls' = /ŋ<u>ee</u> ph<u>o</u>mō dŚ<u>ee</u>qō ńīī/.

Ordinal numeral + adjective + noun + possessive pronoun:

– the general pattern is exemplified by 'my second beautiful girl' = /ŋ<u>ee</u> ph<u>o</u>mō dŚ<u>ee</u>qō ńīīpā/.

Cardinal numeral + adjective (implied noun):

– the general pattern is exemplified by 'two black ones' = /n<u>a</u>qPō ńīīpō/.

Ordinal numeral + adjective (implied noun):

– the general pattern is exemplified by 'the second white one' = /kārpō ńīīpā/.

Cardinal numeral + adjective + possessive pronoun:

– the general pattern is exemplified by 'my two black ones' = /ŋ<u>ee</u> n<u>a</u>qPō ńīīpō/.

Ordinal numeral + adjective + possessive pronoun:

– the general pattern is exemplified by 'your second white one' = /khẹ̄rāān qhī kārpō ńiipā/.

Cardinal numeral + adjective + adjective + noun:

– the general pattern is exemplified by 'two little black stones' = /do̱ na̱qPō tŚūŋtŚūŋ ńii/ (i.e. 'little black stone two').

Distributive numeral + cardinal numeral + adjective + noun + possessive pronoun:

– the general pattern is exemplified by 'each of my three big houses' = /ŋe̱e̱ qhāŋPā tŚīŋpō sūm re̱ re̱ la̱/ (i.e. 'my house big three one by one' = 'my three big houses each').

Distributive numeral + cardinal numeral + adjective + possessive pronoun:

– the general pattern is exemplified by 'each of my two black ones' = /ŋe̱e̱ na̱qPō ńiipō re̱ re̱ la̱/ (i.e. 'my black two one by one' = 'my two black ones each').

Temporal ordering:

– 'today' = /tha̱rī/, 'yesterday' = /qhẹ̄ẹ̄sā/, 'the day before yesterday' = /khīńin/, 'two days before yesterday = /mēēńin/; 'tomorrow' = /sāńin/, 'the day after tomorrow' = /nāānńin/, 'two days after tomorrow' = /śe̱ēńin/, 'three days after tomorrow' = /qṳ̄ūnin/; 'today' and 'yesterday' are the major lexicalized points of division.

Multiplication of the verb object is expressed by means of a cardinal numeral and the verbal noun.

The informant differentiated between 'show me each of your two houses' and 'show me your two houses each' by putting /re̱ re̱ dŚe̱/ (i.e. 'each of') either at the beginning or at the end of the given phrase, in the way directly comparable to the English one.

TAMANG

Informant: Indra Man, male aged 33, born in panchayat Kapre Jilla, village Parsel, district Kaṭhmandu, zone Bagmati in Nepal; he has spent 8 years at his birth place and 25 years in Kaṭhmandu; he is married, his both parents' and wife's native language is Tamang. The questionnaire has been filled out by myself.

Notes on the notation: aspirated consonants are denoted by means of a following /h/ (which is a segment in this dialect on independent grounds, cf. e.g. /hacarkii^{h}/ below), and so-called breathy vowels are denoted by means of a superscript /^{h}/, as they must be viewed as *lax* in comparison with clear vowels, which are *tense*, because the former cause automatic *laxness* and *voicing* of the consonants preceding them, and these are the only attestations of voiced consonants in the given dialect; on the other hand, aspirated consonants are analysable as sequences with /h/ as they behave in the same way as /h/ does by not allowing lax vowels to follow within the same morpheme; on the basis of the same line of reasoning, [c] is assumed not to equal /ts/, but rather /c/, as it can be followed by /h/ whereas /s/ cannot be; long vowels are phonologically sequences; there is a distinctive [+high] tone, implemented as falling, and a [-high] tone, implemented as level – the former is denoted by means of (‘) preceding the morpheme-initial syllable, and the latter is left without any mark.

Cardinal numerals:

1 /‘kii^{h}/
2 /‘ŋii^{h}/
3 /‘som/
4 /‘plii^{h}/
5 /‘ŋaa^{h}/
6 /‘tuu^{h}/
7 /‘ŋis/
8 /‘pree^{h}/
9 /‘kuu/
10 /‘cui/
20 /‘po^{h}khaalkii^{h}/
30 /‘po^{h}khaalki^{h}se ‘cui/
40 /‘po^{h}khaalŋii^{h}/
50 /‘ph^{h}khaalŋii^{h}se ‘cui/
60 /‘po^{h}khaalsom/
70 /‘po^{h}khaalsomse ‘cui/
80 /‘po^{h}khaalplii^{h}/
90 /‘po^{h}khaalplii^{h}se ‘cui/
100 /kyarcakii^{h}/
200 /kyarcaŋii^{h}/
1000 /hacarkii^{h}/.

The intervening numerals are present, too.

The Tamang numeral system is a vigesimal one, with ‘twenty’ as a basic building block.

Ordinal numerals:

the first = /‘ŋa^{h}cala/ (i.e. ‘the front one’)
the second = /‘ku^{h}nteela/ (i.e. ‘the middle one’)
the third = /‘li^{h}ćala/ (i.e. the back one’)
the fourth = /‘plii^{h}la/ etc.

Distributive numerals:

one each = /‘kar ‘kar/
two each = /‘ŋii^{h}‘ŋii^{h}/
three each = /‘som ‘som/ etc.

Multiplicative numerals:
once = /‘kii^{h}r(y)em/
twice = /‘ŋii^{h}r(y)em/
three times = /‘somr(y)em/ etc.
only = /cu^{h}ten/
both = /‘ŋii^{h}non/.

Cardinal numeral + noun:
– the general pattern can be exemplified by
‘one woman’ = /mriincuku ‘kii^{h}/ or /ko^{h}rkii^{h} mriincuku/
‘two women’ = /mriincuku ‘ŋii^{h}/ or /ko^{h}rŋii^{h} mriincuku/
‘three women’ = /mriincuku ‘som/ or /ko^{h}rsom mriincuku/ (cf. also the discussion of hypothesis C which will be presented below).

Ordinal numeral + noun:
– the general pattern can be exemplified by
‘the first woman’ = /‘ŋa^{h}cala mriincuku/
‘the second woman’ = /‘ku^{h}nteela mriincuku/
‘the third woman’ = /‘li^{h}cala mriincuku/
‘the fourth woman’ = /‘plii^{h}la mriincuku/ etc.

Distributive numeral + noun:
– the general pattern can be exemplified by ‘one woman each’ = /‘kar ‘kar mriincuku/.

Cardinal numeral + noun + possessive pronoun:
– the possessive pronouns are: ‘my’ = /ŋala/, ‘your’ = /yela/, ‘his=her=its’ = /thela/, with the same forms for the corresponding plural possessive pronouns;
– the general pattern can be exemplified by ‘my two goats’ = /ŋala raah ‘ŋii^{h}/.

Ordinal numeral + noun + possessive pronoun:
– the general pattern can be exemplified by ‘my second goat’ = /ŋala ‘ku^{h}nteela raa^{h}/.

Distributive numeral + noun + possessive pronoun:
– the general pattern can be exemplified by ‘each of your boys’ = /yela ‘kar ‘kar ‘kola/.

Multiplicative numeral + noun + possessive pronoun:
– the general pattern can be exemplified by ‘my only goat’ = /ŋala raa^{h} ‘ki^{h}ce/.

Cardinal numeral + adjective + noun:
– the general pattern can be exemplified by ‘one beautiful woman’ = /ko^{h}rkii^{h} mriincuku ‘cheepa/ (i.e. ‘one woman beautiful’), but /ko^{h}rkii^{h} ‘cheepa mriincuku/ is possible as well.

Ordinal numeral + noun + possessive pronoun:

– the general pattern can be exemplified by ‘the first beautiful woman’ = /‘ŋa^{h}cala mriincuku ‘cheepa/, but /‘ŋa^{h}cala ‘cheepa mriincuku/ is possible as well.

Cardinal numeral + adjective + noun + possessive pronoun:

– the general pattern is exemplified by ‘my two beautiful women/girls’ = /ŋala mriincuku ‘ŋii^{h} ‘cheepa/ or /ŋala ko^{h}rŋii^{h} mriincuku ‘cheepa/ or /ŋala ko^{h}rŋii^{h} ‘cheepa mriincuku/.

Ordinal numeral + adjective + noun + possessive pronoun:

– the general pattern can be exemplified by ‘my second beautiful girl’ = /ŋala ‘ku^{h}nteela mriincuku ‘cheepa/or /ŋala ‘ku^{h}nteela ‘cheepa mriincuku/.

Cardinal numeral + adjective (implied noun):

– the general pattern can be exemplified by ‘two black ones’ = /ko^{h}rŋii^{h} mlaŋca/.

Ordinal numeral + adjective (implied noun):

– the general pattern can be exemplified by ‘the second white one’ = /‘ku^{h}nteela ‘tarca/.

Cardinal numeral + adjective + possessive pronoun:

– the general pattern can be exemplified by ‘my two black ones’ = /ŋala ko^{h}rŋii^{h} mlaŋca/.

Ordinal numeral + adjective + possessive pronoun:

– the general pattern can be exemplified by ‘your second white one’ = /yela ‘ku^{h}nteela ‘tarca/.

Cardinal numeral + adjective + adjective + noun:

– the general pattern can be exemplified by ‘two little black stones’ = /ko^{h}rŋii^{h}ca^{h}ca mlaŋ ‘yuŋpa/.

Distributive numeral + cardinal numeral + adjective + noun + possessive pronoun:

– the general pattern can be exemplified by ‘each of my three big houses’ = /ŋala ‘karkarlasi ‘ti^{h}m ‘som ‘kre^{h}n/

Distributive numeral + cardinal numeral + adjective + possessive pronoun:

– the general pattern can be exemplified by ‘each of my two black ones’ = /ŋala ‘karkarlasi ko^{h}rŋii^{h} mlaŋ/ or /ŋala ‘karkarlasi ŋii^{h} mlaŋ/.

Temporal ordering:

– ‘today’ = /‘tiini/, ‘yesterday’ = /‘tiila/, ‘the day before yesterday’ = /oyanlakonu/, ‘two days before yesterday’ = /oyanlaŋa^{h}calakonu/, ‘three days before yesterday’ –; ‘tomorrow’ = /naŋkar/, ‘the day after tomorrow’ = /reenlekonu/, ‘two days after tomorrow’ = /reenŋii^{h}latiri/, ‘three days after tomorrow’ = /naŋkarlasomreli^{h}ca/ etc. further regularly derived.

Multiplication of the verb object is expressed by means of a multiplicative numeral.

The informant differentiates between ‘each of your two houses’ and ‘your two houses each' by placing /'karkarlasi/ preceding /'ti^{h}m/ (i.e. 'house') in the former case, and following it in the latter.

With respect to the hypotheses A, B and C, the following conclusions can be drawn:

- hypothesis A is trivial for a fully developed numeral system such as that of Tibetan; in Tamang, spatial denotations were originally used instead of ordinal numerals, and derivation of ordinal numerals from the corresponding cardinal ones is an innovation; hypothesis A is trivial for the newly derived Tamang system, and unrefuted for the old one;
- hypothesis B remains unrefuted in the revised form for Tibetan, and also for Tamang in this sense that Tamang has lexicalized forms for 'today', 'yesterday', 'the day before yesterday', and 'tomorrow', and the derived forms take this asymmetry of lexicalization into account;
- hypothesis C remains unrefuted for Tibetan, whereas Tamang is in the process of change in this sense that a numeral as a determiner follows the noun only if it contains new information in comparison with that expressed by the noun as far as the frame of reference of the given sentence goes. As new vs. nonnew information is expressed by means of noninitial vs. initial word order, we find examples of the following type (produced by my informant and a Tamang friend of his of the same age and from the same village):

1. /ko^{h}rplii^h mriincuku 'ti^{h}m 'ti^{h}mri korpamula/ — '(The) four women went from house to house.'
   Four woman house house-to went.

* /mriincuku 'plii^h 'ti^{h}m 'ti^{h}mri korpamula/

2. /'ti^{h}m 'ti^{h}mri mriincuku 'plii^h korpamula/ — 'From house to house went four women.'
   House house-to woman four went.
3. /'ti^{h}m 'ti^{h}mri ko^{h}rplii^h mriincuku korpamula/ — 'From house to house went (the) four women.'
   House house-to four women went.
4. /yela namsari 'ti^{h}m 'plii^h mula/ — 'There were four houses in your village.'
   Your village-in house four were.

* /yela namsari ko^{h}rplii^h 'ti^{h}m mula/.

A Tamang speaker aged 21 from the same village appeared to place the numeral only preceding the noun, never following it. He may be considered a representative of the next stage of the word order change due to Nepali influence, by which a determiner always precedes the noun.

Hypothesis C remains unrefuted for Tamang, because ordinal numerals do not have the possibility of following the noun as the cardinal ones have, illustrated by 2 and 4 above.

3.3.2. Sgaw Karen, Jinghpaw Kachin, Ashö Chin and Burmese as spoken in Burma

Due to official regulations, I have no personal data on the informants, only their language data and the place of origin.

SGAW KAREN

The informant's place of origin is Rangoon. As to the notation, the tones of Sgaw Karen are represented as follows: /^{1}/ = low, /^{2}/ = mid low, /^{3}/ = mid high, /^{4}/ = high; so-called 'low glottal-stopped' tone of the script is represented as /^{1}ʔ/, and so-called 'high glottal-stopped' tone as /^{4}ʔ/.

The Sgauw Karen vowels are represented as follows; /i/, /e/, /ẹ/, /a/, /o/, /ọ/, /u/, and the nonback round ones /ɸ/ (= close) and /ö/) (= open); note that in a toneless syllable, /a/ is pronounced as [ə].

Like all the investigated Burmese languages, Sgauw Karen has a fully elaborated numeral system, for which I shall mention only the first ten numerals, in an exemplificatory way.

Cardinal numerals:

1 /^{4}tö/
2 /^{4}khi/
3 /^{4}θö/
4 /^{1}lwi/
5 /^{1}ye/
6 /^{4}xü/
7 /^{4}nwi/
8 /^{4}xoʔ/
9 /^{4}khwi/
10 /ta^{4}shi/.

Ordinal numerals:

the first = /a^{4}sho ka^{1}ta/
the second = /^{4}khi^{4}sü ta^{4}sü/
the third = /^{4}θö^{4}sü ta^{4}sü/
the fourth = /^{1}lwi^{4}sü ta^{4}sü/ etc.

Distributive numerals:

one each = /ta^{3}γa ta^{4}kha/
two each = /ta^{3}γa^{4}khi^{4}kha/
three each = /ta^{3}γa^{4}θö^{4}kha/ etc.

Multiplicative numerals:

once = /ta^{4}blo/

twice = /^{4}khi^{4}blọ/
three times = /^{4}θö^{4}blo/ etc.
only = /^{4}the . . . ^{4}blo/
both = /. . . ^{4}blo ka^{1}lọ/.

Cardinal numeral + noun:

– the general pattern can be exemplified by 'one woman' = /^{1}pọʔ^{1}mü ta^{3}γa/
'two women' = /^{1}pọʔ^{1}mü^{4}khi^{3}γa/
'three women' = /^{1}pọʔ^{1}mü^{4}θö^{3}γa/;

the last morpheme, /^{3}γa/, is a so-called numeral classifier, which are in general used for classifying a set of terms, i.e. expressions with a referential meaning in the sense of Dik (1978), on the basis of a common feature of meaning; /^{3}γa/ is the numeral classifier for human beings; on the basis of the numeral classifier, more classes can be distinguished than on the basis of the highest ranking features only, as relevant in the Tibeto-Burman languages of Nepal discussed above (for example, terms with round appropriate referents (the latter in the sense of Ebeling (1978)) form one class in Sgaw Karen characterized by the numeral classifier /^{2}phlö/).

Ordinal numeral + noun:

– the general pattern can be examplified by 'the second woman' = /^{1}pọʔ^{1}mü^{4}khi^{3}γa ta^{3}γa/.

Distributive numeral + noun:

– the general pattern can be exemplified by 'one woman each' = /^{1}pọʔ^{1}mü ta^{3}γa^{2}khe/.

Cardinal numeral + noun + possessive pronoun:

– the possessive pronouns are: 'my' = /ya/, 'your' = /na/, 'his=her=its' = /a/, 'our' = /pa/, 'your, plural' = /na/, 'their' = /a/;
– the general pattern can be exemplified by 'my two goats' = /ya^{4}meʔ ta^{4}leʔ ta^{4}dü/.

Ordinal numeral + noun + possessive pronoun:

– the general pattern can be exemplified by 'my second goat' = /ya^{4}meʔ ta^{4}leʔ a^{2}khọ ^{4}khi^{4}dü ta^{4}dü/.

Distributive numeral + noun + possessive pronoun:

– the general pattern can be exemplified by 'each of their boys' = /a^{1}woʔ^{4}khwa^{4}phọ ta^{3}γa^{2}sẹ/.

Multiplicative numeral + noun + possessive pronoun:

– the general pattern can be exemplified by 'my only goat' = /ya^{4}meʔ ta^{4}le^{4}the ta^{4}dü/.

Cardinal numeral + adjective + noun:

– the general pattern can be exemplified by 'one beautiful woman' = /^{1}pọʔ^{1}mü^{4}xi^{3}la^{4}phọ ta^{3}γa/.

Ordinal numeral + adjective + noun:

– the general pattern can be exemplified by 'the first beautiful woman' = /^{1}pọʔ^{1}mu^{4}xi^{3}la a^{2}kho^{4}thiʔ ta^{3}γa/.

Cardinal numeral + adjective + noun + possessive pronoun:

– the general pattern can be exemplified by 'my two beautiful women' = /ya^{1}pọʔ^{1}mü^{4}xi^{3}la^{4}khi ta^{3}γa/.

Ordinal numeral + adjective + noun + possessive pronoun:

– the general pattern can be exemplified by 'his fourth big house' = /a^{2}ti^{2}dọ^{1}lwi^{2}phlö ta^{2}phlö/ (note that e.g. 'eye', 'pot', 'house' and 'stone' have the same numeral classifier).

Cardinal numeral + adjective (implied noun):

– the general pattern can be exemplified by 'two black ones' = /a^{4}θü^{4}khi^{4}kha/.

Ordinal numeral + adjective (implied noun):

– the general pattern can be exemplified by 'the second white one' = /a^{4}war^{4}khi^{4}kha ta^{4}kha/.

Cardinal numeral + adjective + possessive pronoun:

– the general pattern can be exemplified by 'my two black ones' = /ya a^{4}θü^{4}khi^{4}kha/.

Ordinal numeral + adjective + possessive pronoun:

– the general pattern can be exemplified by 'your second white one' = /na a^{4}war^{4}khi^{4}kha ta^{4}kha/.

Cardinal numeral + adjective + adjective + noun:

– the general pattern can be exemplified by 'two little black stones' = /^{1}lö a ^{4}θü^{4}pho ta^{2}phlö/.

Distributive numeral + cardinal numeral + adjective + noun + possessive pronoun:

– the general pattern can be exemplified by 'each of my three big houses' = /ya^{2}ti^{2}dọ^{4}θö^{2}phlö a^{4}kla ta^{2}phlö/.

Distributive numeral + cardinal numeral + adjective + possessive pronoun:

– the general pattern can be exemplified by 'each of my two black ones' = /ya^{1}ta a^{4}θü^{4}khi^{4}kha a^{3}wu ta^{4}kha^{2}se/.

Temporal ordering:

– counting days in the future starts from 'tomorrow', and in the past, from 'yesterday', as follows: 'today' = /ta^{3}ni^{3}pi/, 'yesterday' = /^{1}mü^{4}tar^{1}köʔ/, 'the day before yesterday' = /^{1}mü^{4}tar ta^{3}ni^{1}köʔ/, 'two days before yesterday' = /^{1}mü^{4}tar^{3}pu^{1}kwiʔ^{4}khi^{4}θo/, etc.; 'tomorrow' = /^{4}khe^{1}mü^{2}khwẹ/, 'the day after tomorrow' = /^{4}khe ta^{2}khwẹ/, 'two days after tomorrow' = /^{4}khe^{1}mü^{2}khwẹ^{3}pu^{1}kwiʔ^{4}khi^{4}θo/.

Multiplication of the verb object is expressed either by means of a multiplicative or of a distributive numeral.

The informant does not differentiate between 'each of your two houses' and 'your two houses each', or any of the comparable expressions.

JINGHPAW KACHIN

The informant's place of origin is Kutkai in Northern Shan State. As to the notation, Kachin tones are represented as follows: /^{1}/ = low, /^{2}/ = mid, /^{3}/ = high, and /^{31}/ = high falling. In my material, the falling tone /^{31}/ occurs only on morphemes which are constantly preceded by a high-tone morpheme, such as /^{3}lă^{31}ngai/ 'one', /^{3}lă^{31}khong/ 'two', /^{3}na^{31}ta/ 'house, and there are no instances of a low-tone unglottalized morpheme preceded by a high-tone morpheme. Within the limited scope of the numeral data, it is possible to view the tone sequence /$^{3\ 31}$/ as an implementation of /$^{3\ 1}$/, but the informant was not available for an extra session in order to investigate this, so I shall leave /^{31}/ in the notation in order not to omit possibly relevant information.

As to the vowels, Kachin has a distinction between /ə/ (written as /ă/ in the Kachin Latin alphabet which, by the way, does not render any tones) and /a/. It is in this respect different from Karen, in which [ə] is a toneless variant of /a/.

Like all the investigated Burmese languages, Jinghpaw Kachin has a fully elaborated numeral system, for which I shall mention only the first ten numerals, in an exemplificatory way.

Cardinal numerals:

1 /^{3}lă^{31}ngai/
2 /^{3}lă^{31}khong/
3 /^{1}mă^{2}shum/
4 /^{1}mă^{2}li/
5 /^{1}mă^{2}nga/
6 /^{3}kruʔ/
7 /^{1}să^{1}nit/
8 /^{1}mă^{3}sat/
9 /^{1}tšă^{1}khu/
10 /^{2}ši/.

Ordinal numerals:

the first = /^{2}šong/ (i.e. 'the front one')
the second = /^{1}lă^{2}pran/ or /^{1}ka^{2}ang/ (i.e. 'the middle one)
the third = /^{1}tšă^{2}thum (i.e. 'the last one').

Distributive numerals:

one each = /^{3}lă^{31}ngai^{1}phraʔ/

two each = /^{3}lă^{31}khong^{1}phraʔ/
three each = /^{1}mă^{2}shum^{1}phraʔ/.

Multiplicative numerals

once = /^{1}kă^{1}lang/
twice = /^{3}lă^{31}khong^{1}lang/
three times = /^{1}mă^{2}shum^{1}lang/
only = /^{1}ša/
both = /^{3}lă^{31}khong^{2}yen/.

Cardinal numeral + noun:

– the general pattern can be exemplified by

'one woman' = /(^{1}ă)^{2}num^{3}lă^{31}ngai/
'two women' = /(^{1}ă)^{2}num^{3}lă^{31}khong/
'three women' = /(^{1}ă)^{2}num^{1}mă^{2}shum/, or
'one goat' = /^{1}bai^{2}nam^{3}lă^{31}ngai/
'two goats' = /^{1}bai^{2}nam^{3}lă^{31}khong/
'three goats' = /^{1}bai^{2}nam^{1}mă^{2}shum/ etc.

(Note that Kachin has no numeral classifier; only the noun stem /^{2}num/ or /^{1}bai^{2}nam/ etc. is used.)

Ordinal numeral + noun:

– the general pattern can be exemplified by 'the first woman' = /^{2}šong^{3}na ^{2}num/ (lit. 'front-in woman').

Distributive numeral + noun:

– the general pattern can be exemplified by

'one woman each' = /^{2}num^{1}kă^{1}ša^{3}lă^{31}ngai^{1}phraʔ/
(lit. 'woman only one each), or
'two women each' = /^{2}num^{1}kă^{1}ša^{3}lă^{31}khong/

Cardinal numeral + noun + possessive pronoun:

– the possessive pronouns are: 'my' = /^{3}ngeʔ/, 'your' = /^{3}naʔ/, 'his=her=its' = /^{3}šiʔ/, 'our' = /^{3}an/, 'your, plural' = /^{3}nan/, 'their' = /^{3}šan/;
– the general pattern can be exemplified by 'my two goats' = /^{3}ngeʔ^{1}bai ^{2}nam^{3}lă^{31}khong/.

Ordinal numeral + noun + possessive pronoun:

– the general pattern can be exemplified by 'my second goat' = /^{3}ngeʔ^{1}lă ^{2}pran^{3}na^{1}bai^{2}nam/ or /^{3}ngeʔ^{1}kă^{2}ang^{3}na^{1}bai^{2}nam/ (lit. 'my the middle-in goat').

Distributive numeral + noun + possessive pronoun:

– the general pattern can be exemplified by 'each of your boys' = /^{3}naʔ ^{2}la^{1}kă^{1}ša^{3}lă^{31}ngai^{1}phraʔ/.

Multiplicative numeral + noun + possessive pronoun:

– the general pattern can be exemplified by 'my both goats' = /^{3}ngeʔ^{1}bai ^{2}nam^{3}lă^{31}khong/.

Cardinal numeral + adjective + noun:

– the general pattern can be exemplified by 'one beautiful woman' = /^{2}num ^{1}som^{1}gă^{1}ša^{3}lă^{31}ngai/ (lit. 'woman appearing-be-only one').

Ordinal numeral + adjective + noun:

– the general pattern can be exemplified by 'the first beautiful woman' = /^{2}šong^{3}na^{2}num^{1}som^{1}gă^{1}ša/.

Cardinal numeral + adjective + noun + possessive pronoun:

– the general pattern can be exemplified by 'my two beautiful women' = /^{3}ngeʔ^{2}num^{1}som^{1}gă^{1}ša^{3}lă^{31}khong/.

Ordinal numeral + adjective + noun + possessive pronoun:

– the same type as that of ordinal numeral + adjective + noun, with the possessive pronoun preposed.

Cardinal numeral + adjective (implied noun):

– the general pattern can be exemplified by 'two black ones' = /^{3}ă^{2}čang ^{3}lă^{31}khong/.

Ordinal numeral + adjective (implied noun):

– the general pattern can be exemplified by 'the second white one' = /^{1}lă^{2}pran^{3}na^{1}phro^{2}ai/ or /^{1}ka^{2}ang^{3}na^{1}phro^{2}ai/.

Cardinal numeral + adjective + possessive pronoun:

– the general pattern can be exemplified by 'my two black ones' = /^{3}ngeʔ ^{2}čang^{2}ai^{3}lă^{31}khong/.

Ordinal numeral + adjective + possessive pronoun:

– the general pattern can be exemplified by 'your second white one' = /^{3}naʔ^{1}lă^{2}pran^{3}na^{1}phro^{2}ai/ or /^{3}naʔ^{1}kă^{2}ang^{3}na^{1}phro^{2}ai/.

Cardinal numeral + adjective + adjective + noun:

– the general pattern can be exemplified by 'one big white horse' = /^{1}gum^{1}ra^{1}phro^{1}gă^{1}ba^{3}lă^{31}ngai/ (lit. 'horse white big one'); one of the adjectives may also precede /^{1}gum^{1}ra/ (i.e. 'horse'), but then it must be followed by /^{2}ai/, which can be analysed as defining a set (cf. 'your three white ones' = /^{3}naʔ^{1}phro^{2}ai^{1}mă^{2}shum/, which can be paraphrased as 'of your white ones, three').

Distributive numeral + cardinal numeral + adjective + noun + possessive pronoun:

– the general pattern can be exemplified by 'each of my three big houses' = /^{3}ngeʔ^{3}na^{31}ta^{1}gă^{1}ba^{1}mă^{2}shum^{1}phraʔ/.

Distributive numeral + cardinal numeral + adjective + possessive pronoun:

– the general pattern can be exemplified by 'each of my two black ones' = /^{3}ngeʔ(^{1}aʔ) ^{2}čang^{2}ai^{3}lă^{31}khong^{1}phraʔ/ (lit. 'my-of black two each').

Temporal ordering:

– 'today' = /^{1}dai^{3}ni/, 'yesterday' = /^{3}mă^{3}ni/, 'the day before yesterday' = /^{3}mă^{1}niʔ^{1}šong^{1}šă^{3}ni/; 'tomorrow' = /^{3}phot^{3}ni/, 'the day after tomorrow' = /^{3}phot^{1}din^{3}ni/.

Multiplication of the verb object is expressed by means of a multiplicative numeral.

The informant does not differentiate between 'each of your two houses' and 'your two houses each', or any of the comparable expressions.

ASHÖ CHIN

The informant's place of origin is Thayet in Central Burma. In relation to the script, Ashö Chin tones are represented as follows: /^{1} _ ʔ/ = low glottalized, /^{2}/ = mid falling, /^{3}/ = high, and /^{3}_ʔ/ = high glottalized. Ashö Chin distinguishes the following vowels: /i/, /ẹ/, /e/, /a/, /o/, /ọ/, /u/, /ɵ/ and /ʉ/ (the latter two are central unround, mid and high, respectively); in addition to these, the following vowel sequences are found: /ei/, /ai/, /au/, /ui/, /uei/ and /uai/. There are vocalic sonorants in addition, denoted by means of a dot underneath. Within a phrase, a continuant segment is implemented as voiced following a voiced segment, and as voiceless elsewhere (including /ʔ/ –.)

Ashö Chin has a fully elaborated numeral system, for which I shall mention only the first ten numerals, in an exemplificatory way.

Cardinal numerals:

1 /^{3}oʔ/
2 /^{3}hṇi/
3 /^{3}thun/
4 /^{3}hṃḷi/
5 /^{3}hṇgọ/
6 /^{3}shọʔ/
7 /^{3}shi/
8 /^{1}sheʔ/
9 /^{1}kọʔ/
10 /^{3}hṇga/ etc.

Ordinal numerals:

the first = /^{3}siʔ^{3}siʔ/
the second = /^{2}pun^{3}hṇi^{3}mlọʔ/
the third = /^{2}pun^{3}thun^{3}mlọʔ/
the fourth = /^{2}pun^{3}hṃḷi^{3}mlọʔ/ etc.

Distributive numerals:

one each = /^{2}pun^{3}oʔ^{3}si/
two each = /^{2}pun^{3}hṇi^{3}si/
three each = /^{2}pun^{3}thun^{3}si/ etc.

Multiplicative numerals:

once /^{3}khọʔ^{3}oʔ/
twice = /^{3}khọʔ^{3}hṇi/
three times = /^{3}khọʔ^{3}thun/ etc.
only = /^{2}pun^{3}oʔ^{2}də/
both = /^{2}pun^{3}hṇi^{2}don/.

Cardinal numeral + noun:

– the general pattern can be exemplified by 'one goat' = /^{2}mẹ^{3}sʉn^{3}oʔ/
'two goats'= /^{2}mẹ^{3}sʉn^{3}hṇi/
'three goats'=/^{2}mẹ^{3}sʉn^{3}thun/
etc.

where /^{3}sʉn/ (pronounced here as [^{3}zʉn] according to the general rule stated above) is the numeral classifier for animals.

Ordinal numeral + noun:

– the general pattern can be exemplified by 'the first goat' = /^{3}siʔ^{3}siʔ^{2}me/.

Distributive numeral + noun:

– the general pattern can be exemplified by 'one goat each' = /^{2}mẹ^{3}sʉn^{3}oʔ ^{3}si/.

Cardinal numeral + noun + possessive pronoun:

– the possessive pronouns are: 'my' = /^{2}čei/, 'your' = /^{2}naun/, 'his=her=its' = /^{2}phọ/, and the same respective forms for the plural;
– the general pattern can be exemplified by 'my two goats' = /^{2}čei^{2}mẹ^{3}sʉn ^{3}hṇi/.

Ordinal numeral + noun + possessive pronoun:

– the general pattern can be exemplified by 'my second goat' = /^{2}čei^{3}sun ^{3}hṇi^{3}mlọʔ^{2}mẹ/ (lit. 'my classifier second goat').

Distributive numeral + noun + possessive pronoun:

– the general pattern can be exemplified by 'each of your boys' = /^{2}naun ^{3}khlaun^{3}sau^{3}lui^{2}də/ (lit. 'your boy classifier-of only').

Multiplicative numeral + noun + possessive pronoun:

– the general pattern can be exemplified by 'my only goat' = /^{2}čei^{3}sʉn^{3}oʔ ^{3}lai^{1}ləʔ^{2}mẹ/ (lit. 'my classifier one and only goat').

Cardinal numeral + adjective + noun:

– the general pattern can be exemplified by 'one long rope' = /^{2}yuei^{2}shau ^{3}yun^{3}oʔ/ (lit. 'rope long classifier one').

Ordinal numeral + adjective + noun:

– the general pattern can be exemplified by 'the third white cloth' = /^{2}pun^{3}thun^{3}mlọʔ^{1}piʔ^{1}bọʔ/ (lit. 'the third cloth white').

Cardinal numeral + adjective + noun + possessive pronoun:

– the general pattern can be exemplified by 'his three big houses' = /^{2}phọ^{2}ẹn^{3}hḷen^{2}lʉn^{3}thun/ (lit. 'his house big classifier three').

Ordinal numeral + adjective + noun + possessive pronoun:

– the same pattern as that of ordinal numeral + adjective + noun, with the possessive pronoun preposed.

Cardinal numeral + adjective (implied noun):

– the general pattern can be exemplified by 'two black ones' = /a^{3}niʔ^{2}lʉn ^{3}hṇi/ (with the classifier /^{2}lʉn/, referring to round things).

Ordinal numeral + adjective (implied noun):

– the general pattern can be exemplified by 'the second white one' = /^{2}pun^{3}hṇi^{3} mlọ a^{1}ḅoʔ/.

Cardinal numeral + adjective + possessive pronoun:

– the general pattern can be exemplified by 'your three white ones' = /^{2}naun a^{1}bọʔ^{2}lʉn^{3} thun/ (lit. 'your white classifier three').

Ordinal numeral + adjective + possessive pronoun:

– the general pattern can be exemplified by 'your second white one' = /^{2}naun^{2}pun^{3}hṇi^{3}mlọʔ a^{1}bọʔ/

Cardinal numeral + adjective + adjective + noun:

– the general pattern can be exemplified by 'two little black stones' = /a^{2}lʉn^{3}niʔ^{3}saụ^{2}lʉn^{3}hṇi/ (lit. 'stone little black classifier two').

Distributive numeral + cardinal numeral + adjective + noun + possessive pronoun:

– the general pattern can be exemplified by 'each of your three big houses' = /^{2}naun^{2}ẹn^{3}hlen^{2}lʉn^{3}thun^{3}duʔ^{2}ka^{2}lun^{3}oʔ^{3}si/.

Distributive numeral + cardinal numeral + adjective + possessive pronoun:

– the general pattern can be exemplified by 'each of your five red ones' = /^{2}naun a^{3}shen^{2}pun^{3}hṇgọ^{3} dʉʔ^{2}ka^{2}pun^{3}oʔ^{3}si/ (I am not able to state whether the difference btweeen /^{3}dʉʔ/ here and /^{2}dɵ/ e.g. in the example 'each of your boys' above is a matter of positional variation, or a distinctive difference).

Temporal ordering:

– 'today' = /^{3}tʉ^{1}hṇuʔ^{3}ka/, 'yesterday' = /^{3}yan^{2}da^{3}a/, 'the day before yesterday' = /^{3}un^{3}ni^{3}a/, 'two days before yesterday' = /^{3}un^{3}hṃwai^{3}a/; 'tomorrow' = /^{1}huʔ^{2}ta^{3}a/, 'the day after tomorrow' = /^{3}čɵʔ^{3}tɵ^{2}a/, 'two days after tomorrow' = /^{1}kauʔ^{3}tɵ^{2}a/, 'three days after tomorrow' = /^{3}tšhen^{3}tɵ^{2}a/ (note that the different tone on the final morpheme as either /^{3}a/ or /^{2}a/ is rendered as such in the script (which is for Ashö Chin derived from the Burmese one, with a notation of tone and of vowel qualities typical of Ashö Chin)).

Multiplication of the verb object is expressed by means of a multiplicative numeral.

The informant distinguishes between 'show me each of your two houses' = /^{2}naun^{2}ẹn^{2}lʉn^{3}hṇi^{3}duʔ^{2}ka^{2}lʉn^{3}oʔ^{3}si^{3}mphla^{3}shon^{2}ei/ vs. 'show me your two houses each' = /^{2}naun^{2}ẹn^{2}lʉn^{3}hṇi^{3}si^{3}mphla^{3}shon^{2}ei/.

BURMESE

The informant's place of origin is Rangoon. In the notation of Burmese, I follow Benedict (1972: 87), who marks the high creaky tone as / ´ /, the high falling tone as / ` /, and leaves the low level tone unmarked. These tones are distinctive only in morphemes which end in a voiced segment (i.e. a vowel or a nasal), and not in those which end in a glottal stop. Burmese has the same rule as Ashö Chin for voicing of continuant segments following a voiced segment, and not following a glottal stop. This rule holds within a phrase. The remaining conventions are the usual ones.

Burmese has a fully elaborated numeral system, for which I shall mention only the first ten numerals, in an exemplificatory way.

Cardinal numerals:

1 /tiˀ/
2 /hṇiˀ/
3 /θọ̀n/
4 /lẹ̀/
5 /ngà/
6 /tšauˀ/
7 /khuniˀ/
8 /šiˀ/
9 /kọ̀/
10 /tăshe/ etc.

Ordinal numerals:

the first = /păthămá/
the second = /dutăyá/
the third = /tátăyá/
the fourth = /sădọ́thá/
the tenth = /dáθămá/.

Distributive numerals:

one each = /tăkhúsi/
two each = /hṇăkhúsi/
three each = /θọ̀nkhúsi/ etc.

Multiplicative numerals:

once = /tăkha/
twice = /hṇăkha/
three times = /θọ̀nkha/ etc.
only = /lẹ̀kha/
both = /tăkhadè/.

Cardinal numeral + noun:

– the general pattern can be exemplified by

'one woman' = /mìnkhălẹ̀ tăyauˀ/
'two women' = /mìnkhălẹ̀ hṇăyauˀ/
'three women' = /mìnkhălẹ̀ θọ̀nyauˀ/
'one goat' = /shiˀ tăgaun/

'two goats' = /shi? hṇăgaun/ etc.
(i.e. in the order noun + numeral + numeral classifier).

Ordinal numeral + noun:

– the general pattern can be exemplified by 'the first woman' = /păthămá mìnkhălẹ̀/.

Distributive numeral + noun:

– the general pattern can be exemplified by 'two goats each' = /shi? hṇăgáunsi/ (i.e. 'goat two classifier each').

Cardinal numeral + noun + possessive pronoun:

– the possessive pronouns are: 'my' = /tšănó/, 'your' = /khămyà/, 'his=her=its' = /θú/, 'our' = /tšănó/, 'your, plural' = /khămyàdó/, 'their' = /θudó/;
– the general pattern can be exemplified by 'my two goats' = /tšănó shi? hṇăgaun/.

Ordinal numeral + noun + possessive pronoun:

– the general pattern can be exemplified by 'my second goat' = /tšănó dutăyá shi?/.

Distributive numeral + noun + possessive pronoun:

– the general pattern can be exemplified by 'each of your boys' = /khămyá kaunlẹ ăθìθì/.

Multiplicative numeral + noun + possessive pronoun:

– the general pattern can be exemplified by 'my only goat' = /tšănó tăgaundè θo shi?/ (with the classifier between the morphemes denoting 'only').

Cardinal numeral + adjective + noun:

– the general pattern can be exemplified by 'one beautiful woman' = /mìnkhălẹ̀ hḷáhḷá tăyau?/.

Ordinal numeral + adjective + noun:

– the general pattern can be exemplified by 'the first beautiful woman' = /păthămá mìnkhălẹ̀ hḷáhḷá/.

Cardinal numeral + adjective + noun + possessive pronoun:

– the general pattern can be exemplified by 'my two beautiful girls' = /tšănó mìnkhălẹ̀ hḷáhḷá hṇăyau?/.

Ordinal numeral + adjective + noun + possessive pronoun:

– the same pattern as that of ordinal numeral + adjective + noun, with the possessive pronoun preposed.

Cardinal numeral + adjective (implied noun):

– the general pattern can be exemplified by 'two black ones' = /ămè hṇăkhú/.

Ordinal numeral + adjective (implied noun):

– the general pattern can be exemplified by 'the second white one' = /dutăyá ăphyu tăkhú/.

Cardinal numeral + adjective + possessive pronoun:

– the general pattern can be exemplified by 'my two black ones' = /tšănó ămè hṇăkhú/.

Ordinal numeral + adjective + possessive pronoun:

– the general pattern can be exemplified by 'your second white one' = /khămyà dutăyá ăphyu tăkhú/.

Cardinal numeral + adjective + adjective + noun:

– the general pattern can be exemplified by 'two little black stones' = /tšau?khè ămè θẹ̀θẹ̀ lẹ̀hṇălọ̀/ (lit. 'stone black little of-two-classifier').

Distributive numeral + cardinal numeral + adjective + noun + possessive prounoun:

- the general pattern can be exemplified by 'each of my three big houses' = /tšǎnó ẹntšì θọnlọn dègá tǎlọnsi/.

Distributive numeral + cardinal numeral + adjective + possessive pronoun:

- the general pattern can be exemplified by 'each of my two black ones' = /tšǎnó ǎmè hṇǎkhú dègá tǎkhúsi/.

Temporal ordering:

- more lexicalized forms for the future than for the past, i.e. 'today' = /dinẹ́/, 'yesterday' = /mǎnẹ́gá/, 'the day before yesterday' = /tǎmyannẹ́gá/; 'tomorrow' = /neˀphyan/, 'the day after tomorrow' = /θǎbékha/, 'two days after tomorrow' = /phìnwèga/, 'three days after tomorrow' = /mìnθǎbeˀ/ (the last form is not any more used by the younger generation).

Multiplication of the verb object is expressed by means of a multiplicative numeral.

The informant distinguishes between 'show me each of your two houses' = /tšǎnógo khǎmyà ẹn hṇǎlọn dègá tǎlọnsi pyába/ vs. 'show me your two houses each' = /tšǎnógo khǎmyà ẹn hṇǎlọnsi pyába/ (note the different placement of the plural suffix /-si/, either following 'one (+classifier)' or 'two (+classifier)').

Conclusions with respect to the hypotheses A, revised B, and C:

- hypothesis A is trivial for a fully developed numeral system such as that of Karen, Ashö Chin, Burmese, and also Kachin with fully developed cardinal numerals;
- hypothesis B in the revised form is refuted in so far as the designations for 'today', 'yesterday' and 'tomorrow' are lexicalized in all cases, and the remaining ones are derived from 'yesterday' and 'tomorrow', respectively, or lexicalized, too; in all cases of derivation, 'today' is left out of the consideration, even though the verb system takes present and future together as nonpast; on the other hand, the original hypothesis B, by which the number of spatial denotations used as ordinal numerals sets the upper limit to lexicalized temporal designations, remains unrefuted for Kachin, whereas it is unapplicable to the other investigated languages of Burma; it is in this respect noteworthy that Kachin has three spatial designations used as ordinal numerals, for which it may be assumed that the features accounting for them, namely *front* vs. *nonfront,* and *back* vs. *nonback,* are mutually asymmetrically ordered such that the former is dominating and the latter, subordinate, and that it is due to presence of ordering among the spatial designations that a relation with temporal ones holds; let this be a hypothesis for further research;
- hypothesis C remains unrefuted, as a possessive pronoun always precedes the noun, and an ordinal numeral precedes whereas a cardinal one follows *ceteris paribus.*

This investigation of numerals and numeral constructions has shown that Kachin stands at the linguistic 'crossroads' of Tibeto-Burman indeed, as correctly observed by Benedict (1972: 5): its using spatial denotations for ordinal numerals and its not using numeral classifiers makes it different from the Burmese Tibeto-Burman languages investigated here, and similar to the Nepalese ones.

3.4. The Bantawa Rai Numerals Elaborated

A real test case for the hypotheses formulated at the end of 3.2.1. about a language-specific cut-off point in numeral decay as related to the conceptual basis of the system is provided by Bantawa, for which three conceptual types have been attested, and decay without overt reference to them, as illustrated by the following examples:

	Bantawa Raniṭar Panchthar	Bantawa Chungbang Dhankuṭa	Bantawa Sarangdanḍa Panchthar	Bantawa Chhinamakhu Bhojpur
1	/ʉkṭa/	/ʉkte/	/ʉkṭa/	/ʉkṭak/, /ʉkpok/
2	/hʉsaṭ/	/hʉsak/, /husak/	/husaṭ/	/hʉapok/
3	/sumkaṭaṭ/	/sumka/	/sumka/	/sumkapok/
4	/reṭkaṭaṭ/	/goda/, /gonda/	/bhanka/	–
5	/ʉkchuk/	/nasi/	/hanka/	–
6	/ʉkchuk ʉkṭa/	/phansi/	/minka/	–
7	/ʉkchuk hʉsaṭ/	/epci/	/sanka/	–
8	/reṭkaṭaṭ/	/ṭupci/	/reṭka/	/reṭkapok/
9	(/ʉkchuk reṭkaṭaṭ/, cf. 3.2. above)	/nusi/	/nanka/	–
10	/hʉachuk/	/ʉkbom/	/nanṭa/	–
20	/cuppabhung/ ('small hundred')	/husabom/	/ʉkbhung/	–
21	/cuppabhung ʉkṭa/	/husaʉk/	/ʉkbhungʉk/	–
30	–	/sumkabom/	/ʉkbhungʉkkek/	–
40	–	/gondabom/	/huwabhung/	–
50	–	/nasibom/	/huwabhungʉkkek/	–
90	–	/nusibom/	/bhankabhungʉkkek/	–
100	/ʉkbhung/	/ʉkbobom/	/hankabhok/	–

Bantawa from Raniṭar has a system based on 'five', from Chungbang, based on 'ten', from Sarangdanḍa, based on 'twenty', and from Chhinamakhu, a decaying system.

The Chungbang attestation is the only one of the decimal type, and the Sarangdanḍa attestation, the only one of the vigesimal type. On the basis of the forms used, both may be considered relatively original in comparison with the quinary type found in Rumṭar and in various other places in Panchthar, Taplejung, Ilam and Jhapa. (Note that several of the Chungbang forms resemble Limbu ones, for which there is also dialectal variation in the order of the forms above five, but I have not been able to investigate any possible Limbu influence on the Chungbang system vs. its originality because the informant had died a few days before I could have started working with him in January 1984.)

The relevant points as to the innovative status of the quinary type are:

- the form for ‘five’, which is not derived from the common Tibeto-Burman root *nga (established as such by Benedict (1972: 94);
- the absence of a fully elaborated system, pointing to partial decay in comparison with what was presumably the original system, and
- the usage of a form based on /reṭka/ either for ‘eight’ or for ‘four’, whereas in the fully preserved systems (presented also in 3.2. above) it is used only as the form for ‘eight’; Bantawa from Chhinamakhu shows that the shift of the form based on /reṭka/ was not a linear one – but consequently a conceptual one.

Apparently, in the process of decay Bantawa had a stage at which the conceptual unit was that of ‘five’. From that stage on, either further decay, or innovation based on ‘five’ as the conceptual unit could take place. (Note that this way of reasoning is in accordance with what W. von Humboldt had understood in 1836 (§ 8: LIX) already, namely that only the generative rules are determined, but that the extent and in some measure also the way of generating remains undetermined for a language.)

The original Bantawa system was not based on ‘five’. The Chhinamakhu type, having a form based on /reṭka/ for ‘eight’, and the Annapurna type mentioned in 3.2.1. above, having the same form for ‘four’, show that there was a shift (and a downward one, in view of comparative evidence) by which the meaning of the form based on /reṭka/ was reinterpreted so as to equal ‘one half of the original one’. This diminishing by one half can be seen as indirectly indicative of a change of the conceptual unit by diminishing it by one half. And if the result is a unit equalling ‘five’, then the original one must have been ‘ten’.

But why do we observe the given shift of the form for ‘eight’ onto ‘four’, and not of ‘ten’ onto ‘five’?

I think that the answer must be seen in the relation between numeral preservation in the lexicon and number preservation in the grammar. Apparently, language systems with three numbers in the grammar also treat the first three numerals in the lexicon as basic. ‘Four’ is the first numeral in the row which is conceptually a derived one, i.e. ‘4 = 2 x 2’, or perhaps ‘4 = 3 + 1’. And it is there that change and decay are observed.

The hypothesis stating that the cut-off point reflects the conceptual basis of the system is strictly speaking inapplicable to Bantawa from Bhojpur. But on the basis of this type of Bantawa we can derive a new hypothesis that whenever there is number ordering in the grammar (as there is one with *singular* vs. *dual* vs. *plural*, but not necessarily with *singular* vs. *plural* only, as shown in 2.2 above), then the first three numerals form the basic elements of the numeral system, and the cut-off point at the last stage of numeral decay is determined by them.

But now back to the quinary system. Can it be shown that the cut-off point in the eastern districts is determined by 'five' as the conceptual unit indeed? And can the presence of a quinary conceptual basis be shown without circularly pointing back to the forms based on 'hand' for 'five'?

The answer is: 'yes, it can', on the basis of the following data collected for the Linguistic Survey of Nepal:

	Bantawa Phungatappa Ilam	Bantawa Cilingdin Panchthar	Bantawa Kobna Jhapa
1	/ʉkṭa/	/ʉkṭa/	/ʉkta/
2	/hʉsa/	/hʉaṭa/	/hʉaṭa/
3	/sumkaṭa/	/sumk̇aṭa/	/sumk̇aṭa/
4	/carkabok/	/reṭkaṭa/	/reṭkaṭa/
5	/panckabok/	/panck̇aṭa/	/ʉk̇chuk̇/
6	–	–	–
7	–	–	–
8	–	–	–
9	–	–	–
10	–	–	–

These examples show that the cut-off point is determined by the conceptual unit of 'five' indeed, even if associated with the Nepali forms for 'four' and 'five' (as in Phungatappa) or only for 'five' (as in Cilingdin).

Another piece of evidence for a quinary innovation in the process of decay, with a transitional stage at which both a unit based on 'ten' and one based on 'five' could have coexisted, can be found in Raniṭar's usage of 'small hundred' for 'twenty' (i.e. 'hundred divided by five') vs. 'big hundred' for 'thousand' (i.e. 'hundred multiplied by ten'), mentioned in 3.2. above. Apparently, there is an association of 'small' with 'five', and of 'big' with 'ten' – but this piece of evidence is an indirect one indeed.

Starting from the stage at which the conceptual unit based on 'five' was present in the way in which Bantawa speakers conceived of counting, the new form for 'five' was introduced and the system was further elaborated by making use of the new sign for 'five' as shown by the Raniṭar data presented in 3.2. above.

Another fact must be mentioned here: establishment of the quinary system, with the new conceptual unit equalling 'five', preceded the conceptual downward shift of the form based on /reṭka/ from 'eight' onto 'four', as can be shown by the following Bantawa data from Durdimba in Panchthar:

	Bantawa Durdimba Panchthar
1	/ʉkbok/
2	/husaṭ/
3	/sumka/
4	–
5	/ʉkchuk/
6	–
7	–
8	/reṭkabok/
9	–
10	/hʉachuk/
20	–
100	/bhung/.

This shows that the Bantawa conceptual downward shift of the form based on /reṭka/ took place against the background of the newly relevant conceptual unit based on 'five' in the system indeed. And apparently the new conceptual unit acquired the function of a sign with the meaning of a basic unit only after the new form based on 'hand' was associated with it.

The Bantawa data thus point to a distinction between simple basic units of meaning (i.e. 'one') and complex basic units of meaning (i.e. 'two', 'three', 'five' and possibly higher ones, such as e.g. 'hundred' in Ranitar), which participate in the ordered part of the numeral component of the lexicon, whereas the remaining units of meaning are derived. The form of the latter is either derived, too, or not any more recoverable as such (i.e. 'lexicalized'), and in connection with the latter, ordering may be observed as a consequence of arbitrary conventionalization.

This investigation of the numeral system leads to the conclusion that the simple basic unit in the lexicon equals a single feature of meaning, and the complex basic unit, an asymmetrically ordered pair (or a set of transitively ordered pairs) of feature oppositions (in the Bantawa case, *'not one'*, which is further subdivided into *'two'* and *'more than two'*, the latter being conventionalized as 'three'). In addition to ordered features, the complex unit may also contain unordered ones (in the Bantawa case, *'more than two, equalling a hand'* is the complex unit for 'five'). Both the extent of ordering and participation of unordered features are language-specific matters.

The distinction between basic units on the one hand, and derived ones on the other, is found at the level of meaning in a parallel way as it is at the level of form. And the basic units at both levels can be either simple or complex.

A simple basic unit consists of a single feature, and a complex one, of asymmetrically ordered features and possibly also one or several unordered ones.

An example of a simple basic unit in grammar is found e.g. in the plural marking of predicatively used adjectives in Russian, where no person or case is marked at the same time, the marked specification of number being the only feature of the given unit of meaning. An example of a complex basic unit in grammar is found e.g. in the Russian marking of number, person and mood by means of /-i/ in the imperative (say, /piší/ 'write, 2nd singular'); the former two features are asymmetrically ordered in Russian, and the latter is unordered.

At the level of form, basic units are the distinctive segments of a language. They can also be simple, i.e. consist of a single feature such as the floating tone, or complex, i.e. consist of asymmetrically ordered features with a possible addition of unordered ones, as we have seen in the first chapter of this study.

The internal organization of units at the level of meaning consequently follows the same principles as that at the level of form.

4. Language Typology in Relation to the System

This study has formulated and tested a theory by which the system of each language consists of an ordered and an unordered part at each of its levels, and the ordered parts of the system impose constraints on variation.

System-internal ordering equals asymmetrical implication, which can be either paradigmatic or syntagmatic. It is established with reference to the entire language system involved.

Paradigmatic ordering holds for pairs of feature oppositions of form on the one hand, and of meaning on the other, whenever there is asymmetrical implication by which the terms of an opposition are distinctive in combination with one term of another opposition, but not with both its terms. Then the former feature opposition is subordinate and the latter dominating.

Syntagmatic ordering holds for pairs of units whenever one unit implies another unit (without making it predictable, though), but not vice versa. At the level of form, we have seen an example of it in diphthongization, where the terms of a feature opposition are distributed in the order 'unmarked, marked' within a segment. The marked term implies the unmarked one, but not vice versa. At the level of meaning, syntagmatic asymmetrical implication is found between any determinandum and its determinatum, e.g. between a unit denoting an entity and one specifying it – as expressed at the level of form a.o. by means of a noun and its determiner – or between a unit denoting an action or state and one specifying it in terms of time or person, gender and number of the participants involved – as expressed at the level of form by means of a verb and its desinences or other deictic units accompanying it.

Asymmetrical implication defines a complex unit of the system. In syntagmatic asymmetrical implication, such a unit is characterized by a fixed order of elements. The fixed order can be crosscut only if two units are formed instead of one. Thus a language with a fixed order between a noun and its determiner (e.g. determiner + noun) can have the opposed order (i.e. noun determiner) only if they occur within two different units of meaning (i.e. noun, determiner). And this grouping of the units of meaning is then expressed by another formal means, most usually by means of intonation.

Language typology evaluates each language element against the paradigmatic and syntagmatic ordered parts of the system in which it occurs. It evaluates whether the element participates in an ordered part of the system. If so, it is part of a complex unit, and its role within it must be determined. If not, it must be evaluated whether it is a unit by itself, or a dependent part of a unit.

A sign consists of a unit of meaning which is in a conventionalized way associated with a unit of form (in the sense of Saussure (1916)). I use here the term 'unit' in the sense of either 'basic' or 'derived', as either of them at the level of meaning can be associated with either of them at the level of form.

Language typology evaluates each language element against the background of the entire language system involved. It is only against the background of the entire system involved that elements of various language systems can be compared with each other. Entire systems can be compared on the basis of the sort and extent of their ordered parts at the level of form, and of those at the level of meaning. This holds both for paradigmatic and for syntagmatic ordering.

In the sound system, paradigmatic and syntagmatic ordering of distinctive features must be taken into account when evaluating any pair of segments or any 'natural class of segments', because its position in the system may be different due to presence vs. absence of ordering, and in the former case, due to its sort and extent. Thus the Polish nasals – which are more 'sonorous' and thus form syllable nuclei more readily than the liquids – differ from the English nasals as discussed in the section on prosodic hierarchy in phonology not because of their greater sonority in comparison with the liquids, but because of the system-internal basis of this sonority, namely distinctive feature subordination with respect to *nonvocalic,* and the fact that the Polish distinctive feature opposition *nasal* vs. *nonnasal* is unordered with respect to *nonvocalic*, whereas the English one is subordinate with respect to *nonvocalic.* This fact, making the Polish nasals 'less nonvocalic' (i.e. 'more sonorous') than the English ones, is due to the existence of nasal vowels in Polish (of which only /ę/ and /ǫ/ in the word-final position must be analysed as distinctively nasal – the remaining ones are analysable as sequences of oral vowel + nasal), and the absence of nasal vowels in English.

In order to establish paradigmatic and syntagmatic ordering, the totality of paradigmatic and syntagmatic relations must be taken into account. Thus the difference between three tonal accents in long syllable nuclei in South-eastern Slavonian Serbo-Croatian and two tonal accents in Neoštokavian

Serbo-Croatian discussed in 1.2. above can be understood properly only if paradigmatic and syntagmatic evaluation of the vowels (i.e. syllable nuclei) characterized by these tonal accents is taken into account. It appears then that long vowels are sequences in Slavonian, and single units in Neoštokavian, as shown in the same section above. This syntagmatic evaluation is related to the paradigmatic one based on the oppositions involved, as shown in a general way by Ebeling (1960) already. And in our case it leads to the conclusion that the three tonal accents in long syllable nuclei of Slavonian Serbo-croatian are due to a differential occurrence of tone as a distinctive feature either on the first or the second vowel of a sequence. Distinctiveness is here crucial for not analysing the tonal accents as tone sequences, but rather as single tones with a differential distribution, and with predictable phonetic pitch on the neighbouring vowel. And distinctiveness equals considering features as signs.

In language comparison, both paradigmatic and syntagmatic establishment of units and of their placement with respect to the ordered part of the system at the given level of form or of meaning, is crucial to the evaluation of these units in the sense of either sameness or difference.

In grammar, i.e. in the signs whose meaning is defined exclusively by relations at the level of meaning, we have seen in the second chapter that the singular and the plural can have a different paradigmatic evaluation, which comes out only when the grammatical feature of number participates in asymmetrical ordering, and that the features of person can have a different paradigmatic and syntagmatic evaluation which comes out in the syntagmatic context of number – as attested in Bantawa of North Bhojpur. These examples show that paradigmatic and syntagmatic relations are mutually interconnected in this sense that any presence of syntagmatic ordering is necessarily connected with a paradigmatically ordered unit, but not vice versa.

In lexicon, i.e. in the signs whose meaning is not exclusively defined by relations at the level of meaning, but it may contain other features of meaning as well, we have seen in the third chapter that the evaluation of each numeral in a system depends on the simple and complex units which are basic to that system. If the complex unit which is basic to that system equals 'five', then e.g. the numeral 'eight' is evaluated as 'five + three' and treated by the language accordingly in the sense of the form which is associated with that meaning. And we have seen also that the ordered parts of the grammar are related to the lexicon, as e.g. the singular, the dual and the plural in a system are related to the first three numerals of that system so that language decay does not affect the numerals without affecting the numbers. Or to take another example, the syntagmatically ordered temporal designations in

Sunwar take 'today' as the starting point for counting forwards, and this is related to the grammatical feature opposition *past* vs. *nonpast*, where *nonpast* includes both present and future. And this is also related to the lexical feature opposition of space *back* vs. *front,* which is used in Sunwar instead of ordinal numerals.

Whereas ordering forms the basis of the typological evaluation of the system itself, the way in which the unordered parts are conventionalized is indicative of the genetic basis of a system, and its geographical and cultural contacts.

Geographically bound sound isoglosses have been mentioned in 3.1. already. Lexical isoglosses are indicative genetically, geographically and culturally, but their participation in the system must be evaluated against the relations between grammatical and lexical ordering as illustrated above. As to grammatical isoglosses, the dimensions along which they are conventionalized must be evaluated against the dimensions which are relevant to that system, and against the ordering in which they participate.

In variants of one language system, same or comparable elements are distributed within the space defined by the same dimensions and which participate in the same ordering, if any. In different language systems, either different elements occur, or they are not distributed within the space defined by the same dimensions, or they do not participate in the same ordering, if there is any present in a given language.

The first condition has been illustrated e.g. by lexicalized temporal designations already, and the third condition by a different evaluation of the singular and the plural e.g. in Old Russian as compared with Modern Russian, which are on the basis of the grammar two different language systems, irrespectively of the fact that the one has developed from the other through language change. In order to illustrate the second condition mentioned above, let me analyse prefixes of complex pronominalized verbs in two dialects of the Kiranti language Limbu, Panchthare and Chattare Limbu, for which I thankfully owe the data to A.K. Weidert.

(66) Complex pronominalization in the verb endings of Panchthare Limbu as spoken in Phidim in Panchthar; the positive paradigm: nonpast/past *hipma* 'to beat':

1st argument	2nd argument 1 sg: ngaˀ	2 sg: heneˀ	3 sg: honeˀ	1du-incl.: antshiˀ	1 du-excl.: antshyaˀ	2 du: hentshiˀ	3 du: huntshiˀ	1 pl-incl.: aniˀ	1 pl-excl.: angyaˀ	2 pl: heniˀ	3 pl: henhaˀ
1 sg: ngaˀ		hipne hipne	hiptungˀ hiptung			hipnetshingˀ hipnetshing	hiptungsingˀ hiptungsing			hipningˀ hipnening	hiptungsingˀ hiptungsing
2 sg: heneˀ	kehippaˀ kehiptang		kehiptuˀ kehiptu		yapmikehip yapmikehipta		kehiptusiˀ kehiptusi		yapmikehip yapmikehipta		kehiptusiˀ kehiptusi
3 sg: honeˀ	hippaˀ hiptang	kehip kehipta	hiptuˀ hiptu	ahipsiˀ ahiptetshi	yapmihip yapmihipta	kehipsiˀ kehiptetshi	hiptusiˀ hiptusi	ahip ahipta	yapmihip yapmihipta	kehiptiˀ kehipti	hiptusiˀ hiptusi
1 du-incl.: antshiˀ			ahipsuˀ ahiptetshu				ahipsusiˀ ahiptetshusi				ahipsusiˀ ahiptetshusi
1 du-excl.: antshyaˀ		hipnetshigyaˀ hipnetshigya	hipsugyaˀ hiptetshugya			hipnetshigyaˀ hipnetshigya	hipsusigyaˀ hiptetshusigya			hipnetshigyaˀ hipnetshigya	hipsusigyaˀ hiptetshusigya
2 du: hentshiˀ	yapmikehipsiˀ yapmikehiptetshi		kehipsuˀ kehiptetshu		yapmikehip yapmikehipta		kehipsusiˀ kehiptetshusi		yapmikehip yapmikehipta		kehipsusiˀ kehiptetshusi
3 du: huntshiˀ	yapmihipsi? yapmihiptetshi	kemihip kemihipta	hipsuˀ hiptetshu	amihipsiˀ amihiptetshi	yapmihip yapmihipta	kemihipsiˀ kemihiptetshi	hipsusiˀ hiptetshusi	amihip amihipta	yapmihip yapmihipta	kemihiptiˀ kemihipti	hipsusiˀ hiptetshusi
1 pl-incl.: aniˀ			ahiptumˀ ahiptum				ahiptumsimˀ ahiptumsim				ahiptumsimˀ ahiptumsim
1 pl-excl.: angyaˀ		hipnetshigyaˀ hipnegya	hiptumbaˀ hiptumba			hipnetshigyaˀ hipnetshigya	hiptumsimbaˀ hiptumsimba			hipnetshigyaˀ hipnetshigya	hiptumsimbaˀ hiptumsimba
2 pl: heniˀ	yapmikehip yapmikehipta		kehiptumˀ kehiptum		yapmikehip yapmikehipta		kehiptumsimˀ kehiptumsim		yapmikehip yapmikehipta		kehiptumsimˀ kehiptumsim
3 pl: henhaˀ	mehippa mehiptang	kemihip kemihipta	mehiptuˀ mehiptu	amihipsiˀ amihiptetshi	yapmimehip yapmimehipta	kemihipsiˀ kemihiptetshi	mehiptusiˀ mehiptusi	amihip amihipta	yapmimehip yapmimehipta	kemihiptiˀ kemihipti	mehiptusiˀ mehiptusi

The notation is phonological. The affricates are phonologically sequences, and so is the velar nasal and are the long vowels. In the Panchthare Limbu material presented in this study, the glottal stop is distinctive only in the syllable coda either directly preceded by a single vowel in the nucleus or with an intervening voiced stop (including nasals) between them. It must be tested, though, whether the restriction to a single vowel in the nucleus is accidental in the presented material, or a general one in the system.

We can observe the following distribution of verb prefixes in Panchthare Limbu:

	first argument	–	second argument
a-	3 sg	–	1 du-incl., 1 pl-incl.;
	1 du-incl.	–	3 sg, 3 du, 3 pl;
	1 pl-incl.	–	3 sg, 3 du, 3 pl;
ami-	3 du	–	1 du-incl., 1 pl-incl.;
	3 pl	–	1 du-incl., 1 pl-incl.;
ke-	2 sg	–	1 sg, 3 sg, 3 du, 3 pl;
	2 du	–	3 sg, 3 du, 3 pl;
	2 pl	–	3 sg, 3 du, 3 pl;
kemi-	3 du	–	2 sg, 2 du, 2 pl;
	3 pl	–	2 sg, 2 du, 2 pl;
me-	3 pl	–	1 sg, 3 sg, 3 du, 3 pl;
yapmi-	3 sg	–	1 du-excl., 1 pl-incl.;
	3 du	–	1 sg, 1 du-excl, 1 pl-excl.;
yapmike-	2 sg	–	1 du-excl., 1 pl-excl.;
	2 du	–	1 sg, 1 du-excl., 1 pl-incl.;
	2 pl	–	1 sg, 1 du-excl., 1 pl-excl.;
yapmime-	3 pl	–	1 du-excl., 1 pl-excl..

All of the prefixes are characterized by syncretism of number along the dimensions of person. Syncretism of number and person is found in *ke-* and *me-* with the first person singular as the second argument involved, but there the desinences are different anyhow as compared with the remaining forms characterized by *ke-* and *me-*. If all the forms, with prefixes and suffixes (including desinences) are taken into account, we can see that full syncretism affects only number, and normally involves the dual and the plural. The only cases in which also the singular is involved – next to the dual and the plural – are the following:

first argument	–	second argument
1 pl-excl.	–	nonpast: 2 sg, 2 du, 2 pl;
2 pl	–	1 sg, 1 du-excl., 1 pl-excl.;
2 sg, 2 du, 2 pl	–	1 du-excl., 1 pl-excl..

Even though it is not fully regular, the system is in all cases constrained by the presence of asymmetrical ordering, *in casu* in the numbers.

The partially irregular, but regularly constrained verb prefixes in Panchthare Limbu correspond with the following ones in Chattare Limbu:

Panchthare	= Chattare	first argument	–	second argument
a-	*a-*	3 sg	–	1 du-incl., 1 pl-incl.;
		1 du-incl.	–	3 sg, 3 du, 3 pl;
		1 pl-incl.	–	3 sg;
a-	–	1 pl-incl.	–	3 du, 3 pl;
–	*a-*	3 sg	–	1sg;
ami-	*an-*	3 du	–	1 du-incl., 1 pl-excl.;
		3 pl	–	1 du-incl., 1 pl-incl.;
ke-	*ka-*	2 sg	–	1sg, 3 sg, 3 du, 3 pl;
		2 du	–	3 sg, 3 du, 3 pl;
		2 pl	–	3 sg, 3 du, 3 pl;
kemi-	*kan-*	3 du	–	2 sg, 2 du, 2 pl;
		3 pl	–	2 sg, 2 du, 2 pl;
me-	*an-*	3 pl	–	1sg;
me-	*mu-*	3 pl	–	3 sg, 3 du, 3 pl;
yapmi-	*a-*	3 sg	–	1 du-excl., 1 pl-excl.;
		3 du	–	1 du-excl., 1 pl-excl.;
yapmi-	*an-*	3 du	–	1 sg;
yapmike-	*ka-*	2 sg	–	1 du-excl., 1 pl-excl.;
		2 du	–	1 sg, 1 du-excl., 1 pl-excl.;
		2 pl	–	1 sg, 1 du-excl., 1 pl-excl.;
yapmime-	*an-*	3 pl	–	1 du-excl., 1 pl-excl..

We can see that Chattare Limbu has the same or comparable verb prefixes as Panchthare Limbu, which are distributed – and in comparison with Panchthare Limbu partially redistributed – within the space determined by the same dimensions and the same asymmetrical ordering. As compared with Panchthare, Chattare's usage of *a-* and *an-* further extends the number syncretism and does so by obeying the number hierarchy involved (i.e. singular, dual, plural)).

Phenomena of this type are characteristic of variants – called dialects – of one language system.

And now consider Puma, a Kiranti Rai language system spoken in Khoṭang and in Udayapur, geographically neighbouring to Chamling to the west and Bantawa to the east. Is Puma a dialect of one of these genetically related Kiranti Rai systems, or a mixture of both, or a language system of its own? And can this be concluded on the basis of its grammar, *in casu* the verb prefixes involved?

The verb prefixes of South Bantawa, which is neighbouring to Puma and at the same time the type of Bantawa which has verb prefixes, have been elaborated in 2.2. above. Let me repeat them here.

South Bantawa verb prefixes (South Bhojpur):

	first argument	–	second argument
tu-	2 sg, 2 du or 2 pl	–	any;
	3 sg	–	2 sg, 2 du or 2pl;
	3 du	–	2 du;

ʉ-	3 sg	– 1 sg (past), 1 du-incl., 1 du-excl., 1 pl-incl., 1 pl-excl. (past and nonpast);
	3 du	– 1 sg (past), 3 sg, 1 du-incl., 1 du-excl., 3 du, 1 pl-incl. (nonpast), 1 pl-excl. (nonpast), 3 pl;
	3 pl	– 3 sg (past and nonpast);
mʉ-	3 du	– 2 sg, 1 pl-incl. (past), 1 pl-excl. (past), 2 pl;
	3 pl	– all except 3 sg.

These prefixes compare with the following Chamling ones (I take Chamling examples from Khoṭang, collected for the Linguistic Survey of Nepal, in order to compare them with the Puma ones, also from Khoṭang).

Chamling verb prefixes (Khoṭang):

	first argument	– second argument
ta-	2 sg, 2 du or 2 pl	– any;
	3 sg, 3 du or 3 pl	– 2 sg, 2 du, 2 pl;
pa-	3 sg, 3 du or 3 pl	– 1 sg, 1 du-incl.; 1 du-excl., 1 pl-incl., 1 pl-excl.;
mi-	3 sg, 3 du or 3 pl	– 3 pl.

Whereas Chamling has syncretism of number, South Bantawa has syncretism of both number and person in a way which cannot be said to follow from the asymmetrical ordering involved in a predictable way so that it could be considered a part of the same language system. Bantawa and Chamling are consequently two different language systems. And how about Puma?

Puma verb prefixes (Khoṭang):

	first argument	– second argument
to-	2 sg, 2 du or 2 pl	– 1 sg, 3 sg, 3 du, 3 pl;
khato-	2 sg, 2 du or 2 pl	– 1 du-excl., 1 pl-excl.;
po-	3 sg	– 1 sg, 3 sg, 3 du, 3 pl;
nipo-	3 du or 3 pl	– 1 sg;
nito-	3 du or 3 pl	– 2 sg, 2 du, 2 pl;
khama-	3 du or 3 pl	– 1 du-incl., 1 du-excl., 1 pl-incl., 1 pl-excl..

Note that the prefixes can further be analysed in terms of their constitutive grammatical signs *to-*, *po-*, *ma-* (which does not occur in isolation in Puma, but it does (as *mʉ*) in South Bantawa, overlapping with the Puma one in only one point of the space of the second argument, namely that of the first person plural, both inclusive and exclusive), *kha-* and *ni-*.

Puma has syncretism of both number and person as well, but in a way more regular than the South Bantawa one, and related to feature ordering in a way which cannot be established for South Bantawa. Namely, Puma has syncretism of person only in the singular, and only between the first and the third person. Through syncretism it eliminates hierarchy of person in connection with the highest ranking marked number, namely the singular. This is indicative of asymmetrical ordering between the dimensions of number and person in Puma, by which the former is dominating and the latter subordinate.

Puma is consequently different from both Bantawa and Chamling by having asymmetrical ordering between the dimensions of number and person, which cannot be established for either of the other two languages.

This fact of Puma's systematic identity is parallelled by its relative lexical identity, which is for Tibeto-Burman languages relatively best revealed by the lexical forms used for body parts and functions. This basic lexicon forms a part of the material collected for the Linguistic Survey of Nepal. I cite it for the districts for which I have cited the verb prefixes.

(67) Lexical expressions for body parts and functions in Bantawa, Chamling and Puma Rai:

	Bantawa South Bhojpur	Chamling Khoṭang	Puma Khoṭang
to comb	/ṭang khutma/	/kato khima/	/tong khima/
head	/ṭang/	/takhle/	/tong/
ear	/nabhak/	/nabro/	/nabre/
eye	/mʉk/	/micung/	/mok/
nose	/nabu/	/nadyipung/	/nabu/
mucus from nose	/nakhʉniwa/	/nakhle/	/nakhiwa/
mouth	/ḍo/	/dyo/	/nga/
cheek	/gala/	–	/khongtangma/
chin	/yobhi/	/dali/	/yon/
saliva	/ṭheṭnungwa/	/khone/	/khothuiwa/
tooth	/kʉng/	/kyung/	/kong/
tongue	/lem/	/lem/	/lem/
language	/yʉng/	/la/	/pima/
finger nail	/tʉngbʉlʉk/	/tungli/	/tongbolok/
toe nail	/tʉngbʉlʉk/	/tungli/	/tongbolok/
foot	/lang/	/philu/	/long/
toe	/buḍi amla/	/budi amla/	/buḍi amla/
hand	/chuk/	/chuk/	/chi/
finger	/amla/	/amla/	/amla/
knee	/ghunṛa/	–	/tumpachok/
arm	/pakhuṛa/	–	/pakhuṛa/
upper back	/deng/	–	/dang/
lower back	/ṭethok/	–	–
buttocks	/kengṭang/	/khilam/	/chumayok/
belly	/buk/	/khori/	/khori/
navel	/chumbutli/	/naito/	/naito/
neck	/pot/	/dungse/	/pot/
heart	/mutu/	/mutu/	/cowa/
liver	/lungma/	/lui/	/kolungma/
intestine	/thok/	/cikhli/	/kotho/
body	/jiu/	/bulim/	/bulum/
corpse	/sʉo mʉna/	/syako mina/	/syako/
to drink	/dungma/	/dungma/	/dungma/
to eat	/cama/	/cama/	/cama/
to bite	/ngekma/	/khrama/	/khama/
to cough	/khokma/	/thungma/	/chungma/

to see	/khangma/	/khongma/	/khangma/
to hear	/enma/	/enma/	/enma/
to know	/lema/	/lema/	/lenma/
to laugh	/ima/	/rima/	/rima/
to die	/suma/	/sima/	/sima/
to kill	/setma/	/soima/	/setma/
to swim	/poweilima/	/wapramma/	/wacakma/
to walk	/penma/	/lamthyima/	/lamtima/
to come	/bima/	/benma/	/benma/.

Correspondencies: Bantawa – Puma: 26 out of 45;
Chamling – Puma: 22 out of 45;
Bantawa – Chamling: 19 out of 45.

(Within the correspondencies, differences are due to independently establishable sound changes.)

We can see that the basic lexicon supports the conclusion drawn on the basis of ordering among the features of grammar, according to which Puma is a language separate from Bantawa and Chamling, although belonging to the same language subgroup. It derives both its individuality and its relatedness to the other languages from the way in which the ordered parts at the level of meaning are ordered, and both the ordered and the unordered parts are conventionalized at the level of form.

And now consider a case of a dialect of one language which has in due course converged with another language. The case I have in mind is that of Yakkhaba and its varieties, a Rai language system originally spoken in Sankhuwasabha and spread through migration to the south and east. Yakkhaba is originally a dialect of Yamphe, as can be seen from the following lexical comparison, but a variety of it has merged with Yakkha, as will be shown below.

(68) Lexical expressions for body parts and functions in Yamphe, Yakkha and Yakkhaba Rai:

	Yamphe Sankhuwasabha	Yakkha Dhankuṭa	Yakkhaba Sankhuwasabha
to comb	/ṭang khipma/	/tamphak khipma/	/si khipma/
head	/ningḍawa/	/tukhruk/	/ningḍaya/
ear	/nek/	/naaphak/	/nek/
eye	/mik/	/miik/	/mik/
nose	/naku/	/naaphuk/	/naku/
mucus from nose	/nakwa/	/naagakma/	/nakwa/
mouth	/yabuk/	/muula/	/yabuk/
cheek	/namḍeng/	/namcikheng/	/namḍeng/
chin	/yaphrekwa/	/singsalik/	/yaphrekwa/
saliva	/cepma/	/khenkma/	/cepma/
tooth	/keng/	/keng/	/keng/
molar	/magengwa/	/umakeng/	/magengwa/

tongue	/lem/	/lem/	/lem/
language	/kha/	/ceʔa/	/kha/
finger nail	/senḍuma/	/muk chendi/	/senḍuma/
toe nail	/senḍuma/	/lang chendi/	/senḍuma/
foot	/sarang/	/lang/	/sarang/
toe	/ṭheṭhupma/	/ṭheeṭhu/	/marangma/
hand	/huk/	/muk/	/huk/
finger	/maṛheto/	–	–
knee	/tumruk/	–	/tumruk/
arm	/huk/	–	/huk/
upper back	/sumarik/	/mising/	/enggowak/
lower back	/sumarik/	/mising/	/sumrik/
buttocks	/akyawa/	/maʔyak/	/akyawa/
belly	/rungma/	/phook/	/rungma/
navel	/okne/	/namcukulik/	/oknaik/
neck	/petla/	/khorang/	/petla/
heart	/mutu/	/lungma/	/mutuk/
liver	/rungmajuwa/	/cucua/	/rungmajuwa/
intestine	/sadhok/	/hiʔrua/	/sasok/
body	/jiu/	/thok/	/jiu/
corpse	/murda/	/syaana/	/sigurik/
to drink	/unmia/	/ungma/	/ungma/
to eat	/camia/	/caama/	/cama/
to bite	/hapmia/	/haapma/	/hapma/
to cough	/hepmia/	/hoopma/	/hepma/
to see	/khangmia/	/soopma/	/khangma/
to hear	/khemmia/	/khemma/	/khemma/
to know	/remia/	/niima/	/lema/
to laugh	/yemia/	/yuncaama/	/yicama/
to sleep	/imma/	/imma/	/imma/
to die	/sima/	/siima/	/si khepma/
to kill	/sepmia/	/siima/	/sepma/
to swim	/wabhakmia/	/wacekma/	/wabhakma/
to walk	/ommia/	/laama/	/khepma/
to come	/apmia/	/taama/	/lemma/.

(The missing forms in 68, as in 67, have only the Nepali equivalents.)

Correspondencies: Yamphe – Yakkhaba: 39 out of 47;
Yakkha – Yakkhaba: 11 out of 47;
Yamphe – Yakkha: 9 out of 47.

(Within the correspondencies, differences are due to independently establishable sound changes.)

In this variety attested in Sankhuwasabha, Yakkhaba is in the lexicon clearly a dialect of Yamphe, whereas Yakkha is a different language.

But now consider a variety of Yakkhaba which has migrated to the south 25 years ago. It is Yakkhaba attested in Dharan, which shares in its grammar an important characteristic with Yakkha as represented by the relatively neighbouring Dhankuṭa variety cited above, which makes it quite different from Yamphe.

Whereas Yamphe has the plural marker /-ci/ or /-ji/ in the nominal categories, and in the verb only where it reflects the pronominal elements involved in the complex pronominalized desinences, Yakkhaba of Dharan has the plural marker /-ci/ in the nominal categories in the same way as Yamphe does, also reflected the verb desinences, and it has an additional phenomenon which it shares with Yakkha only, namely an additional plural desinence /-ha/ which is added to the verb desinences in the cases which will be defined below. /-ha/ is otherwise typical of Yakkha, where it functions as the plural desinence both in the nominal categories and the verbs (with /-ci/ restricted to [+human] nouns, if used at all).

(69) Plurality designation in the verb of Yakkha from Dhankuṭa, district Dhankuṭa.

	first argument	– second argument
/-ha / at the end of the verb desinence:	any person in the singular	– any person in the dual or plural
	any person in the dual	– any person in the dual or plural
	any person in the plural	– any person or number except 3 sg.

And now consider the way in which Yakkhaba from Dharan has extended the usage of /-ha/ in the verb desinences, which obviously both in its meaning and form originates from Yakkha. This usage of /-ha/ is not found in the other variety of Yakkhaba incurred in Sankhuwasabha by the Linguistic Survey of Nepal.

(70) Additional plurality designation in the verb of Yakkhaba from Dharan, district Sunsari, originally coming from Ankhibhuin in Sankhuwasabha.

	first argument	– second argument
/-ha/ at the end of the verb desinence:	any person in the singular	– any person in the dual or plural
	1 du-incl.	– 3 du or 3 pl in the past tense
	1 pl-incl.	– any person or number except 3 sg
	remaining cases	– any person in the dual or plural.

(Note that partially overlapping sets of referents of person and number have neither a lexicalized nor a grammaticalized means of expression in the language.)

These data, collected from the same informant as those for the numerals presented in 3.2. above, show an extension of the Yakkha pattern for the plural onto the dual, and an extension of the restriction for the third person singular onto the third person of any number of the second argument if the first argument is dual-inclusive, i.e. if it includes the addressee, and the verb is nonpast. Yakkhaba has consequently extended the Yakkha usage of /-ha/ along the dimensions of number and person, thus making the presence of /-ha/ usual, and its absence determined by the following boundaries set by the distribution of number and person between the two arguments involved:

no /-ha/ occurs if
- the second argument contains a single participant, or
- there is a division into participants *within the speech situation* vs. *outside of the speech situation* (which distinguishes the third person from the remaining ones as defined in 2.2. above) coinciding with the arguments involved, and
- the speaker is involved (within the speech situation) in the first argument with one addressee, and the verb is nonpast.

Yakkhaba from Dharan consequently does not have a different, but only a further-extended pattern by making use of the same dimensions of meaning as Yakkha does. This is why Yakkhaba cannot be considered a separate language on the basis of its grammatical system. It is rather of a mixed type, sharing some characteristics with Yakkha and some with Yamphe, with the preservation of the original pattern underlying these characteristics.

And how about its lexicon? Unfortunately, I have not collected the basic lexicon from the Yakkhaba informant in Dharan, including denotations of body parts and functions, which are known to be the most preservative in Tibeto-Burman, but I do have some lexical items collected for the purpose of numeral constructions, which can be compared with the same ones in Yamphe and Yakkha in order to get some impression of the lexical relations.

(70) Some lexical correspondencies between Yamphe from Sankhuwasabha, Yakkha from Dhankuṭa and Yakkhaba from Dharan:

	Yamphe Sankhuwasabha	Yakkha Dhankuṭa	Yakkhaba Dharan
woman/girl	/metnami/	/metnungma/	/metnungma/
man	/waṛhamba/	/ṭhangsingba/	/wempha/
goat	/yasuba/	/meenduba/	/mendhak/
stone	/runggokwa/	/lunghwak/	/lunghwak/
fire	/me/	/mii/	/mi/
pot	/bhanṛa/	–	/bhanṛa/
mortar	/sumak/	/chumbu/	/chumbu/
hand	/huk/	/muk/	/muk/
finger	/maṛheto/	–	/kheʔwa/
eye	/mik/	/miik/	/mik/
house	/khim/	/pang/	/pang/
cloth	/ce/	/tee/	/teʔ/
rope	/paṛak/	/khibak/	/khibak/

white	/sema/	/phuna/	/phuna/
black	/makhaima/	/makhruna/	/makhruna/
long	–	/kenggena/	/kenggyatna/
big	/epa/	/maakna/	/maṛa/
small	/aṛeppa/	/miina/	/mina/
old	–	/enchona/	–
sweet	/limna/	/limna/	/ulippa/
today	–	/hen/	/hen/
tomorrow	/waga/	/wendeknga/	/wendek(nga)/
yesterday	/asekngа/	/asen/	/asen/.

(For the missing forms, the Nepali ones are used instead.)

Correspondences: Yamphe – Yakkhaba (Dharan) : 8 out of 23;
Yakkha – Yakkhaba (Dharan) : 17 out of 23;
Yamphe – Yakkha: 7 out of 23.

On the basis of this part of the lexicon, this variety of Yakkhaba could possibly be viewed as a dialect of Yakkha. But a full consideration of the basic lexicon is needed in order to state this.

Neither on the basis of its grammar nor on the basis of its lexicon can Yakkhaba of Dharan be considered a separate language, as it does not have the necessary identity in comparison with the neighbouring related language systems, which are each characterized by an identity of their own.

The data presented in this chapter show that grammatical relations in a language take place within a multidimensional space indeed, and that it is typologically of crucial importance whether the involved dimensions are mutually ordered or not.

The lexicon contains an ordered part which is related to the grammatical dimensions of the language – and together they reveal the system on the basis of which typological classification takes place.

5. Conclusions

The aim of this study has been to develop a theory about the principles of organization of language system and to investigate direct and indirect testability of this theory and of theories of language in general. This aim is in fact a threefold one: developing a part of a theory of language, developing procedures for evaluating a theory of language (in the sense of Popper's (1968, 5th: 106 etc.) *testing the basic statements which constitute a theory*), and developing procedures for analysing language data in terms of a theory without circularity. Against the background of the knowledge that *"the critical problem for grammatical theory today is not a paucity of evidence but rather the inadequacy of present theories to account for masses of evidence that are hardly open to serious question"*, as Chomsky (1965: 20f.) put it, and on the basis of evidence that language variation and change is not random but rather constrained by the system in which it occurs, this study has aimed at developing a theory of language system which is relatable to variational data through a set of hypotheses and in this way partly directly and partly indirectly refutable by the data. And this study has aimed at developing procedures for evaluating such a theory by showing how hypotheses can and must be constructed on the basis of a theory, and how they can be put to the test through various types of language data, all of which apparently fit into the same pattern.

Even though it is agreed with e.g. Hjelmslev (1943: 14) that construction of a theory is in itself independent of experience, and that a theory only introduces certain premisses concerning which the theoretician knows from preceding experience that they fulfill the conditions for application to certain experimental data, the results of this investigation show that one must disagree with Hjelmslev's statement that *"the experimental data can never strengthen or weaken the theory itself, but only its applicability"*. Rather, the results of this investigation show that experimental data can lead to a modification of a statement of a theory, thus strengthening its explanatory power.

The theory of the principles of organization of language system developed here states that among the logically conceivable and also factually present relations among language elements, asymmetrical relations are crucial to language system. They are found whenever one language element implies another element, but not *vice versa.* An asymmetrical relation can hold either between two opposed terms which are patterned within the same dimension, or between dimensions consisting of pairs of terms. The former asymmetrical relation equals markedness, and the latter, hierarchy, consisting of a dominating and a subordinate dimension. This holds both for the level of form and for the level of meaning as expressed by the form. And at both levels, the extent of asymmetrical patterning is a language-specific matter. Only its principle is universal.

On the basis of this theory, a hypothesis has been deduced by which a change of a dominating dimension triggers a change of its subordinate one or ones, whereas a change of a subordinate or unordered dimension need not have consequences for the rest of the system. This was further translated into a number of derived hypotheses based on specific properties of the various parts of the investigated language systems, and tested by observable variation and change there.

The fact that testing was possible showed not only that the testing method was a correct one, but also that the theory reveals a relevant principle of organization of language system and its functioning, and can consequently be evaluated by it.

Only a theory which is translatable into hypotheses to be tested by the full set of language data can increase our understanding of the object under investigation.

References

Andersen H. (1972). "Diphthongization", *Language* 48, 1, 11-50.
– (1973). "Abductive and deductive change", *Language* 49, 4, 765-793.
– (1975). "Variance and invariance in phonological typology", Phonologica 1972 (Dressler W.U. and F.V. Mareš, eds.), München/Salzburg: W. Fink Verlag, 67-78.
Anderson S.R. (1978). "Syllables, segments, and the Northwest Caucasian languages", Syllables and segments (Bell A. and J.B. Hooper, eds.), Amsterdam: The North Holland Publishing Company, 47-58.
Basbøll H. (1981). "Remarks on distinctive features and markedness in generative phonology", Theory of markedness in generative phonology (Belletti A., L. Brandi and L. Rizzi, eds.), Pisa: Scuola Normale Superiore, 25-64.
Belić A. (1950). Istorija srpskohrvatskog jezika; knj. II, sv. 1: reči sa deklinacijom, Beograd: Naučna knjiga.
Bell A. and J. B. Hooper (1978). "Issues and evidence in syllabic phonology", Syllables and segments (Bell A. and J.B. Hooper, eds.), Amsterdam: The North Holland Publishing Company, 3-22.
Benedict P.K. (1972). Sino-Tibetan, a conspectus, Cambridge: Cambridge University Press.
Bieri D. and M. Schulze (1971). Sunwar phonemic summary, revised version, Kirtipur: Tibeto-Burman phonemic summaries IX.
Bista D.B. (1980). People of Nepal, Kathmandu: Ratna Pustak Bhandar.
Blom J.G. and J.Z. Uys (1966). "Some notes on the existence of a 'universal concept' of vowels", *Phonetica* 15, 65-85.
Borkovskij V.I. i P.S. Kuznecov (1963), Istoričeskaja grammatika russkogo Jazyka, Moskva: Izdatel'stvo Akademii Nauk.
Breidaks A. (1972). "Latgalisko izlokšńu prosodijas jautājumi", Veltījums akadēmikim Jānim Endzelīnam (Grab R., ed.), Riga: LPSR Zinātńu Akad. Andreja Upīsa valodas un literatūras institūts, 89-108.
Bright W. (1976). Variation and change in language, Stanford: Stanford University Press.
Brøndal V. (1943), Essais de linguistique générale, Copenhagen: Munksgaard.
Brozović D. (1967), "Some remarks on distinctive features, especially in Serbo-Croatian", To Honor Roman Jakobson, The Hague/Paris: Mouton, 412-426.

Chang K. and B. Shefts (1964). A manual of spoken Tibetan (Lhasa dialect), Seattle: University of Washington Press.
Chomsky N. (1964). Current trends in linguistic theory, The Hague/Paris: Mouton.
– (1965). Aspects of the theory of syntax, Cambridge: The MIT Press.
Chomsky N. and M. Halle (1968). The sound pattern of English, New York/Evanston/London: Harper and Row Publishers.
Cohen A. (1966). "Errors of speech and their implication for understanding the strategy of language users", *Zeitschrift für Phonetik* 21, 177-181; also in Speech errors as linguistic evidence (Fromkin V.A., ed.), The Hague/Paris: Mouton.
Cohen A., C.L. Ebeling, K. Fokkema and A.G.F. van Holk (1969). 4th. Fonologie van het Nederlands en het Fries, The Hague: M. Nijhoff.
Cohen A. and J. 't Hart (1967). "On the anatomy of intonation", *Lingua* 19, 177-192.
Collier R. and J. 't Hart (1978). Cursus Nederlandse intonatie, Eindhoven: Instituut voor Perceptie Onderzoek manuscript 333.
Cook Th. (forthcoming). The phonology and inflectional morphology of Efik.
Dik S.C. (1978). Functional grammar, Amsterdam: The North Holland Publishing Company.
Ebeling C.L. (1960). Linguistic units, The Hague/Paris: Mouton.
– (1967). "Some premisses of phonemic analysis", *Word* 23, 122-137.
– (1968). "On accent in Dutch and the phoneme /ə/", *Lingua* 21, 135-143.
– (1978). Syntax and semantics, Leiden: Brill.
Foley J. (1977). Foundations of theoretical phonology, Cambridge: Cambridge University Press.
Fromkin V.A. (1971). "The nonanomalous nature of anomalous utterances", *Language* 47, 27-52; also in Speech errors as linguistic evidence (Fromkin V.A., ed.), The Hague/Paris: Mouton.
– (1974). "On the phonological representation of tone", The tone tome, *UCLA working papers in phonetics* 27, 1-17.
Goldsmith J. (1976). "An overview of autosegmental phonology", *Linguistic Analysis* 2, 22-68.
Greenberg J.H. (1966). "Synchronic and diachronic universals in phonology", *Language* 42, 508-517.
Greenberg J.H. and D. Kaschube (1976). "Word prosodic systems: a preliminary report", *Stanford working papers on language universals* 20, 1-18.
Grierson G.A., ed. (1909). Linguistic Survey of India, vol. III, part 1; repr. in 1967, Delhi: Motilal Banarsidass.
Gvozdanović J. (1980a). Tone and accent in Standard Serbo-Croatian, with a synopsis of Serbo-Croatian phonology, Wien: Österreichische Akademie der Wissenschaften.
– (1980b). "Features, markedness and the role of empirical data in phono-

logical analysis", Studies in Slavic and General Linguistics 1 (Barentsen A.A. *et al.*, eds.), Amsterdam: Rodopi, 125-160.
– (1982). "On establishing restrictions imposed on sound change", Papers from the 5th International Conference on Historical Linguistics (Alhqvist A., ed.), Amsterdam: John Benjamins Publishing Company, 85-97.
– (1983a). "Patterning of distinctive features in relation to variability", Proceedings of the 13th International Congress of Linguists (Hattori Sh. and K. Inoue, eds.), Tokyo: Gakushuin University, 611-617.
– (1983b). "Distinctive feature constraints on speech errors", Sound and structure, studies presented to A. Cohen (Broecke M.P.R., V.J. van Heuven and W. Zonneveld, eds.), Dordrecht: Foris, 129-140.
– (1983c). "Variability in relation to the language system", General Linguistics, studies presented to Th.F. Magner (Schmalstieg W., ed.), 49-63.
– (1983d). "Typological characteristics of Slavic and non-Slavic languages with distinctive tonal accents", Dutch Contributions to the 9th International Congress of Slavists, Linguistics (Holk A.G.F. van, ed.), Amsterdam: Rodopi, 53-108.
– (1983e). "On the relation between segmental and prosodic analysis", *Folia Linguistica* 17/1-2, 25-49.
– (1984a). "Theories of sound change fail if they try to predict too much", Papers from the 6th International Conference on Historical Linguistics (Fisiak J., ed.), Amsterdam: John Benjamins Publishing Company (to appear).
– (1984b) "Markedness and ordering at various levels", Studia linguistica diachronica et synchronica (Pieper U. and G. Stickel, eds.), Berlin/New York/ Amsterdam: Mouton (to appear).
Hale A. ed. (1973). Clause, sentence and discourse patterns in selected languages of Nepal, Norman: SIL, University of Oklahoma.
Halle M. and K. Stevens (1971). "A note on laryngeal features", *MIT Quarterly Progress Report* 101, 198-213.
Harlow R.B. (1983). "Some phonological changes in Polynesian languages", Papers from the 5th International Conference on Historical Linguistics (Alhqvist A., ed.), Amsterdam: John Benjamins Publishing Company, 89-109.
Hart J. 't (1982). "The stylization method applied to British English intonation", Working group on intonation, The 13th International Congress of Linguists, Tokyo (mimeographed), 23-34.
Hattori Sh. (1973). "What is the prosodeme, i.e. 'word accent', and what are its distinctive features", *Sciences of Language* 7, 1-61.
Hjelmslev L. (1935). La catégorie des cas, Aarhus: Universitetsforlaget.
– (1943). Omkring sprogteoriens grundlaeggelse, København: Munksgaard.
– (1961), 2nd. Prolegomena to a theory of language, Wisconsin: University of Wisconsin Press.
Hockett Ch. (1955). Manual of phonology, Bloomington: Indiana University Press.

Hooper J.B. (1976). An introduction to natural generative phonology, New York/San Francisco/London: Academic Press.
Humboldt W. von (1836). Über die Verschiedenheit des menschlichen Sprachbaues, Berlin; Facsimile 1960, Darmstadt: Wissenschaftliche Buchgesellschaft.
Hyman L.M. and T. Tadadjeu (1976). "Floating tones in Mbam-Nkam", Studies in Bantu tonology, *Southern California Occasional Papers in Linguistics* (Hyman L.M., ed.), 3, 52-112.
Ivić M. (1961). "On the structural characteristics of the Serbocroatian case system", *International Journal of Slavic Linguistics and Poetics* 4, 38-47.
Ivić P. (1958). Die serbokroatischen Dialekte, ihre Struktur und Entwicklung I: Allgemeines und die štokavische Dialektgruppe, The Hague/Paris: Mouton.
– (1968). "Procesi rasterećenja vokalskog sistema u kajkavskim govorima", *Zbornik za filologiju i lingvistiku* 11, 57-69.
Ivšić Stj. (1911). "Prilog za slavenski akcenat", *Rad Jugoslavenske Akademije Znanosti i Umjetnosti* 196, 133-208.
– (1913). "Današńi posavski govor", *Rad Jugoslavenske Akademije Znanosti i Umjetnosti* 196, 124-254, 197, 9-138.
Jakobson R. (1936). "Beitrag zur allgemeinen Kasuslehre: Gesamtbedeutungen der russischen Kasus", *Travaux du Cercle Linguistique de Prague* 6, 240-288, also in 1971, 23-71.
– (1939). "Zur Struktur des Phonems", *Vorträge an der Universität von Kopenhagen;* also in 1962, 280-310.
– (1941). Kindersprache, Aphasie und allgemeine Lautgesetze, Uppsala: Språkvetenskapliga Sällskapets Förhandlingar, also in 1962, 328-401.
– (1948). "Russian conjugation", *Word* 4, 155-167; also in 1971, 119-129.
– (1949). "On the identification of phonemic entities", *Travaux du Cercle Linguistique de Prague* 5, 205-213; also in 1962, 418-425.
– (1962). Selected Writings I (phonological studies), the Hague/Paris: Mouton.
– (1971). Selected Writings II (word and language), The Hague/Paris: Mouton.
Jakobson R., E.C. Cherry and M. Halle (1953). "Toward the logical description of languages in their phonemic aspect", *Language* 29, 34-46; also in 1962, 449-463.
Jakobson R., G. Fant and M. Halle (1952). Preliminaries to speech analysis, Cambridge: The MIT Press; also in 1962, 449-463.
Jakobson R., and M. Halle (1956). Fundamentals of language, The Hague/Paris: Mouton; also in 1962: 464-504.
Jakobson R. and L. Waugh (1979). The sound shape of language, Brighton: The Harvester Press.
Jespersen O. (1922). Language: its nature, development and origin, London: George Allen & Unwin.
Jurišić B. (1966). Rječnik govora otoka Vrgade, Zagreb: Jugoslavenska Akademija Znanosti i Umjetnosti.

Kálmán B. (1972) "Hungarian historical phonology", The Hungarian language (Benkő L. and S. Imre, eds.), The Hague/Paris: Mouton, 49-83.

Kean M.-L. (1980). The theory of markedness in generative grammar, Bloomington: The Indiana University Linguistics Club.

– (1981). "On a theory of markedness: some general considerations and a case in point", Theory of markedness in generative grammar (Belletti A., L. Brandi and L. Rizzi, eds.), Pisa: Scuola Normale Superiore, 559-604.

Keijsper C.E. (1983). "Comparing Dutch and Russian pitch contours", *Russian Linguistics* 7, 101-154.

Kiparsky P. (1981). "Remarks on the metrical structure of the syllable", *Phonologica* 1980 (Dressler W.U., O.E. Pfeiffer and J.R. Rennison, eds.), Innsbruck: *Innsbrucker Beiträge zur Sprachwissenschaft,* 245-256.

– (1982). Explanation in phonology, Dordrecht: Foris.

– (1983). "From cyclic phonology to lexical phonology", The structure of phonological representations (Hulst H. van der and N.S.H. Smith, eds.), Dordrecht: Foris, 131-175.

Koopmans-van Beinum F. (1980). Vowel contrast reduction; an acoustic and perceptual study of Dutch vowels in various speech conditions, Amsterdam: Academische Pers.

Kuipers A.H. (1960). Phoneme and morpheme in Kabardian, The Hague/ Paris: Mouton.

Labov W., M. Yaeger and R. Steiner (1972). A quantitative study of sound change in progress, Philadelphia: The University of Pennsylvania.

Ladefoged P. (1975). A course in phonetics, New York/Chicago/San Francisco/Atlanta: Harcourt Brace Jovanovich.

Lehiste I. (1970). Suprasegmentals, Cambridge: The MIT Press.

Lessen Kloeke W.U.S. van (1981). "How strident is raspberry? Likely, unlikely, and impossible feature configurations in phonology", Theory of markedness in generative grammar (Belletti A., L. Brandi and L. Rizzi, eds.), Pisa: Scuola Normale Superiore, 363-406.

Lindau M. (1975). "Phonetic mechanisms of vowel harmony in African languages", paper read at the 8th International Congress of Phonetic Sciences, Leeds.

Marsack C.C. (1962). Teach yourself Samoan, London: English Universities Press.

Martin Ph. (1978). "Questions de phonosyntaxe et de phonosémantique français", *Linguistic Investigations* 2, 93-125.

Martinet A. (1955). Economie des changements phonétiques., Berne: Francke.

Meringer K. (1908). Aus dem Leben der Sprache, Berlin: Behr's Verlag.

Morin Y.-Ch. and J. Kaye (1982). "The syntactic bases for French *liaison",* *Journal of Linguistics* 18, 291-330.

Morton J. (1964). "A model for continuous language behaviour", *Language and Speech* 7, 40-70.

Nespor M. and I. Vogel (1980). "Prosodic hierarchy and speech perception", paper presented at the Conference on the Perception of Language, Florence.

– (1983). "Prosodic domains of external sandhi rules", The structure of phonological representations (Hulst H. van der and N.S.H. Smith, eds.), Dordrecht: Foris, 225-263.

Nooteboom S.G. (1969). "The tongue slips into patterns", Leyden Studies in Linguistics and Phonetics", The Hague Paris: Mouton, 114-132; also in Speech errors as linguistic evidence (Fromkin V.A., ed.), The Hague/Paris: Mouton.

Popper K.R. (1968), 5th. The logic of scientific discovery, London: Hutchinson & Co.

Rigler J. (1967). "Pripombe k pregledu osnovnih razvojnih etap v slovenskem vokalizmu", *Slavistična revija* 15, 1-2, 129-152.

Rubach J. (1977). Changes of consonants in English and Polish; a generative account, Wrocław/Warszawa/Kraków/Gdańsk: Zakład Narodowy Imienia Ossolińskich, Wydawnictwo Polskiej Akademii Nauk.

Saussure F. de (1916). Cours de linguistique générale, Lausanne/Paris: Klincksieck.

Selkirk E.O. (1980a). On prosodic structure and its relation to syntactic structure, Bloomington: The Indiana University Linguistics Club.

– (1980b). "The role of prosodic categories in English word stress', *Linguistic Inquiry* 11, 3, 563-605.

– (1982). On the major class features and syllable theory, Cambridge/ Amherst: MIT and University of Massachusetts.

Shafer R. (1966). Introduction to Sino-Tibetan, part I, Wiesbaden: Otto Harrassowitz.

Shattuck-Hufnagel S. and D. Klatt (1979). "The limited use of distinctive features and markedness in speech production: evidence from speech error data", *Journal of Verbal Learning and Verbal Behavior* 18, 41-55.

Smith N.S.H. (1981). "Foley's scales of relative phonological strength", Phonology in the 1980's (Goyvaerts D.L., ed.), Ghent: Story – Scientia, 587-595.

Sonderegger S. (1979). Grundzüge deutscher Sprachgeschichte; Diachronie des Sprachsystems, Band I: Einführung – Genealogie – Konstanten, Berlin/New York: Walter de Gruyter.

Steriade D. (1982). Greek prosodies and the nature of syllabification, Cambridge: MIT Ph. Diss.

Thurneysen R. (1946). A grammar of Old Irish, Dublin: The Dublin Institute for Advanced Studies.

Toporišič J. 1967. "Pojmovanje tonemičnosti slovenskega jezika", *Slavistična revija* 15, 1-2, 64-108.

Trubetzkoy N.S. (1939). Grundzüge der Phonologie, *Travaux du Cercle Linguistique de Prague* 7; repr. in 1958, Göttingen: Vandenhoeck und Ruprecht.

Vennemann Th. and P. Ladefoged (1973). "Phonetic features and phonological features", *Lingua* 32, 61-74.

Vogel I. (forthcoming). "External sandhi rules operating across sentences",

Sandhi phenomena in the European languages (Andersen H., ed.), Berlin/New York/Amsterdam: Mouton (to appear).

Vogel I. and S. Scalise (1982). "Secondary stress in Italian", *Lingua* 58, 213-242.

Wang W.S.-Y. (1967). "Phonological features of tone", *International Journal of American Linguistics* 33, 93-105.

Ward I. (1933). The phonetic and tonal structure of Efik, Cambridge: Heffer.

Weidert A.K. (1979). "The Sino-Tibetan tonogenetic laryngeal reconstruction theory", *Linguistics of the Tibeto-Burman area* 5, 1, 49-127.

Weijnen A.A. (1968). Het schema van de klankwettten, Assen: Van Gorcum.

Welmers Wm. E. (1973). African language structures, Berkeley/Los Angeles/London: University of California Press.

Winter W. (1959). "Über die Methode zum Nachweis struktureller Relevanz von Oppositionen distinktiver Merkmale", *Phonetica*, Suppl. ad Vol. 4, 28-44.

– (1982). "O markirovannosti, sootvetstvii norme, i 'estestvennosti'", *Voprosy jazykoznanija* 31, 4, 72-77.

– (1984). Distribution of languages and sublanguages in Eastern Nepal, Kirtipur: Tribhuvan University.

– (forthcoming). "Differentiation within Rai: nonlexical isoglosses", Publications of the Linguistics Department, University of Kiel (to appear).

Indexes

Index of Subjects

Index of Languages

Index of Authors